Contemporary Japanese Architecture

Contemporary Japanese Architecture presents a clear and comprehensive overview of the historical and cultural framework that informs the work of all Japanese architects, as an introduction to an in-depth investigation of the challenges now occupying the contemporary designers who will be the leaders of the next generation. It separates out the young generation of Japanese architects from the crowded, distinguished, multi-generational field they seek to join, and investigates the topics that absorb them, and the critical issues they face within the new economic reality of Japan and a shifting global order. Salient points in the text are illustrated by beautiful, descriptive images provided by the architects and from the extensive collection of the author. By combining illustrations with timelines and graphics to explain complex ideas, the book is accessible to any student seeking to understand contemporary Japanese architecture.

James Steele is an architect who received both his bachelor's and master's degrees from the University of Pennsylvania, and practiced in the Philadelphia region before accepting a position at Dammam University in Saudi Arabia where he taught for eight years. He then served as Senior Editor at Academy Editions, and taught at the Prince of Wales's Institute of Architecture in London before relocating to the University of Southern California School of Architecture in 1991, receiving a PhD in Urban Planning and Development at USC in 2002. Professor Steele has taught history and theory as well as design studio, and also organized the first Foreign Studies Program for architecture students in Malaysia in 1998. He administered it up through its fifteenth and final session in 2013 and then founded and became the director of a new undergraduate program in South America, based in Sao Paulo, Brazil. He has written extensively on contemporary architecture and has been a guest critic and speaker at numerous universities in the United States and internationally.

"James Steele has written an immensely well researched, insightful and scholarly work on the genealogy of contemporary Japanese architecture and in the process of unravelling this, he demystifies the architecture and explains in depth the 'whys', the 'hows' and the 'whats' of modern Japanese architecture since the Second World War. The book is not just invaluable for architects seeking to understand Japanese architecture, it is *sine qua non* for those in the humanities seeking to understand the Japanese mind and culture through the medium of architectural studies."—*Ken Yeang (Dr.), Principal, T.R.Hamzah & Yeang Sdn. Bhd. (Malaysia)*

Contemporary Japanese Architecture

Tracing the next generation

James Steele

Routledge
Taylor & Francis Group

LONDON AND NEW YORK

First published 2017
by Routledge
2 Park Square, Milton Park, Abingdon, Oxon OX14 4RN

and by Routledge
711 Third Avenue, New York, NY 10017

Routledge is an imprint of the Taylor & Francis Group, an informa business

British Library Cataloguing-in-Publication Data
A catalogue record for this book is available from the British Library.

Library of Congress Cataloging-in-Publication Data
Names: Steele, James, 1943- author.
Title: Contemporary Japanese architecture : tracing the next generation /
James Steele.
Description: New York : Routledge, 2017. | Includes bibliographical
references and index.
Identifiers: LCCN 2016036737| ISBN 9781138941243 (hb : alk. paper) |
ISBN 9781138941250 (pb : alk. paper) | ISBN 9781315673813 (ebook)
Subjects: LCSH: Architecture – Japan – History – 21st century. |
Architecture – Japan – Themes, motives.
Classification: LCC NA1555.6 .S74 2017 | DDC 720.952/0905 – dc23
LC record available at https://lccn.loc.gov/2016036737

ISBN: 978-1-138-94124-3 (hbk)
ISBN: 978-1-138-94125-0 (pbk)
ISBN: 978-1-315-67381-3 (ebk)

Typeset in Adobe Caslon
by Florence Production Limited

Printed and bound in the United States of America by Sheridan

For my sons Christopher and Casey
and
my granddaughter Remi

Contents

Acknowledgments		xi
Introduction: the (dis)continuities of Japanese architecture		1
Part I: An enduring cultural framework		**7**
1	The land and its people	9
2	History and religion	19
3	Paroxysm and change	31
Part II: From modernity to Modernism: 1868–1940		**41**
4	The search for knowledge and its consequences	43
5	Modernism sidetracked on the road to war: 1930–1940	57
Part III: From re-birth to economic collapse		**71**
6	Post-war reconstruction, from survival to recovery: 1945–1950	73
7	The Le Corbusier syndrome	85
8	Metabolism revisited	97
9	Expo '70: a joyful vision of a new world	111
10	The Shinohara School	121
11	Postmodernism: apostasy or prophesy?	129
12	A decade of excess: life inside the bubble	141

Part IV: Transitional figures   **151**

13   Witness to war: Fumihiko Maki, Yoshio Tanaguchi and Arata Isozaki   153

14   Conflicting identities: Tadao Ando, Itsuko Hasagawa, Toyo Ito, Riken Yamamoto,
      Chiaki Arai and Shin Takamatsu   165

15   Relief and rebuilding: Kazuo Sejima, Kengo Kuma and Jun Aoki   187

Part V: The next generation   **199**

16   Doing more with less   201

        Atelier Bow Wow, Yoshiharu Tsukamoto and Momoyo Kajima: Office in Tokyo
        TNA, Makoto Takei and Chie Nabeshima: Mosaic House
        Ryue Nishizawa: House and Garden
        Hideyuki Nakayama Architecture: 2004 House
        Shuhei Endo: Springtecture

17   On the surface   207

        Togo Murano: Morigo Office building
        Takaharu and Yui Tezuka; Tezuka Architects: Echigo-Matsunoyama Museum
            of Natural Science
        Shuhei Endo: Environmental Education Center in Hyogo and the Tsunami
            Disaster Prevention Center in Minamiawaji Ciy
        Hitoshe Abe: F-Town and the Kanno Museum in Shiogama
        Kumiko Inui: Dior, Ginza and Shin-Yatsushiro Pavilion
        Jun Aoki and Associates: Louis Vuitton Matsuya Ginza Facade Renewal
        Hiroshi Nakamura: Lanvin Boutique
        Kiichiro Sako and Takeshi Ishizaka; Sako Architects: Romanticism shop in
            Hangzhou, China
        Masahiro and Mao Harada: Mt. Fuji Architects Studio, Sakura House
        Masaki Endoh and Masahiro Ikeda: Endoh Design, Natural Ellipse
        Hideyuki Nakayama Architecture: House SH

18 Interstitial space: the new engawa   219

        Jozan Ishikawa: Shisendo
        Tomohiro Yokomizo: Tomihiro Hoshino Museum and NYH House
        Sou Fujimoto: Musashino Library and House N, Oita
        Hitoshi Abe: Yomiuri Miyagi Guest House and Reihoku Town Hall
        Makoto Tanijiri, Suppose Design Office: House in Buzen

19 Reinventing Modernism   229

        Kumiko Inui: Apartment house
        Tomohiro Yokomiz: NYH House

Kiichiro Sako and Takeshi Ishizaka; Sako Architects: BUMPS and BEANS
Hiroshi Nakamura: Lotus Beauty Salon, Mie
Makoto Tanijiri; Suppose Design: Otake, Bishamon and Kitakumakura houses
Hitoshi Abe: Miyagi Stadium, Sendai and Sasaki-Gishi office building
Waro Kishi: Nihonbashi and Nakagyo houses

20 Technology as nature   247

Makoto Takei and Chie Nabeshima, TNA Architects: Ring House, Karuizawa
Hiroshi Nakamura and NAP: Dancing Trees, Singing Birds
Takaharu and Yui Tezuka; Tezuka Architects: Fuji Kindergarten
Junya Ishigami Office: Kanagawa Institute of Technology
Sou Fujimoto: NA House
Masahiro and Mao Harada; Mt. Fuji Architects Studio, Tree House

21 Searching for the sublime   257

Sou Fujimoto: Tokyo Apartments, Wooden House, Kumamoto, Children's
    Center for Psychiatric Rehabilitation
Hitoshi Abe, Bouno House
Akihisa Hirata: Saragaku, Tokyo

Glossary   265
Bibliography   271
Index   283

Acknowledgments

As Senior Editor at Academy Editions in London, in the early 1990s, prior to accepting a position at the University of Southern California School of Architecture in Los Angeles, it was possible to meet, interview and attend lectures and symposia by many Japanese architects, and to edit their work for both the books and the articles we were publishing about them. Among this group, Kisho Kurokawa, Arata Isozaki and Fumihiko Maki were most helpful in providing an initial introduction into the complexities of contemporary architecture in their own context, and the transcripts of the lectures that Kurokawa and Isozaki gave at that time have proven to be especially useful primers ever since.

The USC School of Architecture had no foreign studies presence in Asia and very little cultural diversity of any kind in its curriculum when I first arrived there in 1991, and so it seemed necessary to establish a base in that region, and to include more relevant material on it in the history-survey sequence and by creating several elective offerings. Although financial, logistical and linguistic issues finally dictated that the new full semester Program in Asia be based at the University of Malaysia, in Kuala Lumpur, it also included a substantial segment in Japan.

For the next 15 years, from its inauguration in 1998 until it ended in 2013, the first two weeks of that program were spent exploring Japan, seeing and analyzing significant architecture of all periods there as well as visiting architects' offices, and generally immersing myself in its richly textured history and culture. These annual visits were augmented with several additional personal trips each year and as connections increased, cultural knowledge did as well, in a multi-layered way. Yo-ichiro Hakomori was instrumental in helping to organize the early phase of that program in Japan.

A preparatory course was one of the required prerequisites for the Asia Program, to familiarize students with each of the countries they would experience prior to departure. In teaching this as well as the history-survey series with its added content on Japan, and a new elective on contemporary Asian architecture, which I introduced when the Foreign Studies initiative in the region was launched, it became obvious that no overarching text existed that covered all of the material that had to be taught. This extended to include the dearth of comprehensive coverage of the youngest generation of Japanese architects as well, which interested and engaged the students most. It became necessary to patch together readings from a variety of sources, as well as articles and field notes from office and site visits that started to accumulate, and these became touchstones for this project.

As the idea of actually attempting this project started to coalesce, Yuki Hirai helped me to select the members of the younger architects who best represent their generation.

Many people were helpful to me during the long and arduous course of completing it, both during the years that the USC Foreign Studies Program in Asia operated in Japan and the extended period of time in preparation after it ended. Among the earlier generations of architects presented here, several have been especially instructive in that regard. Kisho Kurokawa and Fumihiko Maki, mentioned earlier in the context of Academy Forum activities, continued to offer valuable advice, in addition to Hitoshi Abe, Jun Aoki, Tadao Ando, Shuhei Endo, Isao Hashimoto, Toyo Ito, Kazuhiro Ishii, Gary Kamemoto, Kazuo Sejima, Kengo Kuma and Kulapat Yantrasast, who worked for Tadao Ando at the time, but now practices in Los Angeles. Hiroko Goto, in Abe's Atelier, and Kyoko Kawahata with Jun Aoki, have been particularly helpful, as well.

The latest cohort of Japanese architects, which are the focus of this book, have been unfailingly kind in providing access to their offices and offering information about their work. They are: Yoshiharu Tsukamoto and Momoyo Kajima of Atelier Bow Wow, Hitoshi Abe, Shuhei Endo, Sou Fujimoto, Masahiro and Mao Harada, Kumiko Inui, Junya Ishigami, Hideyuki Nakayama, Hiroshi Nakamura, Ryuji Nakamura, Keiichiro Sako, Makoto Takei and Chie Nabeshima of TNA, Makoto Tanijiri, Takaharu and Yui Tezuka, Makoto Yokomizo and Shiro Doi, of Aida-Doi Architects.

During the final stages of this effort, Chiaki Arai also provided invaluable guidance, not only in helping me understand his own work, but also in putting the current scene in Japanese architecture in perspective.

Noriko Miyagawa has been invaluable as a liaison in helping me gain access to those offices and in maintaining contact with them. Noriko was initially associated with our USC Foreign Studies program as a member of the team in Japan, using her considerable skills as a tactician, during a majority of the 15 years of our two-week visits to ensure things ran smoothly. She then agreed to specifically assist on this book but, due to the pressures of her full-time job, delegated that role to Makiko Yonemura. Over the next three months, she and her colleague Fidel Toru Takahashi then helped me to make initial contact with, visit and interview most of the "next generation" firms included here. Nobuko Fujioka was extremely helpful during that early stage, and Chizuko Shimazaki assisted.

Thanks also to the many photographers who have provided images for this publication. Among those in Japan, Tomio Ohashi has been outstanding for both his extraordinary talent, and his in-depth knowledge of all of the protagonists in this narrative, as well as Daichi Ano, Ryota Atanashi, Katsuhisa Kida, Takuma Ota, Toshiyuki Yano, Haruo Shirane and Kenichi Suzuki. Among the international photographers that have contributed, I would especially like to thank Iwan Baan and Christoffer Rudquist for their wonderful images.

During the early stages of the USC program's presence in Japan, Mira "Mimi" Locher and David Stewart also made significant contributions to my understanding of the country and its architects past and present and Stewart's lectures, augmenting readings from his *The Making of a Modern Japanese Architecture* were particularly instructive at that time, providing a platform for future knowledge, as were informative sessions with Peter Popham in London and Kevin Nute, in Los Angeles.

Many others have played a critical role in numerous ways in bringing this project to fruition, including Yuki Hirai, who assisted in surveying firms at the start, Midori Mazuzawa, Nobu Fujioka and Yifei Wu who helped with research while they were students at USC, and Makoto Kanatani for his extensive knowledge of Kyoto, who helped me with logistics there.

Miki Fujiwara has also provided sustained assistance, primarily in maintaining contact with offices in Japan, image gathering and in providing photographs of her own, which have contributed substantially to this publication as well as by offering encouragement during difficult periods. Her indefatigable energy and enthusiasm have proven to be an invaluable antidote to occasional indecision and doubt. I am very indebted to her for her unwavering loyalty to this project.

Fran Ford of Taylor & Francis demonstrated seemingly infinite patience while the complex proposal for this project evolved, and I am also grateful to Grace Harrison, who has also assisted in nudging me along toward its completion.

Introduction
The (dis)continuities of Japanese architecture

Japan entered the modern world in 1868, with the advent of the Meiji Restoration, which was initiated in response to the very real threat of foreign colonization. Although the word "feudal" is controversial among historians today, the nation had operated under a social structure that fits our conventional understanding of that word during the Tokugawa Shogunate, and remained deliberately isolated and unchanged for hundreds of years. In rapid succession over the course of the next two generations, it careened through social, cultural and technical transformations of unprecedented speed and scope, starting with an embrace of Western ideas and values, followed by a reflexive, xenophobic retrenchment enveloped in hyper-nationalism and militarization, a devastating World War, the foreign occupation it had originally feared, rapid recovery and re-building, an economic bubble, a stock market collapse, and finally regression, stagnation and self-doubt.

The power of the media

A new generation now confronts an unbounded but also uncertain and troubling future, along with the possibility of equally dramatic upheavals, due to the geopolitical shifts now underway in both the region and the world, as well as within their own country. The young architects of that cohort, at the bottom of an inflexible ancestral hierarchy, are the standard bearers of a proud, carefully conceived heritage, incrementally crafted during these previous periods of unprecedented change, as a collective expression of difference. That fragile image, in turn, is also rooted in a profoundly complicated national tradition, overlaid by what is undoubtedly the most technically advanced and densely saturated information society in the world.

Multiple forms of media constantly bombard the senses in endless competition for visual and mental attention in this "empire of signs" that French theorist Roland Barthes has described so well. It is evident that its youngest generation of architects are extremely proficient in using its latest digital iteration to both separate themselves from the crowded field of new personalities that enter the profession each year, and in leveraging the smallest, seemingly insignificant projects into larger ones, with incrementally extensive global reach. By strategically using the Internet and social media, as well as the surprisingly effective device of mini-exhibitions that now seem to be constantly on offer throughout Tokyo and other major cities in Japan, they are able to amplify the typical range of small, entry-level projects available to young architects into substantial reputations and international fame.

While the use of the media is a time-honored way for architects to get noticed, ever since Adolf Loos launched *Das Andere,* and Le Corbusier followed suit with *L'Esprit Nouveau,* this phenomenon of capitalizing on the nexus between electronic hype and a complicit curatorial underground that provides frequent, small, pop-up exhibitions certainly is.[1]

The latest generation that is the final focus of this investigation must navigate an incredibly complicated cultural landscape, but they also stand a chance of finally being able to break free of many of the most repressive parts of its gravitational pull, which have ancient roots but started to coalesce at the beginning of the Meiji Restoration a century and a half ago. To bring the challenges they face into proper perspective and in order to fully appreciate the disjunctions that confront them, it is necessary to analyze the complex legacy of the entirety of the proud public consciousness that they represent. Among the many other, less daunting options available, this elusive goal inevitably indicated a roughly chronological, historically based framework, to position the next generation within a wider context, culminating in a review of the most legible issues that seem to characterize the work of young architects in Japan today. The dendritic path of discovery that ensued uncovered several recurring themes, which in no specific order include the following.

Sempai-Kohai: senior–junior relationships and professional genealogy

While apprenticeship continues to represent an important part of an architect's education throughout the world today, it is especially important to consider the aesthetic and stylistic lineage that derives from such relationships in Japan when trying to critique individual projects within the context of the culture they represent. Japanese architects continue to observe the age-old *Giri-On*, or superior-subordinate protocol, between a teacher, or *Sensei* and student or a master and an apprentice, which have remained intact in spite of the rejection of the past fostered by the Meiji Restoration. In fact, it has now become evident that the well-established, deeply entrenched hierarchical relationships between those engaged in the building trades not only survived this sudden, profoundly radical collective bifurcation, but have also provided a critical framework for future change.

This narrative of the venerable practice of apprenticeship in all trades and crafts has also extended to architects, because of the unique way that the profession has evolved over time and is still viewed in Japan today. Architects have historically been considered to be just one of the many categories of *Kenchikushi* or construction trades, and there is still no legal distinction between them. While expressing respect for this traditional habit of designers becoming builders, the Japan Institute of Architects has voiced its concern about the dangers posed by what could be construed as a conflict of interest, eerily echoing a similar debate that raged within the American Institute of Architects until very recently, in which architects that also participated in the building process were considered to be somehow tainted by commercial interests and suspected of compromising their values.

Giri-On relationships, as one of the hierarchies that continue to both compartmentalize and standardize social experience in Japan, are still perpetuated through mutually reinforcing rituals, and it will be instructive to track the ways in which they guide future careers.[2]

Doken Kokka: the Construction State

Another closely related challenge facing the next generation is how to navigate the seemingly implacable legacy of the trilogy of politicians, financial institutions and contractors commonly referred to as the *Doken Kokka*, or Construction State, which can be traced back to the Meiji Restoration, and the fact that Japanese architects have evolved, over the last century and a half, in a symbiotic relationship with the political and economic forces that have transformed their nation. The so-called "big five" group of general contractors in Japan today, who are part of this triumvirate, are the Kajima Corporation, Shimizu Kentetsu, Obasyashi Gumi, Taisei Kentetsu and Takenaka Komuten, who counted 70,000 employees between them in 2006, all have very large design departments and all started as carpenters' guilds at the end of Tokugawa rule, or soon afterward. Kajima Iwakichi started his "Kaisha" or firm in 1840, Shimizu Kisuke in 1804, Obayashi Yoshigoro in 1892, Taisei begun as Okura Kihachiro in 1887, and Takenaka, which is the oldest, established by Takenaka Tobei Masataka, in 1610.[3] Each of these, and other smaller firms that were formed at that time and have thrived as their country has developed, were able to quickly adapt from using traditional methods of wood construction to the industrial material, such as steel, glass and concrete, which the new, modern buildings that were in demand required.

Because Japan tied its economic, if not its existential fate to the rising American star right after World War II, it quickly became the first developed nation in the Asia Pacific region. Due to Article 9 in its newly adopted Constitution, which limited its defense budget to a token amount to be spent for domestic protection, Japan was also able to funnel the majority of the money that would have otherwise been spent on a defense budget into development. As soon as the Occupation ended, architects were needed to re-design and re-build an urban landscape that had essentially been eradicated by war, and they were soon surfing on the providential wave of prosperity provided by this deficit as well as economic windfall provided by the Marshall Plan, and were able to convert its war-time industries, the Zaibatsu, to the production of military supplies that the United States needed in the Korean War.

Within a mere three decades, and in spite of a chronic shortage of raw materials of its own that forced it to become an export economy, trade deficits disappeared and Japan managed to leverage these advantages into becoming the world's second largest per capita GDP, with an average annual economic growth rate of 4 to 5 percent and a reputation as a global leader in technological excellence. In a scenario that echoes Chinese growth today, trade surpluses increased and the real estate market not only expanded domestically, but Japanese investors also began to purchase foreign properties on a large scale. This "miracle" was realized incrementally through three periods of Post War expansion. The first was the "Iwato Boom" or "high economic growth period" of the late 1950s, of 10 per cent per year, that occurred once basic infrastructure was finally established, and the national focus shifted to technology. The second boom was fueled by Prime Minister Kakuei Tanaka's "Re-modeling the Japanese Archipelago" Program, which was launched in 1972 but cut short by the "oil shocks" that followed soon afterward. The third phase of this expansion was the Heisei Boom from 1987 to 1990, followed by the crash of the Japanese "Bubble Economy" the next year.[4]

The *Doken Kokka*, or Construction State, evolved exponentially during these three phases of growth, from initially addressing the essential need of replacing and improving missing infrastructure to a financial behemoth supporting the entire Japanese social safety net. Despite a radically altered economic landscape during the "Lost Decade" that followed this collapse, in which surpluses morphed into huge deficits, a well-established pattern of massive public works projects continued, mostly because they were seen as a way to reverse decline and stave off unemployment. At the beginning of the crash, more than 40 percent of the Japanese annual national budget was being funneled into construction.[5]

Due to their close, essentially indistinguishable association with contractors, and their mutual reliance on official approvals and largesse, architects were inextricably caught up in this addictive cycle as it transitioned from infrastructure to "extra-structure" as a make-work system that continued to enrich all concerned. The latest generation of their number has inherited this nightmare, which threatens not only financial but environmental disaster as the relentless leveling of the archipelago rolls on.[6]

Revisiting the future

Modernism is another recurring issue that has once again engaged the next generation of architects in Japan, just as it seems to have absorbed their predecessors and many others throughout Asia today. Those who rebuilt Japan after World War II may have literally had to begin from the ground up, but they did have the benefit of a sound theoretical framework to start with. Modernism, with both a large and small "m," along with the wholesale adoption of Western styles and values that accompanied it, had been introduced almost 80 years earlier, during the Meiji Restoration in 1868, and to contextualize that framework, the debate that followed between the advocates of tradition and those for change is presented in some detail here. Modernism, with a capital "M" was eventually deemed to be too liberal and revolutionary to serve a war-time Imperial purpose, but after that enormously destructive period ended it re-emerged as not only the symbol of progress that it had been during the Meiji era, but also as a political statement about the victory of freedom and democracy over Fascism.

The choice of Kenzo Tange, along with Sachio Otani and Takashi Asada, to design the Hiroshima Peace Center and to rebuild this devastated city, and the selection of Tange to also design the Olympic Complex in Tokyo for the Games that were held there in 1964 underscored the unmistakable national message that not only a modern re-birth but also recovery had finally been achieved and that Japan had finally returned from the ashes.

Modernism permeates the architecture that followed as well. Historian Ioanna Angelidou has perceptively noted that the Giri-On ritual also played an important role in this transition since, rather than resisting Western innovation, "the relation of master and disciple fostered the acceptance of modernist principles as representative of progress and the subsequent idealization of modern architecture" and, subsequently, "the discussion over tradition and adaptation nurtured an architectural culture of dialogical manifestation through a combination of practice and representation."[7]

That intense and obdurate sense of national pride, and the competitive hope of finally being able to technically and economically prevail over a Western foe, not only seems to have softened considerably, but has arguably disappeared entirely. There is a new level of sophistication in evidence that indicates that both the memory of traditional constructs and the envy of foreign forms is now irrelevant and that the seemingly relentless cycle of assimilation and rejection of Western values and aesthetics has finally ended.

A noticeable indicator of this new self-confidence is an almost unanimous rejection of parametric modeling, in favor of the less predictable heuristic discoveries made possible by graphic investigation. The child-like joy found in the first sketches that many young Japanese architects use to reveal their ideas to themselves and others, regardless of the technical difficulty of the final scheme, is noticeably absent in the impersonal computer graphics and lack of conceptual investigation that seem to pass for design elsewhere in the developed world today. They have courageously resisted the lure of the electronic imperative in the early stages of project evolution, in spite of the high level of technological skill they possess, in the understanding that algorithms do not easily equate with tradition, and are unable to translate the rich cultural heritage they represent.

New environmental imperatives: re-inventing nature

Empathy with and a reverence for nature and sensitivity to its rhythms, further enhanced by geography that heightens the poignancy of each of its four seasons, is an integral part of that heritage, and has historically inspired and informed both the spiritual and aesthetic life of the Japanese people. That leitmotif also runs throughout each of the chapters that follow, culminating in a polemical, structured commentary about the very real prospect of a future in which, in spite of this awareness, technology wins and nature is gone for good. The early twentieth-century American poet Joyce Kilmer famously said that "only God can make a tree," but that hasn't deterred many of the young architects presented here from trying to create suitable metaphors of their own in anticipation of a time when real trees disappear.[8]

The historical imperative

All of these topics revolve around one of the biggest issues confronting Japanese architects today, which is their own history and how to assess, unravel and negotiate it, and how to assimilate it in a way that allows them to confront outside influences as well. And, since this is Japan, where events that took place thousands of years ago, and the architecture that resulted from them are a daily source of discussion and reference, no serious critique of the ways in which they are managing to do that would be complete without at least an annotated overview of that complex past.

As this narrative unfolds, it eventually becomes obvious that no matter how distanced the work of any of the architects discussed here seems to be from that collective legacy, it remains to be discovered, in various permutations, at different depths just below the surface, and in spite of denials it can be shown to inform all of the creative decisions they make.

This proof is more challenging with the latest generation, who ostensibly seem to be the most distanced from their heritage and talk and write far less about it than their predecessors have. And yet, it is there, and open to discovery to those with a critical eye and willingness to look for it. The danger here, of course, is falling into the trap of confirmatory bias, in which one seeks information that is consistent with personal beliefs or stereotypes, and selects accordingly, to confirm them. And yet, the evidence presented speaks for itself.[9]

Notes

1   Ioanna Angelidou, "Intertwinements," *MAS Context*, 9, Networks.

2   Brian J. McVeigh, *The Nature of the Japanese State*, London: Nissan Institute/Routledge Japanese Studies Series, 1998.

3   Hiroshi Shimizu, *Japanese Firms in Contemporary Singapore*, Singapore: NUS Press, 2008, p. 153.

4   Shigenori Shiratsuka, "The Asset Price Bubble in Japan in the 1980s: Lessons for Financial and Macro-economic Stability," IMF-BIF Conference on Real Estate Indicators and Financial Stability, International Monetary Fund, Washington, D.C. October 27–28, 2003, p. 43.

5   Gavan McCormack, "Breaking Japan's Iron Triangle," *The New Left Review*, 13, January–February 2002, p. 11.

6   Gavan McCormack, *The Emptiness of Japanese Affluence*, M.E. Sharpe, 2001, p. 62.

7   Ioanna Angelidou, "Intertwinements," *MAS Context*, 9, Networks.

8   Joyce Kilmer, *Trees and Other Poems*, New York: George H. Doran Co., 1914, p. 19.

9   Raymond Nickerson, "Confirmation Bias: A Ubiquitous Phenomenon in Many Guises," *Review of General Psychology*, 2, 2, 1998, pp. 175–220.

PART I

An enduring cultural framework

CHAPTER 1

The land and its people

History is never far away in Japan, to an extent that is rare elsewhere in the world. A thousand years seem like yesterday and the past is always foremost in the national subconscious. This keen awareness of a unified memory is even more evident among each generation of its architects, who constantly refer to it, making at least a rudimentary understanding of the entirety of their cultural recollection an absolute necessity.

A belief in divine origins

An essential component of any cohesive cultural entity is a binding foundation myth, and it is difficult to surpass a belief in a divine origin as a collective claim to authority. As in other mythologies, such as the Hindu *Ramayana*, or the *Theogony* by Hesiod, which codified the Hellenic pantheon or the *Prose and Poetic Edda* and Icelandic sagas, which did the same for the Norse and Germanic cosmology, the deities described in the Japanese equivalent, *The Kojiki or Record of Ancient Matters*, have a tantalizing combination of supernatural and distinctly human traits, making it seem almost possible that the stories are partially based on real people.

The collective narrative in the *Kojiki* begins with a God and a Goddess on a bridge (Ama-no-uki-hashi) who have descended from Takama-ga-hara or "the high plain of heaven."[1] They are named Izanagi (he who invites) and Izanami, (she who invites) and after they dipped a lance into the primordial ocean below them,

the droplets from the tip formed Onogoroshima, which they then inhabited and populated.

Kagu-tsuchi, the God of Fire, who was the last of their children, fatally burned Izanagi during childbirth. This and the subsequent journey of Izanami to the "Land of the Dead" mark a critical turning point in the Kojiki, from creation to destruction, similar to the expulsion of Adam and Eve from the Garden of Eden in the Judeo-Christian tradition.[2]

The descent into Yomi

In passages that also echo similar motifs in other myths, Izanagi followed his wife to the underworld, to bring her back, but found she could not return because she had "eaten at the hearth of Yomi." He begged the Gods to release her, but then, when he finally saw her horribly disfigured body he ran away.[3] A chase ensued, first by Izanami's female followers, then by the Goddess herself, but Izanagi reached the gateway of Yomi first, and rolled a boulder across it, sealing them inside. In washing away the stench of death, Izanagi gave birth to the Goddess of the Sun, Amaterasu Omikami (literally: "shining over heaven, great spirit") the God of the Moon, Tsukiyomi-no-mikoto (Moon Counting, or Moonlit night), and the God of Summer Storms and the Sea, Susano-o-no-Mikoto ("his swift, impetuous, male-augustness").

His father banished Susanoo-no-Mikoto from Takama-ga-hara for both his neglect of his duties and his bad behavior, but before leaving he asked to say good-bye to his sister Amaterasu. During their final meeting, Susano-o suggested that he prove the sincerity of his intentions by producing more male deities than she could, after each of them chose something belonging to the other. Susano-o took his sister's jewelry, and after eating it, gave birth to five sons. Amaterasu, in turn, shattered and ate Susano-o's sword, and produced three daughters. Amaterasu claimed the sons as her own, however, because they were born from her necklace, causing her brother to leave in anger. He returned later and as one renowned translator recounts, broke "a hole in the roof of the hall in Heaven where his sister is sitting at work with the celestial weaving-maidens," and tossed in "a heavenly piebald horse, which he had flayed with a backward flaying."[4]

Ama no Iwato: the rock cave of heaven

To escape this attack, Amaterasu retreated into Ama-no-Iwato, "the heavenly rock cave" casting the world into darkness and ushering in a time when evil freely roamed the earth. Then, according to the Nihon Shoki or "Chronicles of Japan," which followed the Kojiki, the heavenly deities met and agreed upon a course of action, to dig up a Sakaki tree from Mt. Kagu, hang a string of Yasaka jewels on the upper branches, a mirror in the middle and blue and white colored offerings below, and then to recite a liturgy. These offerings, along with a highly erotic dance by Ame-no-Uzume-mikoto ("Her Augustness Heavenly Alarming Female"), who was wearing only a moss belt and Sasaki-leaf headdress, finally enticed Amaterasu to roll away the rock door and step outside.[5] Once she did this, a rope was placed across the mouth of the cave and Amaterasu was forbidden to re-enter. This rope is now recalled in the shimenawa marking the entrance to sacred Shinto shrines.

Susano-o on Earth

In exile in Izumo for causing this mayhem, Susano-o rescued the daughter of an elderly couple he encountered by slaying the dragon *Yamata-no-orochi* ("eight-forked serpent"). After slicing it open, he found the "Sword of the Gathering Clouds of Heaven" inside.

He presented this to Amaterasu as a peace offering, and she subsequently passed it, along with the necklace and mirror, to her son Ame no oshihomimi, who then bequeathed it to her grandson Ninigi. The legend continues to recount that Ninigi in turn brought them to earth, and they were subsequently passed to Jinmu Tenno, who was the first recorded Emperor of Japan.

Symbolism and significance

In 707, the Empress Genmei commissioned court poet Ōno Yasumaro to complete an existing compilation of stories, the Kojiki and the Nihon Shoki, about imperial genealogy as well as other myths and legends begun by the Emperor Temmu, and his son Prince Toneri.[6] Genmei and Yasumaro fastened on the theme of rice agriculture to clearly set Japan apart from China, and selectively chose myths and legends that would allow the Yamato regime to claim ownership of it. The Sun Goddess Amaterasu played a key role in this construct as both the symbol of fertility and originator of rice cultivation, and the progenitor of the Japanese Imperial line.

Taken together, these histories parallel other profoundly significant socio-theological and philosophical texts, such as the Quran, Torah, Bible, Bhagavad Gita, Analects, and the Tao Te Ching because they establish the foundation of Shinto, which is a singularly Japanese religion. Although generally described as animistic and translated as "the Way of the Gods," from the Chinese *shen dao*, or "way of the spirits," Shinto revolves around "kami" which are invisible spiritual essences, or "hidden sources."[7]

The Kojiki and Nihon Shoki create a chronology that effectively binds the Shinto pantheon to Yamoto authority, describing how Ninigi no Mikoto, who was the grandson of Amaterasu, was sent to earth to teach people to cultivate the land. Ninigi's great-grandchild Yamato Iwarehiko became the first Yamoto ruler and was re-named Jinmu. Rather than the inheritance of the "three treasures" of the sword, necklace and mirror, that are now the symbols of Imperial power in Japan, the most important legacy that Amaraterasu gave to Jinmu and the Yamoto people was both the physical sustenance and symbolic authority that came with the gift of rice.[8]

Ideology aside, both the Kojiki and Nihon Shoki also provide compelling insights into the socio-cultural mores of the time in which they were written. In the first of many stark contrasts between Eastern and Western belief systems that will subsequently be presented here, the description of the interactions between Izanagi and Izanami and Amaterasu and Susano-o not only reveal an overt male chauvinism, if not blatant misogyny, but also a marked suspension of moral judgment, in favor of more abstract, amoral, situational ethics.[9]

Two sacred Shinto shrines at Izumo and Ise

The spirits of Amaterasu and Susano-o still remain physically separated in the earthly realm, with his being evoked at Izumo Taisha in Shimane, and hers specifically enshrined at Ise-shi in Mie Prefecture. Although Izumo is officially dedicated to Susano-o's son-in-law Ōkuninushi it radiates the presence of "his swift impetuous, Male-Augustness" because it is the oldest and largest shrine in Japan. In 2009, the oldest stone implements on the archipelago were found near here, pushing back the date of origin to about 120,000 years ago. Its initial construction is shrouded in mystery, but it is mentioned in the Nihon Shoki that the Empress Saimei ordered it to be repaired. It is known to have been periodically re-built every 60 years in its exact form until 1744, and only renovated whenever necessary since then.[10] The Honden, or main hall, which is the most sacred part of the complex, and is considered to be where the spirit of the deity or kami resides, has a square plan with a pillar in the center. This recalls the passage in the Kojiki that describes the descent of Izanagi and Izanami to Onogoroshima, and flirtingly circling around a single column, the Ama-no-mihashira or "pillar of heaven," before they united, had children and built a palace on top of it.[11]

Recent archeological investigation has revealed that there were originally nine clusters of three tree trunks each, with each tree being one meter in diameter. In addition to the central pillar cluster, each of the walls of the square Honden had two equally spaced column clusters. The Honden was also once 48 meters high, elevated on a platform accessible only by a ramp.

The Shrine of Amaterasu at Ise has an equally quasi-mythological timeline, but an apocryphal history maintains that the Emperor Sujin relocated a Shrine to the Sun Goddess that already existed on the grounds of his Palace to Kasunui, close to Tawaramoto, in Nara Prefecture near where the Buddhist temple of Jinraku-ji is now located. The next, equally quasi-mythical Emperor Suinin, subsequently sent his daughter, Princess Yamatohime-no-mikoto, to find an even more suitable location for the Shrine, and after 20 years of searching, she had a vision, in which Amaterasu appeared to her and directed her to Ise. The Princess encircled the site she had selected with chimes, which is why the river that demarcates it is named "Isuzu" or "fifty bells."[12]

In spite of this ancient fourth-century BC lineage, however, the first Shrine, or Naiku dedicated to Amaterasu, did not appear until the Asuka period, during the reign of the Emperor Tenmu, (672 to 686 AD). There must have been an earlier structure here however, even if only a sacred column, or shin-no-mihashira, (tree of heaven, or heart column) of cryptomeria or Sakaki wood because Geku, which is a second outer Shrine dedicated to Toyouke Omikami, the Goddess of Grain meant to serve Amaterasu, is thought to have been built by the Yamoto Emperor Yuryaku, between 456 and 479 AD (Figure 1.1).

In addition to the Honden, or Shoden, as it is referred to at Ise, which is thought to be inhabited by the kami, each of these Shrines consists of several subsidiary structures, used as treasuries, all surrounded by three successive rows of fencing. Each of these is also built from Japanese cypress, or Hinoki, prized for its straightness, fine grain, ability to be easily split, distinctive scent and resistance to rot. Large columns at each end of the main ridge beam support the roof and walls of the Shoden. These recall the central "heart column" and also touch the ground with no footings, to better serve as conduits to transport the kami from heaven to earth. In spite of being rot-resistant, Hinoki does start to seriously decompose in about two decades, and so 16 separate structures as well as the Uji bridge over the Isuzu River that provides access to them are torn down and replaced in a reconstruction ceremony called the "Shikinen sengu" that has taken place with only a few interruptions every 20 years since the first rebuilding by Tenmu's wife, the Empress Jito in 692 AD. The most

Figure 1.1 Ise Shrine
Source: Haruo Nakano

serious gaps occurred during the Onin War from 1467 to 1477 and the most difficult part of World War II, during the bombing raids which lasted from 1944 until Japan surrendered on September 2, 1945, but otherwise these reconstructions have been carried out for over 1,300 years.

A series of rituals mark various stages of the reconstruction sequence, beginning with Okibiki hajime-shike, or pulling the first of thousands of logs to be used in the building of Naiku up the Isuzu river and carting others for Geku to its site. The 500-year-old Hinoki trees needed to produce the logs of the diameter required for the construction of these shoden were once readily available on site, but now must be brought in from elsewhere.

The Sengyo, which is one of the most profoundly moving of these ceremonies, involves the relocation of an ancient mirror, only at night and enclosed by white sheets to protect it from view, from the old shoden to the new one. The go-shintai, or "sacred body" of Amaterasu is believed to be captured in it, echoing a taboo held in many traditional societies today, that capturing one's image also captures the soul. Rather than being glass this is an ancient bronze disc similar to those produced during the Spring and Autumn period and Han Dynasty in China, and traded into Japan between 200 BC and 200 AD. They have a very high tin content, allowing one side to be polished and reflective, while the other side was left rough and decorated in high relief. In addition to the wooden structures of each of the shrines, more than 1,600 "treasures" are also reproduced, but this mirror has never been replicated.[13]

The closest historical parallel to Ise is the Parthenon in Athens, built between 438 and 432 BC. Like Ise, which was intended to strengthen the legitimacy of the Emperor, it was also designed to enshrine a deity that not only embodied the socio-political entity she represented, but also proclaimed a desire for Imperial hegemony. Recent extensive attempts to discover how this marble masterpiece was built, however, clearly illustrate the difference between the two. In spite of the fact that Ise is made of highly perishable materials, the method of construction used today is essentially the same as it was 1,300 years ago, because, unlike the Parthenon, it has been passed down during a 20-year cycle that matches the passage from one generation to the next. Small groups accomplish this transfer. These include older, more experienced carpenters and young apprentices, with each group focusing on a different part of the structure. The actual process of construction only takes place during the last three years of the cycle, preceded by an initial planning and material gathering stage, and the fabrication of all elements that can be made ahead.

Unlike the Izumo Shrine, which has a decidedly non-rural curved roof, with an entrance on the shorter front end of its rectangular plan, the doors of the Ise Shrines are in the center of the long side of the rectangle, and the roofs are emphatically straight, emphasizing their Japanese-ness. They are also built of locally accessible materials, such as Hinoki, and Kaya reeds, surrounded by a carpet of white river stones, as well as more sophisticated decorative features made of precious metal and enamel. This contrast establishes a dialectical tension between the simple and the complex, the native and imported that recalls the deliberate adoption of Chinese culture initiated by Prince Shotoku during the Taika Reforms in 645 AD.[14]

Ise is one of several traditional buildings that are constantly referred to by architects of all generations of Japan. It has generated a great deal of discussion and debate, and has been the subject of many books, due to both its significance and provenance. Kisho Kurokawa has perhaps best described its deeper meaning, saying that

although the visible, material object, its physical existence, might be destroyed every twenty years, it was believed that its heritage was transmitted and the tradition preserved as long as the invisible tradition that lay behind the object, with its aesthetic and sense of order, was passed on spiritually from generation to generation. In contrast to the materialistic aesthetic of Western civilization, which sought eternity for its architectural monuments, we can call the Japanese a more spiritual aesthetic.[15]

The Jomon and the Yayoi

The question of the origin of the first population of Japan is polemical, given the extent of ongoing scientific research and new archeological discoveries, as well as the profound socio-political implications involved. Distinctive, flame-like pottery shards, dating back to at least 10,000 years ago, have given this indigenous population the name "Jomon", or "cord-marked" because rope was pressed into the wet clay of free-formed pots before they were fired to decorate them.

They lived in wood frame and thatched houses during the winter, which were excavated to about six feet into the earth to preserve heat and stabilize temperatures during the bitterly cold winter months, alternating with cooler, elevated platforms in the summer. Their houses were circular, about 12 to 15 feet in diameter, with a hard earth floor and a hearth on a stone circle in the center (Figure 1.2). Their settlements were concentrated in central Honshu, especially near Toyama Bay, and along the eastern coast, and bone hooks found in them indicate that they were hunter-gatherers, subsisting mainly on fish. As they advanced toward the Neolithic age, they also farmed and planted rice, but not to a large extent.

Then, a new population entered Japan about 300 BC, probably across the narrow strait that separates South Korea from Kyushu. Its pottery is clearly differentiated from Jomon samples, based on smooth-sided containers found in the Yayoi district in Bunkyo-ku, Tokyo Prefecture, near the Hongo Campus of Tokyo University in 1884, giving this group its name.

The Jomon and Yayoi cultures co-existed for about 500 years and although skilled in other ways, the Yayoi first adopted the subterranean Jomon house as their own.[16] The Yayoi, however, concentrated on growing rice and created a barn to protect this valuable labor-intensive commodity from moisture and vermin. This Austronesian typology, which is still used throughout Asia, is basically a long, rectilinear wooden storage space, raised about six to eight feet above the ground on two ranks of round wooden columns, and covered with a steeply sloped roof thatched with rice straw (Figure 1.3). The designation, which is based on ethnographic, anthropological and archeological similarities, has now been expanded to identify formal similarities in the vernacular architecture of Taiwanese Indonesian, Malay, Melanesian, Micronesian, and Polynesian sub-groups. The tripartite horizontal division of both of the Ise shrines, with their columnar

Figure 1.2 Jomon house
Source: Hartmut Poeling

Figure 1.3 Jomon Rice Barn
Source: Midori Mazuzawa

Figure 1.4 Minka farm house
Source: James Steele

base, elevated box-like body and wide-eaved overhanging roof, strongly resembles this rice-barn typology.[17]

This early, Jomon-Yayoi house form is recalled today in the Minka farmhouse, (Figure 1.4) with its heavily thatched roof, and has been reinterpreted by Makoto Tanigiri in a partially submerged residence that he has designed (Figure 1.5). They initially clustered in the lowlands and marshy areas and in fields that could be easily cleared to be able to plant rice and their initial population, estimated to have been about 1,000,000,

grew quickly. Their knowledge of wet-rice cultivation and metallurgy provided them with the refined skills needed to dig the irrigation ditches and prepare the fields for planting. The 1-meter wide, 260-meter long Kaerumataike Dam on the Yodo River, in the Kansai region near Nara, which was built in 162 AD, is an impressive example of the vast engineering effort they expended to grow rice.

The anthropological term for what followed is a "socio-technological complex"; the ability to impose the

Figure 1.5 Pyramid House
Source: Makoto Tanagiri

hierarchical system of organization required to implement rice farming on a large scale, based on the control of the human capital necessary for such a labor-intensive endeavor. Because of the high degree of social cooperation in rice farming and harvesting, it came to shape the entire Yayoi populace, creating a "shame culture" which ostracized those who shirked or did not assist, as opposed to the "guilt culture" that evolved in tandem with Christianity in the West, and also came to symbolize their identity and helped them to become a viable presence within the rapidly changing dynamic of the powerful entities that surrounded them.[18]

They found that increasing the number of laborers increased the yield, making multiple plantings of at least one rice harvest and other crops possible each year. With so much social capital invested in rice production, the protection of land and water rights understandably became more important, which explains the walls, moats and watchtowers found at archeological sites today, mostly excavated recently.[19]

These finds indicate that, after establishing a foothold at Harunotsuji on Iki, an island in the Korea Strait, and then in Fukuoka, at Kojindani, Hirabaru and Yoshinogari, in Saga Prefecture, the Yayoi advanced into the Jomon heartland to the north-east. Successive sites, at Ikegami-Sone, Izume, near Osaka, Karako Kagi, in Tawaramoto, Nara Prefecture, Yamaki Toro, in the Suruga Ward in Shizuoka City, about 80 miles south of Tokyo, mark that determined trajectory.[20]

During the Ch'in and Han Dynasties Chinese metal artifacts, including bronze weapons, were traded into Japan, and at that point, their advances put the Yayoi in a better position to acquire and copy them. At the dawn of the Iron Age, the Yayoi had also perfected weapons using this new material, and from the third century AD onward their hegemony expanded rapidly.

Notes

1   Roy Starrs, "The *Kojiki* as Japan's National Narrative" in *Asian Futures, Asian Traditions*, Edwina Palmer (Ed.) Folkestone, KT: Global Oriental, 2005.

2   Basil Hall Chamberlain, *Kojiki: Records of Ancient Matters*, Presented at the Asiatic Society of Japan, Kobe, 1882. Re-printed by Tuttle Publishing, 1981, p. 64.

3   Ibid.

4   Ibid.

5   Patricia Monaghan, *Encyclopedia of Goddesses and Heroines, Africa, Eastern Mediterranean, Asia*, Vol. 1, Greenwood, ABC-CLIO, 2010, p. 141.

6   Sakamoto Taro, *The Six National Histories of Japan*, Vancouver: UBC Press, 1991, p. 17.

7   Sokyo Ono, *Shinto: The Kami Way*, Tokyo: Tuttle, 1992. And Sonoda Minoru, *The World of Shinto*, International Shinto Foundation, Tokyo, 2009.

8   William George Aston, *Nihongi; Chronicles of Japan from the Earliest Times to A.D. 697*, in *Collected Works of William George Aston*, Ganesha, 1997, p. 66.

9   Kenneth Henshall, *A History of Japan from Stone Age to Superpower*, Basingstoke: Palgrave, 1994, p. 7: "an avoidance of moral judgement as to good or evil, behavior is accepted or rejected depending on the situation, not according to any obvious set of universal principles."

10   William George Aston, op. cit., p. 42.

11   Robert Treat Paine and Alexander Soper, *The Art and Architecture of Japan*, New Haven and London: Yale University Press and Pelican History of Art, 1958, p. 275.

12   Brian Bocking, *The Oracles of the Three Shrines: Windows on Japanese Religion*, Richmond, Surrey: Curzon Press, 2001, p. 51.

13   Cassandra Adams, "Japan's Ise Shrine and Its Thirteen-Hundred-Year-Old Reconstruction Tradition," *Journal of Architectural Education*, 1998, pp. 46–60. Estimated to have cost $320 million for the 1993 Sengu.

14   Ibid., p. 50.

15   Kisho Kurokawa, "Architecture," Wiley, 1993, p. 38.

16   Robert Treat Paine and Alexander Soper, op. cit., p. 23.

17   Ezrin Arbi, "Austronesian Vernacular Architecture and the Ise Shrine of Japan: Is There Any Connection?" Department of Architecture, Faculty of the Built Environment, University of Malaya, Kuala Lumpur. See also: Roxana Waterson, *The Living House: An Anthropology of Architecture in South-East Asia*, 3rd Edition, Thames and Hudson: Oxford University Press, 1997; and Peter Bellwood, James J. Fox, and Darrell Tryon, (Eds.) *The Austronesians, Historical and Comparative Perspectives*, Canberra: Australian National University Press, 1995.

18   Emiko Ohnuki-Tierney, *Rice as Self: Japanese Identities Through Time*, Princeton University Press, 1993. Quoted by Nold Egenter in "Rice in Japan: You Are What You Eat," *The Economist*, December 24, 2009:

> the planting of rice has an intimate bearing on Japan's indigenous religion, Shintoism. The religion makes a virtue of the idea of subordination of self-interest to the well being of the group. Scholars believe this may stem from the traditional labour-intensity of rice cultivation, in which all members of the village were required to help sow, weed and harvest, and water had to be shared out with scrupulous fairness (even today, two-thirds of Japan's water goes to its paddies). Those who did not co-operate risked being shunned, in a chilling village practice known as *murahachibu*; it could lead to ostracisation of a farmer and his descendants. There may be traces of this in the striking conformity that visitors to Japan notice today.

19   Mark Hudson and Gina L. Barnes, "Yoshinogari. A Yayoi Settlement in Northern Kyushu," *Monumenta Nipponica* Vol. 46, No. 2 (Summer, 1991), pp. 211–235.

20   A. Goto, *The Japanese People Seen from the Sea Side: History of Japan with a Focus on the People Living in the Coastal Areas*, Tokyo: Kodansha, 2010.

CHAPTER 2

History and religion

The social norms and characteristics of every culture are both embedded in and revealed by their written history, and those accustomed to a clear, linear, chronological sequence of historical events and a constant, easily recognizable cast of characters will be especially frustrated by any re-telling of this earliest period of Japan's distant past. It is replete with quasi-mythical figures with unverified inter-related progeny that become kings and queens, constant unresolved arguments about identity, mysterious invaders of unknown origin that eventually become dominant, conflicting dates, and a disputed layering of historical periods with different names depending on which academic you believe.

History is indeed written by the victor, and in this case it is the Yamato rather than the Jomon or Yayoi versions that are reflected in these atavistic myths. They strengthened their legitimacy and were a defensive mechanism against increasingly powerful neighbors. Sociologists classify such taxonomies as being either mixed, or "rhizotic" or bounded and discrete which they refer to as "cladistic," like the Yamato; conforming to a tribal model derived from a belief in an identifiable family tree.[1]

Transition from Yayoi villages to a Yamoto state

The real story here, then, is of the critical transition that took place during a second, final historically important appropriation of power, by the Yamoto, and so we start there.

It is even less perfectly understood than the first, but one possibility is an invasion. Two options are the "horse-rider" theory proposed by Egami Namio in 1948, or that the Baekje Kingdom, which was in an expansionist phase in the middle of the fourth century, also spilled over into Japan. Both the Nihon-ji and the Korean Samguk-sagi, mention an emissary to the Yamato court in 397, indicating that the Emperor Ojin, who originated in Kyushu, may have been the founder, leading to a first wave of Paekche immigration, then another during the reign of Yuriaku in 463.[2]

It is also possible that one of the indigenous Yayoi clans, or Uji, became more powerful than the others. However, there are significant differences between this new, Yamato entity and the Uji they subjugated. The Yayoi were essentially crafts-based farmers and metalworkers, quite literally had a grassroots, bottom-up federated organization concentrated around a ceremonial culture led by a Shaman. An early example is Queen Himiko, recorded in the Chinese text Wei Zhi in 240 AD, as having ruled Yamatai, perhaps Yoshinogari, in Fukuoka, until her death in 248 AD.[3]

The Yamoto, by contrast, were a top-down, control-oriented, institutionally based and highly stratified society entirely focused on social status and land ownership. They organized their territory into provinces and districts each governed by a royal estate that paid taxes to a central authority. Their social organization mirrored the exclusionary class distinctions of the Korean "bone-rank" system, using the kabana, or family name code of hereditary titles. Unlike the Yayoi, the Yamato rulers also used laborers from Korea to boost rice production. This allowed them to expand previous engineering projects, such as diverting the Ishikawa river to irrigate 2,000 acres of the upper and lower districts of both Suzuka and Toyura in Kawachi, in the fourth century and the 10.5-kilometer long, 20-meter wide Furuichi-omizo canal in Osaka prefecture around 592.[4]

The Kofun or "Ancient Graves" Period: 250 to 645 AD

The accrued wealth, and technological advances provided by increased rice yields translated into military organization and the ability to build the Kofun (from *kōen-fun,* meaning "ancient tombs") for which this period is named. By 391 AD the Yamato also felt strong enough to help the Paekche battle the Silla and Goguryeo Kingdoms, before being brutally repulsed by the Goguryeo King Gwanggaeto.[5]

There are more than 200,000 Kofun scattered throughout the southern half of Japan, tracking an equal number of stages of Yamato development, of an early period in the 300s, a middle phase from 400 to 475, and a late period from 475 to 700.

Due to sacred associations, Mt. Miwa, in Nara Prefecture, was the first locus of Yamato activity, as they moved north-east from Kyushu. The Omiwa Jinja there, dedicated to Ōkuninushi, the Shinto god of fertility and son of Susano-o, is believed to be the oldest Shinto shrine in Japan. It has no Honden to house the kami, since the entire mountain is considered to be the home of the god.

The Hashihaka tomb in Sakuri, one of the oldest Kofun sites, originally ascribed to a daughter of Emperor Korei, (ruled from 290 to 342) but now attributed to Himiko, defines the type. Early tombs were located on hills, moving to lowland fields during the Middle period, when the size increased. In each case construction involved moving massive amounts of earth into a circular mound, and then excavating a vertical shaft on top of it, lining the bottom and sides with stones, and lowering the coffin into it, before it was

sealed with capstones or logs and covered over. Wood coffins, replaced by stone sarcophagi in the Middle period, and additional shafts were added for other family members, as needed.

The focal point of government then shifted from Mt. Miwa to Sakai, south of Osaka. The Mozu-Furuichi Tomb cluster of over 220 burial sites demonstrates the enormous power that the Yamato dynasty had amassed by this time. These include the 186-meter long Gobyoyama tumulus of Ojin, (ruled from 270 to 310) the 486-meter long and 35-meter high tumulus of Nintoku (313–399), estimated to have taken 2,000 workers 16 years to complete, the Kofun of Emperor Richu (400–405) which is 360 meters wide and 25 meters tall, and the tumulus of the Emperor Hanzei (406–410) which is 148 meters long.[6]

A new configuration, with an extended corridor and ante-chamber leading into a circular corbeled inner sanctum, similar to the passage graves built in Europe during the Neolithic period, began in the Late Kofun period.[7] Artifacts recovered from tombs not constrained by Imperial restrictions indicate similarity to Goguryo and Chinese iconography. The seventh-century Takamatsusuka mound, in the Asuka region of Nara Prefecture, for example, has frescos showing female courtiers and the four Chinese cosmological symbols denoting the cardinal directions.[8]

The Late Kofun or Asuka Period 475–645 AD

Large tombs became incongruous when Buddhism, with its emphasis on cremation, arrived in 552 AD. A delegation from the Paekche King Syong Myong presented the Yamato Emperor Kimmei a statue of Shakyamuni, some texts and a letter that said in part: "This doctrine is amongst all doctrines the most excellent. But it is difficult to explain and hard to understand." This introduction also coincides with the relocation of the capital to Asuka, giving this final period its name. It changed the political structure of Japan, and eventually transformed its architectural image from that of amorphous Shinto places of worship, to distinct temple compounds.

Soga no Iname, Minister at the court of the Emperor Kimmei, saw that this new religion had the potential to offset the rising stature of the conservative

Mononobe and Nakatomi clans and in 596, he received the Emperor's permission to build a Shrine on his own estate. More religious academic and technical groups from Korea followed, and helped to build this and other Buddhist temples.[9]

Kimmei died in 572, and the succession of Yomei in 585 caused warfare that was a thinly veiled proxy for the power struggle between the Mononobe-Nakatomi faction, representing Shintoism, and Soga no Umako, the son of Iname, as the champion of Buddhism. Yomei's son Umayado no Toyotomimi, or Shotoku, (born 572, died 622) is the key protagonist of the remainder of the Asuka period, as well as the creative force behind its most memorable architecture. After Yomei died in 587, infighting broke out again, and after assassinating several rivals, Soga no Umako installed another relative, Sukiya-hime, as Empress Suiko in 593, and named Shotoku as her regent.[10]

Shotoku Yatsumimi: "From the Land of the Rising Sun"

Shotoku was a devout Buddhist as well as a proponent of Chinese culture, sending students and emissaries there. In quick succession he replaced hereditary ranking with meritocracy in the "19 Article" Constitution, which is the first legal document in Japanese history. It reflects Buddhist and Confucian moral values, such as virtue: toku, benevolence: jin, propriety: rei, sincerity: shin, justice: gi and knowledge: chi, with "greater" and "lesser" grades in each category. With characteristic modesty, he took the second category in the first rank of "lesser virtue" or Shotoku, for himself. He also famously was the first to use the name "Nihon" instead of "Wa" for Japan when addressing the Sui Emperor as an equal rather than a vassal as "the Son of Heaven in the Land of the Rising Sun to the Son of Heaven of the Land of the Setting Sun."[11]

Horyu-ji: The Temple of the Flourishing Law

Horyu-ji, preceded by the Ikaruga temple-palace in 601, is inarguably the most memorable of the many temples attributed to Shotoku (Figure 2.1).[12] The final temple-monastery, completed in 607, is divided into eastern and western precincts. The main western enclosure conforms to the Kudara, or Korean-style ideal north-south, seven-hall temple model. At Horyu-ji, these seven components are the Chumon or central gate, a Pagoda and Kondo or Golden Hall placed side by side in the middle of the courtyard, a Dai-kodo, directly opposite the central gate, on the northern perimeter, a Sutra Repository, or library, a Belfry and covered arcade that surrounds the courtyard.

The 20-by-20-meter square, 32.45-meter high pagoda, which is on the left after entering the court-yard, has five floors and a massive shinbashira, or central column, which was cut and erected in 594, resting on a three-meter deep stone coffer foundation containing a relic of the Buddha. The two-story, rectangular Kondo, on the right, has a double roof and contains the Shaka Triad commissioned by the Empress Suiko shortly after Shotoku died in 622. Tori Busshi sculpted the Buddha in Shotoku's image, flanked by his mother and his wife, as attendants. There is also another likeness of Shotoku, in the oldest gilded camphor wood statue in Japan, known as the Guze, or "world saving" Kannon, sequestered in the octagonal Yumedono, or Hall of Dreams in the eastern precinct of Horyu-ji.

Subtle manipulations elevate this temple above others built at that time, or since, such as its asymmetrical rather than axial arrangement of the Pagoda and Kondo, and instead of just having one entrance, the Chumon is divided into four three column deep bays, creating two distinct aisles, parallel to the Pagoda and Kondo the face. The entry arcade on the eastern side of the Chumon gate is also one bay wider than the western side, to mirror the different widths of the Pagoda and Kondo. These adjustments create the impression of a majestic, reverberating, layered foreground and background scenography, in which carefully balanced horizontal and vertical forms are framed by a gate and arcade, setting the viewer up for what has been aptly described as the "latitudinal panoramic plan."[13]

Excavations carried out in 1938 indicate that Shotoku's palace, the Ikaruga no Miya, was located to the south-east of the Chumon, and subsequent excavation in 1968–9 determined that the attached Wakakusa-Garan temple was destroyed by fire in the mid-600s. This corresponds with the tragic events that followed Shotoku's and Suiko's death, when Soga

Figure 2.1 Horyu-ji
Source: Hartmut Poeling

no Emishi killed Shotoku's son Yamashiro and his family and burned both the buildings down, bringing Shotoku's lineage to an end.[14]

The Taika reforms

Centuries of family in-fighting within the Yamato court came to a head on July 10, 645, when Nakatomi no Kamatari and his followers killed Soga no Iruka in the Imperial Palace in the presence of the Empress Kogyoku. Fearing further retribution for the death of Shotoku's entire family, Iruka's father, Soga no Emishi, committed suicide.

According to Shinto law, the Empress was a living kame, or goddess who had been exposed to a transgression, or tsumi, within her ritual space and was in a state of kegare, in which her life force (ki) had diminished (kare) by witnessing this violent event. She had been defiled by it, so ritual purification or harae was required or it was thought that divine retribution would befall her subjects.

Consequently, Kogyoku abdicated in 645, and her brother, Karu, became Emperor Kotoku. Sensing the dire internal and external threats to his hegemony, he drafted the Taika, or "Great Radiance" edicts to reform the government in 646, based on the Confucian philosophy of social hierarchy to concentrate Imperial power. In addition to neutralizing the Soga, and ending clan warfare, these reforms also helped present a more unified front to Tang ruler Tai-sung, who ushered in a Golden Age in China. His capital of Chang'an had nearly two million occupants in 742, making it the largest city in the world at that time, with extensive land and sea "silk" routes that exponentially increased its prosperity and reach.[15] Kokotu's defensive instincts proved to be prescient, since, after he died, the close blood relationship between the Yamato and Paekche courts drew his successor Saimei into a struggle against a Tang-Silla alliance then attempting to eliminate the Paekche Empire entirely. In the Battle of Hakusuki-no-e in 663, a combined Yamato land and naval force was wiped out on the river Geum in Korea, and thousands of Baekje refugees streamed into Japan; the largest migration from the mainland since skilled workers were brought in to build temples after Buddhism was introduced a century earlier.[16]

Another hint of the crisis mentality within the court came in 720, when the Emperor Temmu, commissioned the Kojiki to distance the Yamato dynasty from its Baekje roots by characterizing it as an indigenous race. Also, in spite of its ancient founding, Temmu and Jito finally constructed the first Naiku shrine at Ise, and she carried out the first ceremonial rebuilding in 692, further enhancing the Imperial claim to ancient lineage.

The Nara Period: 710–794 AD

The Yamato followed the Chinese tradition of relocating their capital after each reign, and Temmu started planning a move from Asuka to Fujiwara-kyo in 682, but died before it could be implemented. Jito completed the re-location in 694, using a city plan based on the gridiron layout of the Chinese capital of Chang'an. Empress Gemmei moved it again to Nara, building the Heijo Palace there in 710.

In 752, the Emperor Shomu confirmed the rising influence of Buddhism within his kingdom and court, as well as the continuing need to deflect foreign intrusion by ordering the construction of the monastery temple of Todai-ji, with arcades connecting its central Daibutsuden, and 62-foot-high bronze Buddha, to a Lecture Hall, refectory and vegetable gardens (Figure 2.2). It was originally 30 percent wider, with 11 instead of 7 bays, which would have made it 86.1 rather than 57 meters wide and was flanked by a pair of 100-meter high pagodas on its east-west axis. In addition to its enormous size, which still qualifies it as the largest wooden building in the world, Todai-ji is also unusual in being intended for secular as well as sacred use. It was laid out on a Chinese feng-shui, north-south axis, with a main approach from the south and its back to the Wakakusa range, to the north. To facilitate this orientation, more than 700 meters of the mountain was excavated into terraces that vary from 10 to 30 meters

Figure 2.2 Todai-ji
Source: Hartmut Poeling

deep, with the main temple precinct on the eastern end of these plateaus, and the Ordination Hall or Kaidan-in on the west.[17]

The Sangatsu-do, or Lotus Sutra Hall, as well as the Nandaimon gate and Shoso-in, also deserve special mention here. The Sagatsu-do and Shosso-in survived both the Taira war in 1180 and the sixteenth-century conflagration and so are important as time capsules of the original temple. The Nandimon, or great southern gate is the first of two that calibrate the main southern approach to Todai-ji. It is six bays wide and three deep, and each of its 21-meter high columns were cut from a single tree. They are stabilized by horizontal tie beams and jointly support roof trusses that end in interlocking Dou-kung brackets, allowing the roof eave to extend five meters beyond the face of the columns. It was burned down during the Taira-Minamoto war, and re-built by the monk Chogen, in 1181.

The Treasury or Shoso-in, which is located 300 meters north-west of the Daibutsu-den, was completed after Shomu's death, in the azenuki style of rough-cut hinoki logs, and is raised up on columns, like the rice barn typology that inspired the Ise Shine. There were originally two adjacent square buildings on the site, but the space between them was enclosed, and the resulting rectangle was then covered in an extended hipped roof, making it 29.7 meters long and 25.7 meters high. It is a paragon of traditional environmental wisdom, because its raised base promotes natural ventilation that kept its precious contents dry, and the interlocking logs expand in the summer and contract in the winter to serve the same purpose: to protect the precious contents, which eventually came to include 9,000 items, from climatic variations.

The Daibutsuden was destroyed again in 1567 causing a second recasting to be sanctioned by the Tokugawa Shogunate in 1707. Subsequent restorations, in 1906 and 1973–80, concentrated on the roof of the Daibutsuden, finally replacing rotten trusses and cracked roof tiles.[18]

Even in its final breathtaking iteration, which is much changed and substantially smaller than its original form, Todai-ji represents an impressive demonstration of the power, wealth and authority of the Nara government to marshal the human and material resources required to build it. Like the Gothic cathedrals in Europe, it involved the entire community, with a vast support system of 1,200 administrators, supervisors and master builders, and 1,500 laborers. This included an Office of Construction broken into separate departments such as design, bronze casting, tile manufacturing, and timber collection, transport, and delivery. This last group alone sourced the 30-meter long trees for the 48 columns of the Daibutsen from mountains around Kobe, and hauled and floated them to the site.

State Buddhism

Todai-ji also represents the apotheosis of State Buddhism, in which the faith had become so powerful that it threatened Imperial stability. Friction between the royal court and the Buddhist establishment started as early as 624, when the Empress Suiko convened the clergy to announce administrative changes to deal with criminal acts.[19] Tensions rose when Buddhist shrines were made mandatory in each house and then, in 741 the powerful priest Roben decreed that each of the 67 provinces must have a Buddhist monastery and nunnery, including a seven-story pagoda, angering Shinto conservatives who were not given the same option.[20]

Then, in 749, Emperor Shomu abdicated in deference to his daughter Takano, who became Empress Koken. He became a Buddhist priest, establishing the practice of Insei, or monastic administration, in which he ruled in absentia. Koken first ruled from 749 to 758, and then abdicated in favor of Junnin, who ruled until 764. She met the monk Dōkyō Uge, during her Insei, in 752 and became infatuated with him. He and several other priests then took advantage of her by enacting statutes that established a Buddhist government in tandem with Imperial civil authority. In 764 Koken replaced Junnin, and elevated Dokyo to a series of increasingly important posts, eventually trying to have him named Emperor in 766. After she died in 770, Dokyo was exiled, and the scandalized court decided to not elect female rulers from that point on.[21]

The Heian period: 794–1185

Kammu made legal attempts to curb the growing number of Buddhist temples and clergy, but, faced with an increasingly powerful religious establishment, he finally decided to move the capital from Heijo to Nagaoka-kyo in 784, without permitting the Buddhist temples or establishment in Nara, to relocate there. He then ordered another relocation to Heian-ko, once again inspired by Chang'an. His Daigokuden palace occupied pride of place at the north end of the Suzaku-Oji, or central spine, with its back to the mountains arcing around and behind it. The wide, central spine terminated at the southern Rashōmon Gate. Small Buddhist temples such as To-ji on the eastern and Sa-ji on the western side of the southern gate were later allowed.

New sects, such as Tendai, introduced by Saicho in 805, and Shingon, by Kukai in 806, then sprang up in the mountains near Mt. Hiei, but unlike State Buddhism, they embraced modesty, humility and abstinence. Because of steeply sloping sites their temples were based on vernacular examples.

The Heian age, encompassing both the Fujiwara and Taira periods, was the longest period of peace in Japanese history before the modern age, because State Buddhism was decisively replaced by an independent State and Chinese influence on the wane and it was characterized by a new found freedom in architecture, literature and other forms of artistic expression. It is also the first of which we have a personal written record, in what is considered to be the first novel, by Murosaki Shikibu, a handmaiden to Princess Akiko. Her *Tale of Genji*, of 1004, recounts daily life at court in detail. Such hedonistic pursuits required the proper setting to enframe them, resulting in new freedom in palace, house and garden design. They can be summarized as substituting heavy materials with wooden columns, floors and screen walls and sliding partitions laid out with the standardized "ken" system, as well as the use of an engawa, or deck and a second "hidden" roof, for added moisture protection. It is also evident in the appearance of the Shisenden, a semi-formal hall borrowed from Chang'an and relocated from its usual position as the last of three axial rooms to the foreground of public view.[22]

The Fujiwara period: 858–1160

The Fujiwara clan gained power in the Heian court through the time-honored tactic of Imperial inter-marriage. Their line began when the Emperor Tenji initiated the title as an honor given to Nakatomi no Kamatari in 645 for ending Soga domination. They became so strong that Fujiwara Yoshifusa, who was not of royal blood, was named regent in 858, starting a dynasty in Heian-kyo that lasted for more than 300 years. Fujiwara Michinaga, who ruled from 995 to 1027, built his residence-temple, the Hojo-in in Uji, now the Phoenix Hall of the Byodo-in, using the Shishinden form of the Imperial Palace as a Shinden-zukuri with a main rectangular structure flanked by two L-shaped wings, with a garden between them.

Kamakura period: 1185–1333

In retrospect, this transfer of power was part of the strategic devolution of the Heian court, from a centralized *ritsuryō* state which mimicked the *lüling* system of Tang China, to an atomized alternative in which a standing conscript army was replaced by local militia, and the number of shoen, or estates which were granted tax-free status dramatically increased. This caused a shift of influence from the capital to the countryside, and as the Heian court became weaker and increasingly unable to curb lawlessness there, it strengthened the power of local warlords. The Minamoto, or Gengi and Taira, or Heiki clans emerged as the strongest of this new rural elite.

In 1068, Go-Sanjo, who was one of the first Em-perors since 857 to have no ties to the Fujiwara clan, tried to restore a strong central government, albeit with selfish intent, and started to investigate the records of existing shoen, mostly controlled by the Fujiwara. After stiff resistance, he retired in favor of his son Shirakawa,

who ruled from 1073 until 1087. They continued to confiscate large estates, creating new shoen for those loyal to their family.

Dueling Samurai clans

In 1155, a short civil war over succession called the Hōgen no Ran erupted between Sutoku and Go-Shirakawa, or Shirakawa II, most significant because it further exacerbated the rivalry between the Minamoto and Taira clans. Sutoku was defeated and sent into exile, and Go-Shirakawa became the new emperor in 1158. In the following year, the Taira and Minamoto clashed again, in the Heiji Rebellion, with Taira Kiyomori finally emerging victorious. Minamoto Yoritomo, who finally ends up as the hero of this complicated narrative, was captured and his father was killed in this battle, and he was sent into exile in Izu province. While there, he met and married Hojo Masako, gaining the support of this powerful family.

Taira Kiyomori was named Prime Minister in 1167, and arranged to have his wife's sister marry Go-Shirakawa, so that their son became the crown prince. Kiyomori's own son became Emperor Antoku in 1180, and he ruled as regent, finally solidifying his hold on power. It was short-lived however, since in 1180, Prince Mochihito, a son of Go-Shirakawa, asked him to offset Taira power. He rallied the Minamoto and established an encampment in Kamakura. He first opposed Kiyomori by undermining his authority, appointing *shugo* (constables) and *jitō* (district stewards) throughout the Kanto and then he and his brother Yoshitsune pushed the Taira back to the Inland Sea, finally destroying them in the Battle of Dannoura in 1185. Yoritomo then turned his attention to the Fujiwara stronghold of Hiraizumi, near Sendai, and conquered it, solidifying his hold on the entire country and bringing Fujiwara domination to an end. By elim-inating the last of the Taira clan, including the emperor Antoku, as well as Fujiwara domination, he established Minamoto supremacy throughout Japan.

The first Shogun

Minamoto Yoritomo returned to Kamakura in 1192, giving this period its name. He was the first to take the title of Shogun, and based his regime on the loyalty of the *shugo* and *jitō*, or tax collectors he appointed, who would soon emerge into a feudal state and what we recognize as the Samurai class today. This was the first of three Samurai-led governments in Japan and so marks an important transition in its history.[23] The term "feudal" isn't exactly accurate in discussing it, however, since, in adopting the hierarchical Confucian system Japanese authority figures also accepted the Chinese concept of the mandate of heaven, or of loyalty to a leader based on his or her moral capacity to claim authority, rather than the European tradition of Roman law. A key difference from the Chinese system, however, was that Japanese officials were selected on the basis of family connections and allegiance, not merit.

Nonetheless, the new Samurai class adopted the Confucian values of loyalty, devotion to duty and moral discipline. At first they were uneducated, and deemed to be unrefined, but they eventually adopted upper-class sensibilities. Unlike medieval knights, they were insensitive to the concept of romantic love but were not disdainful of the fine arts, and poetry.[24]

Yoritomi ordered that many shrines be rebuilt, and revived the Buddhist establishment in Nara, because the Todai-ji and Kofuku-ji factions had supported him during the war. The militant Yorimoto Shoguns rejected the Heian court as being dissipated and weak and this attitude was reflected in their houses, or buke-zukuri, which were less open than the shinden and were clustered together and often surrounded by protective enclosures. They did, however, introduce a new type of residence called the shoin zukuri, or study, which included a bay window to provide natural light.

Zen Buddhism, temples, teahouses and gardens

Eisai, who was one of the religious scholars who started making pilgrimages to China to study at Ch'an

Figure 2.3 Ryōan-ji
Source: James Steele

Figure 2.4 Saiho-ji
Source: James Steele

monasteries just after the start of the Kamakura period, introduced Zen or Ch'an Buddhism into Japan by 1191. Another monk, named Gikai, also surveyed many Zen temples in China, and his drawings survive as a testimony to the interest in the faith and the determination to replicate Zen forms. This ushered in a period of austerity and asceticism, coupled with less revenue at court during the Kamakura period, marking a return to strict monasticism. Zen forms were adopted most faithfully at Nanzen-ji, Daitoku-ji, Sofu-ji and Myoshin-ji, in Kyoto, and the Kencho-ji and Engaku-ji Temples in Kamakura.[25] Subsequent Kamakura rulers lacked the militant discipline of Yoritomo, and symmetrical axial layouts soon started to become more informal. The modest, simply detailed chashitsu, or teahouses also inspired the use of lighter structural elements and materials in residences.

Many exquisite dry stone, or Karesansui Zen gardens, typified by those at Ryōan-ji, and Daisen-in, a smaller temple at Daitoku-ji, accompanied this change. Hosokawa Katsumoto completed Ryoan-ji in 1473, assisted by the monk Soami, who is also famous for his calligraphy and landscape paintings. The Zen priest Kogaku Sōkō founded Daisen-in and its garden, also designed by Soami between 1509 and 1513. Soami was inspired by Song Dynasty calligraphy and used diluted ink to create similarly mystical landscapes. This connection between painting and garden design has its origin in the Chinese confluence of the Buddhist awareness of transience and a Confucian admiration for scholarship, and the idea of a learned refined person seeking refuge from everyday materialism by seeking isolation in a mountain retreat to meditate, write poetry and reflect on the vicissitudes of life and the impermanence of wealth.

During the Tang Dynasty, painters such as Song Zhiwen, Wang Wei and Bai Juyi, best known for their ethereal renditions of the mountain peaks of Guilin, also started to translate them into three dimensional landscapes for wealthy patrons who preferred to forego the hardships of a hut in the mountains by recreating a hermitage on their own property. This started a tradition in which painters and calligraphers became garden designers and Ji Cheng later codified their techniques *Yuanye*, or *The Craft of Gardens* in 1631. Japanese gardens are more organic and less a stylized kit of parts, guided more by the inherent character of each site and often using shakkai, or borrowed scenery to extend their reach, by gradually layering progressively larger trees in front of the viewer.

At Daisen-in, the garden was designed to be a metaphor for the various stages of human existence within a small space. Existential transitions are symbolized by the gravel, which is first raked to look like a stream, flowing from a mountain, then a river and then an ocean, with obvious parallels in human physical and psychological growth, with the gravel, or water, eventually returning to its source, as a reminder of reincarnation, unless nirvana is achieved. Rocks of various shapes are placed alongside and sometimes in the midst of the symbolic water representing attributes such as curiosity, exploration, endurance and strength.

Ryōan-ji, on the other hand, is less literal. The rectangular garden is surrounded by a low, rammed earth wall, which acts as a visual datum against the cherry trees behind it. When the wall was built, each of its layers was sprinkled with oil, which has slowly oozed out, creating subtle iridescent patterns on the surface, protected from precipitation by an overhanging eave. Based on the concept of mie-gakure, or "hide and reveal," there are 15 rocks of various sizes strategically positioned on the gravel field so that one of them is always hidden from view, from any vantage point, symbolizing the invisible aspects of life (Figure 2.3).

Not all Zen gardens use stone, however, and one of the most famous variants is the moss garden of Saihō-ji, outside Kyoto, which was created by Gyōki, on the location of a site associated with Shōtoku during the Nara Period (Figure 2.4).

Notes

1   Mark Hudson, *The Ruins of Identity: Ethnogenesis in the Japanese Islands*, Honolulu: University of Hawaii Press, 1999.

2   Walter Edwards, "Event and Process in the Founding of Japan: The Horse-rider Theory: Archaeological Perspective," *The Journal of Japanese Studies* Vol. 9, No.2, Summer, 1983, pp. 265–295.

3   Wontack Hong, *Relationship Between Korea and Japan in Early Period: Paekche and Yamato Wa*, Pan Korea Books, 1988. Also see his *Ancient Korea-Japan Relations: Paekche and the Origin of the Yamato Dynasty*, Seoul: Kudara, 2012.

4 Graeme Barker and Candice Goucher, (Eds.), *The Cambridge World History: Volume 2, A World With Agriculture, 12,000 BCE–500 C.E.*, p. 376.

5 Delmar M. Brown, *The Cambridge History of Japan, Vol.1: Ancient Japan*, Cambridge: Cambridge University Press, 1993, p. 27.

6 Ibid., p. 310.

7 Gina Barnes, *State Formation in Japan: Emergence of a Fourth Century Ruling Elite*, Abingdon, Oxon: Routledge, 2007 p. 7.

8 Ibid., p. 146.

9 Timothy Insoll, (Ed.), *The Oxford Handbook of the Archaeology of Ritual and Religion*, Oxford: Oxford University Press, 2011, p. 56. Japan was originally not racially homogeneous, beginning with the Yayoi, who formed what has been referred to as a "supra-local elite" with Korean rulers, solidified by a similar material culture that confirmed "group membership." See Richard T. Pearson, "Japan, Korea and China: The Problem of Defining Continuities Asian Perspectives," Vol. 19, No. 1, pp. 176–187. No less an authority than Edwin O. Reischauer has unequivocally stated that:

> the archeological record clearly shows that a large number, if not most, of the early inhabitants of Japan came to the islands from Korea and areas further away in Northeast Asia, and there is indisputable historical evidence that a considerable flow of people from the peninsula into Japan continued until the eighth century A.D. An early eighth century book attributes recent continental origin to more than a third of the aristocratic families of the Japanese court at that time.
> (Edwin O. Reischauer, *Japan: The Story of a Nation*, Tokyo: Tuttle, 1990, p. 10)

10 William E. Deal and Brian Ruppert, *A Cultural History of Japanese Buddhism*, Chichester: John Wiley/Blackwell, 2015.

11 Gary L. Ebersole, *Ritual Poetry and the Politics of Death in Early Japan*, Princeton, NJ: Princeton University Press, 1989, p. 144. Japanese historians Sekino Tadasu and Okakura Kakuzo have further subdivided this period. Sekino claims it ended with the Taika Reform of 646, and used the term Hakuho to refer to the remaining time until the move to Nara, while Okakura used it uniformly through the transfer of the capital to the Heijō Palace in Nara in 710.

12 Shitennōji, Osaka, Chūgūji, Hōkiji (or Ikejiri Dera), Tachibanadera, Kōryūji, Katsuragi Dera, Ikarugadera in Hyōgo Prefecture and Hōrin-ji.

13 J. Edward Kidder, Jr., *The Lucky Seventh: Early Horyu-ji and Its Time*. International Christian University, Hachiro Yuasa Memorial Museum, 1999, p. 42.

14 Louis Frederic, *Japan Encyclopedia*, trans. Kathe Roth, Cambridge, MA: The Belknap Press of the Harvard University Press, 2002, p. 1045.

15 Bruce Batten, "Foreign Threat and Domestic Reform: The Emergence of the Ritsuryo State," *Monumenta Nipponica*, Vol. 41, No. 2 (Summer, 1986), pp. 199–219.

16 J. Edward Kidder, Jr., op. cit., p. 42.

17 William Coaldrake, *Architecture and Authority in Japan*, London: Routledge, 2002, p. 56.

18 Coaldrake, Ibid., p. 56.

19 Jonathan Morris Augustine, *Buddhist Hagiography in Early Japan*, London: Routledge Curzon, 2005, p. 54.

20 John M. Rosenfeld, "Todai-ji in Japanese History and Art," p. 201[AT1].

21 Yoseburo Takokoshi, *The Economic Aspects of the History of the Civilization of Japan*, Vol.1, Allen and Unwin, 1930, reprinted by Routledge 2005, p. 70.

22 Robert Treat Paine and Alexander Soper, *The Art and Architecture of Japan*, Yale University Pelican History of Art Series, 3rd Edition, p. 332.

23 Edwin O. Reischauer, *Japan: The Story of a Nation*, Tuttle, 1990, pp. 37–47.

24 Patrick Smith, *Japan: A Reinterpretation*, New York: Vintage, 1998, p. 186.

25 Paine and Soper, op. cit., p. 384.

CHAPTER 3

Paroxysm and change

In Kyoto, the Emperor Go Horikawa tried to restore Imperial power by overthrowing the Kamakura baefuku in 1221, but Yoritomo prevailed once again, and retaliated by exiling him and moving to Kyoto himself. He died there in 1199, causing yet another succession crisis. His formidable wife, Masako, and the Hojo family assumed authority, killing two of Yoritomo's male heirs to do so, and put a Fujiwara candidate forward instead, reviving the habit of indirect rule. The Kamakura court, now in Kyoto, survived this crisis, but a sequence of Mongol invasions tested it anew. An armada assembled by the Golden Hoard in 1274 turned back due to an impending typhoon but returned in 1281, and finally did make landfall in Kyushu. A second storm wrecked their ships, forcing a final retreat. Even though Kamakura troops were victorious, the invasion drained the Imperial coffers and embittered the local troops that bore the brunt of the action at their own expense, without subsequent reward, sowing the seeds of future rebellion.

In time Yoritomo's Shogunate was fatally weakened by the distance between Kyoto and Kamakura, as well as the passing of its original retainers and the gradual impoverishment caused by the patrimonial system it had inaugurated. The end of the Kamakura period came quite quickly in 1333, when Go-Daigo, a scion of the imperial line, called for it to be re-instated and assumed the title Emperor Kemmu. Sensing a power vacuum, an entrepreneurial Ashikaga Takauji forced him to retreat to Yoshino in 1336, setting up

bifurcated, Northern and Southern principalities and took over control of the government in Kyoto himself in 1338.

The Ashikaga, or Muromachi period: 1333–1573

Takauji established his base in the Muromachi district of Kyoto in 1338, which gives this period its alternative name. By delegating power to provincial leaders and allowing them to control their own troops, Takauji was able to govern fairly effectively, but it wasn't until the rule of the third Ashikaga Shogun Yoshimitsu that things started to settle down. There were 15 Ashikaga Shoguns over the next two and a half centuries, until the Onin War weakened its authority.

The courts remained divided until 1392, when the third Ashikaga shogun, Yoshimitsu, invited the Southern half to join him in Kyoto. He also sanctioned a return to the luxurious lifestyle associated with the Heian court, and aristocrats abandoned the simple buke-zukuri to once again embrace the earlier shinden-sukuri style. He sought to absorb and continue the architectural traditions of the recent past, as a fusion of inherited strains.[1]

Kinkaku-ji and Ginkaku-ji

Yoshimitsu is undoubtedly best known for his "Golden Pavilion" or Kinkaku-ji, in the Kitayama hills north of

Figure 3.1 Kinkaku-ji
Source: James Steele

Kyoto (Figure 3.1). He bought the property, originally called Kitayama-dai, from the Saionji family, in 1397, and transformed it into a particularly legible metaphor of the complex undercurrents rippling through Ashikaga society at the time by projecting each of his layered identities onto its three telescoping stories. Appropriate to his aristocratic status, the ground floor, of natural wood frame and sliding white panels, can be completely opened up to its peripheral balcony and the lake and garden beyond. The equally square second story, which was once covered in gold leaf but is now painted, is also paneled, but less open, as befitting his military stature as a Shogun, superior to other nobility. Both lower stories are then capped with a Chinese-style roof, as if drawing a line above these contiguous responsibilities. The smaller third story has a roof of its own, conveying the image of a separate entity, yet it is also carefully detailed to be part of the ensemble. In spite of being incongruously covered in gold, however, its modest scale and arched windows send the unmistak-

able message that this is the retreat of a ruler in Insei, as a Zen monk.[2]

Gold was discovered at Toi, in the Tagata District, Shizuoka Prefecture, Japan on the west coast of Izu Peninsula facing Suruga Bay in 1370 during the Ashikaga period, followed by other mines at Yugashima and Nawaji. It started to play an important part in architecture, arts and crafts from then on. The Silver Pavilion, or Ginkaku-ji built by the 8th Ashikaga Shogun Yoshimasa, is often thought of as the companion piece to Kinkaku-ji, but was actually built 83 years later, in 1483 (Figure 3.2). Yoshimasa died before it was completed, so it never received its silver coating, but its rustic natural wood sheathing makes it seem much more approachable than its golden relative, and reminds us that Yoshimasa was an aesthetic iconoclast, who rejected formality and artificiality. He dedicated one quadrant of the interior to social events, planned by his tea master Shuko, which were the highlight of his Higashiyama set.

Figure 3.2 Ginkaku-ji
Source: James Steele

The Azuchi-Momoyama period and the three unifiers: 1573–1600

Ginkaku-ji was the Ashikaga swan song, however, because a succession dispute after Yoshimasa died led to the disastrous Onin War, and this, along with the assassination of Ashikaga Yoshiteru in 1565, encouraged Oda Nobunaga, who was the son of Oda Nobuhide, a Daimyo in Owari province, to seize power. He initially put Ashikaga Yoshiteru's brother Yoshiaki forward as a surrogate but then followed a previous pattern of taking over himself. This marks the beginning of the 35-year-long saga of the fatefully intertwined lives of Oda Nobunaga, Hideyoshi Toyotomi and Tokugawa Ieyasu, which eventually led to an end to constant warfare and the final unification of Japan.

Nobunaga is famous for being a brilliant strategist who not only stabilized the government after years of upheaval, but also brought nearly half of the country under his control by neutralizing the power of the Daimyo. He probably would have succeeded in unifying all of it if Akechi Mitsuhide, who was one of his retainers, had not betrayed him. He was caught by surprise with only a small group of defenders at Honno-ji in Kyoto in 1582, and committed suicide to avoid capture.

He also built a castle in Azuchi, near lake Biwa, which, along with another in the Momoyami district of Kyoto housing his successor Hideyoshi Toyotomi, gave this period its name (Figure 3.3). Unlike Nobunaga, Hideyoshi was not of aristocratic birth, first serving as a servant at the Imagawa castle before switching sides and joining the Oda clan in 1557, as Nobunaga's sandal bearer. He was present at the battle of Okehazama when Oda defeated Imagawa Yoshimoto in 1560, and slowly worked his way up through the ranks, impressing Nobunaga with his tireless resourcefulness and ability to convince opposition forces to surrender and join the Oda cause.

Figure 3.3 Hideyoshi Toyotomi
Source: Hartmut Poeling

As a result, Nobunaga promoted him to General in 1570, and also rewarded him with the title of Daimyo and land in Omi Province. Out of loyalty, Hideyoshi revenged Oda's death by defeating Akechi Mitsuhide at Yamazaki, and then prevailed in the subsequent negotiations over succession, eventually assuming leadership of the Oda clan. He built his own castle in Osaka in 1583, based on Nobunaga's fortress in Azuchi, and continued to pacify the provinces that still remained in rebellion after Oda's death. He also confiscated all weapons from those below the rank of Samurai, to thwart further uprisings. After capturing Odawara castle in 1590, he had effectively eliminated all resistance and was finally granted the title of Kampaku, or Imperial Regent, rather than Shogun in 1585. Because he came from the peasant class, he did not have a surname, but had taken the name Hashiba

Hideyoshi for himself. The Emperor granted him the name Toyotomi in 1586, and he built Jurakudai Palace for himself in Kyoto that same year. He retired from the Regency in 1592, and relocated Fushimi castle to Kyoto, relocating many of the interiors from Jurakudai there.

Violence and beauty: the tea ceremony

While ever mindful of the dangers of stereotypical generalization, one well researched trait made famous by anthropologist Ruth Benedict, which has a direct bearing on a majority of the architecture presented here so far, is the parallel capacity for both extreme cruelty and violence on the one hand, and sensitivity to beauty and ability to manifest it in physical form on the other, typified by Hideyoshi Toyotomi.[3]

For example, in 1592, he adopted Hidesugu, the son of his deceased half-brother Hidenaga, because he initially lacked an heir but after his concubine Chacha gave birth to a boy, named Hideyori, he ordered Hidesugu, along with his entire family, with the exception of a one-month old daughter, to be executed. And yet, Toyotomi also promoted cultural treasures such as the tea ceremony, which began to conform to the ritual we recognize today during the Ashikaga Shogunate, but really came to fruition during his Regency.

This complex custom, which is such a potent signifier of and window into Japanese culture, has ancient Chinese and Buddhist, rather than secular roots. According to the Nihon Koki it was introduced into Japan by Eichu, a monk who served sencha, or unground green tea to the Emperor Saga in 815 AD. The Emperor then ordered seedlings to be cultivated in the Kinki region due to its favorable climate, but it wasn't until Luyu, of the Zen Ch'an school, wrote the *Classic of Tea*, that public interest grew. In the twelfth century, the monk Eisai brought more exotic tea seeds from China, crushed the leaves from them into powder, and served the tea at Buddhist monasteries to help them stay awake during long meditations. The Kamakura court adopted the practice, and when the Ashikaga shogun returned to Kyoto he assimilated the fashion and transferred it there.

However, several more iterations were required to transform the ceremony into the event we know today.

In the mid-1400s, Murato Juko founded the chano-yu, or wabi chai style, using natural, indigenous implements. Juko, or Shuko began using understated, locally produced utensils, as did his successor, Jo-o. Shuko had apprenticed with Ikkyu Sojun, or Zenji, in Kyoto who in turn had studied with the Rinzai Zen Abbot Kano at Saikin-ji, and the Kaso at Kenko-en, within the Daitoku-ji complex in Kyoto. It was destroyed during the Onin war and Ikkyu re-built it. In addition to this founding, he is also still renowned as a poet and calligrapher, and brought these disciplines to the Daitoku-ji way of tea.

Sen no Rikyū

Sen no Rikyū, who studied with Takeno Joo, and trained as a Zen monk at Daitoku-ji, finally perfected the ceremony. He became the tea master for Oda Nobunaga and then Toyotomi Hideyoshi after Oda's death in 1582, and is credited with providing a restrained counterpoint to the ostentation of the Azuchi-Momoyama period, and the status conscious fashion of using ornate, expensive Chinese tea utensils, during parties that lasted for several days.

He created smaller tea houses, with a small doorway, or nijiriguchi, to remind guests to practice humility, and continued both Shuko and Jo-o's preference for simplicity, introducing rough Raku bowls named after Hideyoshi's Jurakudai palace, which are shaped by hand, lead glazed and fired at low temperature, as well as unlacquered bamboo utensils.

In addition to enhancing previous sensibilities regarding simplicity and honesty of materials, his key contribution was the concept of "ichi go ichi-e" or the idea of the singularity of time and space within the teahouse, as well as the need for harmony (wa), respect (kei), purity (sei), and tranquility (joku) among the participants sharing this special moment, protected from the travails of life outside. This is tied to the temporality of the teahouse, beginning with the building of a rudimentary hut from whatever natural materials are at hand, such as stones, twigs, branches, clay, leaves, straw or paper. The intention is that the shelter is impermanent, intended for a single gathering of friends, although, inevitably and ironically, many teahouses have become national treasures that are carefully preserved. A personal example that may help illustrate the concept is provided by the tea vendors along the railway sidings in India, who use clay rather than paper cups, intending that they will be thrown back onto the berm after being used, to break and return to their natural state. This aspect of transience and imperfection encapsulates the twin ideals of wabi, or the acceptance of impermanence and imperfection, and sabi, or the appreciation of faded beauty.[4]

Hideyoshi lacked the refined aristocratic elegance of previous advocates of the tea ceremony, and certainly must have tested Sen no Rikyū's sensibilities by commissioning a portable gold covered tea room, inspired by Kinkakuji, in an attempt to impress everyone with his taste and status wherever he went. In 1587, he invited more than 1,000 guests to a mass Tea Ceremony at Kitano, in Kyoto, the Kitano Ōchanoyu, near his Jurakudai Palace in Kamigyo where his peripatetic golden pavilion was finally installed. Guests drew lots to be served by Hideyoshi himself, as well as by Sen no Rikyū, and other tea masters such as Tsuda Sogyu and Imai Sokyu, and Hideyoshi finally cut the event short due to exhaustion.

True to form, he eventually ordered Sen no Rikyū to commit suicide in 1591, for an imagined slight that may have been related to a statue of himself that the Tea Master had erected on the road to Hideyoshi's palace, putting the Regent beneath it as he passed.

The Katsura Palace, and Sukiya

Lacking a male heir, Hideyoshi Toyotomi adopted Hachijo Toshihito, the younger brother of Emperor Go Yozei in 1586, but the relationship cooled after his own son, Hideyori Toyotomi, was born in 1593. In the interim, he gave Toshihito the family title Hachijo no-miya and a large parcel of land on the south side of the Katsura river outside Kyoto, and Hachijo built a small pavilion for viewing the reflection of the full moon on the water there in 1620 (Figure 3.4).

Since he was part of the cash-starved Kyoto Imperial line, he adopted a rustic teahouse, sukiya style for the first house, inspired by a passage in the "The Wind in the Pines" chapter in *Tales of Genji* which says that: "Far away, in the country village of Katsura, the reflection of the moon upon the water is clear and tranquil." As his status at court increased, he dedicated more

Figure 3.4 Katsura Rikyū
Source: James Steele

resources to the house so that, by 1624, he added to the pavilion and completed a garden and pond. Prince Toshihito died in 1629 when his son Toshitada was still an adolescent, but he later decided to restore and expand the house known as the "old shoin" again. In 1641, Toshitada built the main portion, or "middle shoin" of what was referred to as a Villa, as well as adding the teahouses which surround the pond. Moving clockwise from the Chomun gate, these are Geppa-ro, or moon-wave teahouse, the Shokin-tei, after shokin, the sound of a koto or Japanese harp, Shoka-Tei, the Onrindo teahouse and Temple, with its distinctive Jibutsudo tile roof and finally, the Shoiken. Seeking inspiration for his Shugakuin Villa, Emperor Gomino-o visited Katsura in 1658, and Toshidata built the final "new Shoin" for this event.

Among other noteworthy aspects, Katsura is remarkable as a complete synthesis between architecture and landscape, designed in such a way that each outward view is directed toward a perfectly framed composition in the garden around it, just as each view from this peripheral kaiyū-shiki-teien, back to the Rikyū is impeccably composed as well. This differs considerably from the Western notion of landscape as something that serves as a background for architecture, rather than being an integral part of it. Since it was inspired by Murasaki Shibu's *The Tale of Gengi*, it is also quite literally a three dimensional text, and as such, it was as much a stage-set as it was a residence, a backdrop against which the members of the *Hachijo no Miya* court could act out their various hierarchical roles.[5]

The final unifier

Tokugawa Ieyasu, (1543–1616) who finally unified Japan, was originally named Takechiro, and was the son of Matsudaira Hirotade, a Mikawa Daimyo of middle rank (Figure 3.5).

Rivalry with the Oda clan forced his father to ally with the Imagawa, who asked that Takechiro be held hostage at their castle at Sumpu, in return. Oda Nobuhide captured him on the way, however, and used him to try to blackmail his father into joining the Oda. Hirotade coldly refused. Oda let Takechiro live, however, and later released him and after Hirotade and Oda Nobuhide died, he allowed him to finally go to Sumpu. He was only six years old when he arrived. When he turned 16 in 1556, he changed his name to Matsudaira Notoyasu and joined Yosimoto Imagawa to defeat Oda Nobunaga at Terbe. Yoshimoto died at a

Figure 3.5 Tokugawa Ieyasu
Source: Hartmut Poeling

later battle, at Okehazama, and Notoyasu then decided to join Oda Nobunaga, capturing the Imagawa fortress at Kaminogo to prove his loyalty. He changed his name for a final time to Tokugawa in 1566, assuming a thinly conceived Minamoto lineage in the process. When Oda Nobunaga victoriously marched into Kyoto in 1568, Tokugawa was at his side.

The Battle of Sekigahara

Hideyoshi appointed Tokugawa to be one of five regents to protect his son until he became old enough to become Shogun, but infighting between an "eastern" camp led by Tokugawa, and a "western" rival led by Ishida Mitsunari, started immediately after Hideyoshi's death in 1598. The two sides, totaling about 160,000 samurai, met in a driving rain at dawn on October 21, 1600, in the narrow valley of Sekigahara, for a battle that equals Hastings, Waterloo, Yorktown and Normandy in historical significance. It was closely fought for about four hours, with neither the defections from Ishida's side nor the reinforcements from his son Hidetada happening as expected. Ieyasu finally ordered his musketeers to fire at the vacillating stragglers, forcing them to commit to him, and just before sunset events turned in his favor, even though his son's reinforcements had still not arrived. Tokugawa was named Shogun by Emperor Go-Yozei on March 24, 1603 and the unification was just about complete, but his supremacy was still thwarted by the potential succession of Toyotomi Hideyori. Ieyasu finally surrounded Osaka castle in 1615 and forced Toyotomi and his family to commit suicide, except for Hideyori's wife, Senhime, who was Ieyasu's granddaughter. Understanding the true legacy of the Tokugawa Shogunate, then, as one of preparation for, but also a contradiction of the modern period, is important because it puts the triumphs and tribulations of the architects of this time into historical perspective.

Following his victory in the battle of Sekigahara on October 21, 1600, Tokugawa Ieyasu, as the last of the three unifiers of Japan, instituted several sweeping social, political and economic reforms, which were intended to consolidate his control, and bring stability after centuries of civil war. These set the collective course for the next 268 years of his dynasty. He granted varying degrees of status to the Daimyo, based on the extent to which they had helped him win his decisive victory, establishing an inner circle of fudai and a less privileged tozama or "outer lords." He introduced a Confucian-based hierarchical caste system or Shi-Nou-Kou-Shou, of warriors, or samurai, peasant-farmers, craftsmen, and merchants.

The Tokugawa dynasty that Ieyasu founded ruled for the next 163 years, until the beginning of the modern period, and profoundly changed both the rural and urban landscapes of Japan. These changes can be traced to two decisions in particular that aimed to control the military, economic and political power, defined in spatial terms, of the newly unified country. The side that the Daimyo and Samurai chose at Sekigara determined their new status, and size of their allotment, with the "inner Daimyo" or fudai, being most trusted, and the untrusted "outer" lords, or tozama, being sent to the hinterlands. The Gemma or "one castle one town" Edict of 1615, was an attempt to reduce the number of fortresses that had proliferated during the feudal era, and allocate them to one Daimyo each, in specific urban areas. This also included the relocation of the Samurai, who had previously been self sufficient, into these castle towns, with their status determined by proximity to the center. This change essentially transformed them into an administrative class, forced to sell their rice allotments to survive.[6]

One castle one province

Ieyasu also initiated a new policy of ikkoku ichijo rei, or one castle in each province, so that all castles, other than the primary residence of the Daimyo in each province, had to be torn down. This policy also made it mandatory for middle- and lower-class samurai to move to these castle towns, of either their Daimyo, or to Edo if they served the Shogun. They were also allocated a fixed stipend of rice, which they could either sell or use personally, tightening control over them and essentially converting them from self-sufficiency into a class of dependent civil servants. By the time of the Meiji Restoration, these castle towns, or jokamachi, had become a well-organized urban network that allowed government control to be effectively transmitted throughout the country, from the capital of Edo to each province. Even though the city that it ruled has long since been covered over by its modern equivalent, Himeji Castle, with its massive sloping

Figure 3.6 Himeji Castle
Source: James Steele

stone walls and moats, remains and is one of the best preserved of these, providing a vivid example of physical and symbolic power that these bastions conveyed (Figure 3.6). Tokugawa Ieyasu also completed a land-tenure system, or kokudaka, that his predecessor, Toyotomi Hideyoshi, had started in 1584, setting the tax base at the value of a koku or five bushels of rice, as the average fixed proportion of the yield for a specified parcel of land.

Sankin Kotai, the law of alternative residence

Following onto these profound changes, Ieyasu's grand-son, Iemitsu, launched the policy of sankin kotai, or alternative residence in 1635, requiring all Daimyo to establish a household in Edo and occupy it, with full retinue, every other year, or every third year depending on rank, and to leave family members there, as hostages. The intention of this edict was to impoverish the Daimyo, to prevent them from rebelling, since the cost of travel, as well as maintaining two full households, was high. Five main government-controlled post roads, or kaido, were authorized to connect Edo with the outer provinces, and the Tokaido, which connected Kyoto with Edo, now the rail-bed of the Shinkensen train line between the two cities, was the largest. The former post towns of Magome and Tsumago in the Kiso valley segment of the Nakesendo, or Kisokaido post road, which ran through the center of the mountains of Honshu, have recently been restored (Figure 3.7). The combined effect of the one-castle-one-province edict, and the law of alternative residence, was that it brought both the Daimyo and the Samurai, and the artisans and merchants that served them, from the countryside to the city.

During the Togugawa period Edo, as well as Osaka and Kyoto, which were the other members of the Santo, or main urban axis, grew exponentially. Spatial organization became a legible record of social order, in which class lines determined position. The hier-archy started with baefuku, or Shogunate land, followed by the fudai, or inner Daimyo and tozama or outer Daimyo estates, followed by the Confucian division of the Samurai, peasant, artisan and merchant classes, with the land given to Samurai according to their rank.

Ever conscious of retaining control, the Tokugawa baefuku divided zones below the Samurai class into Cho, or neighborhoods of 60 by 60 ken each, with 1,818 meters in a ken, with 300 people in each Cho. These were self-regulating districts, ostensibly controlled by a landlord, but in reality each resident was responsible for the behavior of the others. This discouraged a sense of civic consciousness of the kind found in Renaissance cities like Florence, for example, where the city was viewed as a holistic self-governing entity, as merchants at this time started to take power away from the nobility. Official obsession with control in the Santo particularly extended to public space, which was seen as a threat rather than a public amenity, because poten-tially dangerous large groups could gather there. Green space was also reserved because it was seen as sacred, rather than recreational, leaving the temple grounds as the only option for social gatherings.

Figure 3.7 Tsumago
Source: James Steele

In spite of all of its faults, the Tokugawa regime did effectively manage one of the largest urbanized pre-modern societies in the world at that time, and delivered to the doorstep of modernity a collective entity that had already dealt with many of the problems that would face the Industrialized cities in the west after the Meiji period began.[7]

Notes

1   Robert Treat Paine and Alexander Soper, *The Art and Architecture of Japan*, The Yale University Press Pelican History of Art, 1955, p. 44.
2   Mark Ravina, *Land and Lordship in Early Modern Japan*, Stanford, CA: Stanford University Press, 1999.
3   Ruth Benedict, *The Chrysanthemum and the Sword*, Boston and New York: Houghton Mifflin, 1974.
4. Kakuzo Okakura, *The Book of Tea*. Originally published in 1906, reprinted by Tuttle, 1989, p. 10. "Those who cannot feel the littleness of great things in themselves are apt to overlook the greatness of little things in others."
5   A Shoin is a study, refined during the Muromachi period, with tatami, fusama, or sliding rice paper and wood screens, chigaidana, or staggered shelves, and a tokonoma, or recess for calligraphy. For a complete listing of books and articles about Katsura, see Dana Buntrock, "Katsura Imperial Villa: A Brief Descriptive Bibliography with Illustrations" in *Crosscurrents: East Asian History and Culture Review*, Vol. 1, No. 2, November 2012.
6   Andre Sorenson, *The Making of Urban Japan: Cities and Planning from Edo to the Twenty-first Century*, London and New York: Routledge, 2002, p. 15.
7   Ibid., p. 16.

PART II

From modernity to Modernism: 1868–1940

CHAPTER 4

The search for knowledge and its consequences

Within the course of an average lifetime, Japan was irrevocably transformed from an insular medieval oligarchy to a global powerhouse. This remarkable metamorphosis was instigated by the forced entry of an American naval expedition led by Commodore Matthew C. Perry into Uraga harbor, near Tokyo on July 8, 1853 and his subsequent landing at Yokosuka, six days later. Perry and his delegation then met with representatives of the Tokugawa Shogunate, handing them a letter from American President Millard Fillmore demanding trade concessions. Perry returned in February 1854 with a much bigger fleet and signed the Convention of Kanagawa in March of that same year. It opened up the ports of Shimoda and Hakodate to trade with the United States and brought the Japanese policy of Sakoku, or seclusion, to an abrupt end.

The Tokugawa Shogunate, which had been in power for 268 years by the time of the American incursion, is often mistakenly considered to have been an intractable, obdurate and relentlessly regressive regime, but this one-sided view is now being systematically re-evaluated. It is unquestionably true that what Japan lost while the Tokugawa policy of Sakoku was in place from 1633 until 1853 is inestimable, considering events in the West during this time.[1]

The coming of the *kurofune*, or "black ships"

The entry of the iron-hulled fleet of Commodore Matthew Perry into Uraga Harbor was extremely humiliating for the Japanese, and *kurofune* or "black ships" remains a loaded term, at once synonymous with foreign intervention, the end of isolation and the introduction of new technology. The loss of face that the incursion caused the Shogunate set into motion a plan by leaders of the Satsuma and Choshu provinces to dissolve it and restore the Emperor to power. Their part in instigating this plot is certainly one of the most compelling examples of historical memory, since these leaders were descendants of the *tozama* or "outer lords" who had been exiled to these distant provinces because they had not actively supported Tokugawa Ieyasu at Sekigahara, in 1601. Two hundred and fifty-three years later, their descendants saw this sign of weakness as their chance to even the score. Their candidate, the Emperor Komei, however, died on January 30, 1867, forcing them to pin their hopes on his young son, Meiji, who took the throne four days later. The Boshin War, which was a struggle between forces loyal to each side, soon followed, and after the Imperial army prevailed in 1868, the Emperor Meiji formally announced his supreme authority.

In retrospect, the pro-active Japanese response to this almost certain threat of foreign occupation is astounding, and resoundingly confirms their inherent ability to assimilate ideas from other cultures and adapt to new circumstances. Rather than submitting to colonial rule, as many other nations did, its leaders decided to emulate the colonizer, and become as much like its potential invader as possible. As we now know, they far exceeded their expectations.

The first phase: searching the world for knowledge, 1868–1890

In hindsight, the introduction of and adaptation to new ideas in architecture in Japan evolved in three distinct phases. The first, much less precise socio-cultural phase, which was of the most consequence to architects, has been characterized as one of "defensive borrowing," starting in 1868 and lasting until a second period marked by the onset of the questioning of Western values in 1889–1890. After a second phase of retrenchment, there was a third stage of extremely overt nationalism and aggression, culminating in a proposal for a "Greater East Asian Co-Prosperity Sphere," or Dai-tō-a Kyōeiken, as a euphemism for an expanded Empire, proclaimed by Foreign Minister Hachiro Arita, during the first part of the Showa period, in the Spring of 1940. An alliance with Germany and Italy was finalized in the same year.[2]

The first phase, which lasted from the start of the Restoration in 1868 until around 1878, was in a direct, almost panicked response to what was seen as a foreign threat, leading to the wholesale adoption of Western methods and customs as a way of defraying colonization. The temper of the times is evident in the slogan "Fukoku Kyohei" or "Enrich the country, strengthen the military," which was adopted by the Meiji government, to establish an industrial infrastructure along Western lines. It was expected that this would increase the economic and military profile of Japan, as a bulwark against colonization.

During this decade there was substantial social reorganization and upheaval, including the Japanese Land Reform Act of 1873, which allowed private land ownership and title as an important step in the direction of capitalism, along with tax reforms, the establishment of Tokyo as single capital to replace the dual centers of Kyoto and Edo, and the re-structuring of the restrictive Tokugawa class system, including the elimination of the Samurai. This profoundly changed the pre-existing, feudal structure of the country. The military was also modernized, as new weaponry was introduced and foreign advisors were brought in to train government troops. The construction of an extensive railway system, and a free press, also heralded a plethora of other political and economic changes. One of the most significant domestic consequences of the Meiji Restoration, then, was that it introduced the capitalist model and full-scale, Western-style principles of land ownership and industrial production into Japan, leading to the First Enterprise Boom of 1886–1889, which changed the standard of living of urban and rural areas alike. Individuality, as the primary ingredient of capitalism, however, is another matter, so the model was modified to conform to a well-established social habit of collective consensus.[3]

An inspiring omen of resistance to change

Such rapid change, however, was not readily accepted in a nation so steeped in tradition. One famous dissenter was Saigo Takamori, a former Samurai who formed the Public Party of Patriots or Aikokukoto and withdrew to Kagoshima. Many ex-Samurai followers joined them and the government sent a naval expedition to disarm them in January 1877. The Satsuma Rebellion that followed made it clear that the Samurai were not prepared to go quietly. Resistance against advanced weaponry was futile however, and only lasted until September 24th, when Saigo died in a heroic last stand. Takamori has recently received a posthumous pardon in recognition of his loyalty to traditional values and his statue now occupies a prominent place at the entrance to Ueno Park (Figure 4.1).

The literal appropriation of British Arts and Crafts architecture

As a prelude to this first apprehensive, acquisitive phase, the Meiji government issued the Charter Oath of 1868, and one of its five articles specifically authorized "the seeking of knowledge throughout the world in order to strengthen the country."[4] It eagerly embraced and actively welcomed Western influence and

Figure 4.1
Saigo Takamori
Source: James Steele

values, including issuing invitations to foreign architects to teach new construction methods and styles. This was no mean feat, given the extent to which highly organized and influential carpentry guilds were entrenched within the Japanese social structure at the time. It was not simply a matter of the superficial imitation of foreign fashion, since it also involved the complete reorganization and re-education of these construction trades, which had previously built in wood and rice paper rather than stone, iron and glass. Some sources bemoan the fate of the various groups that perpetuated these skills, but these carpenter guilds then established companies that eventually morphed into the "big five" construction corporations of Kajima, Shimizu, Taisu, Obayashi, and Takenaka Komuten, that eventually went on to control one-third of the construction in Japan.[5]

It is not the purpose here to dwell on "Meiji-style" architecture, which has been documented in great detail elsewhere, but suffice it to say that because it had not been colonized, Japan could not build upon a prior body of classical forms that were gradually refined over a long period of time, resulting in eclectic and awkward foreign styles.

Josiah Conder

There were also a multitude of foreign experts in various fields who were invited to assist in national development, but Josiah Conder was undoubtedly the most influential of these and had the most extensive and lasting impact on the future of contemporary architecture in Japan. He taught as well as practiced, and mentored a cadre of devoted students who then went on to establish the foundation of architecture as a profession. Conder became the first professor in the College of Architecture of the Imperial College of Engineering, or Kobu Daigakko, in Tokyo in 1877, remaining there until he established his own practice in 1888 and, in spite of the difficulties inherent in

Figure 4.2 Tatsuno Kingo Tokyo Train Station
Source: Miki Fujiwara

Figure 4.3 Nakanoshima, Osaka
Source: Hartmut Poeling

being a foreign resident, became an associate member of the RIBA in 1874 and a Fellow in 1884. His many buildings include the Ueno Imperial Museum in 1882, and the Mitsubishi Building, Mitsui Club, and Naval Ministry in 1894, but perhaps most memorable of all, the Rokumeikan or "Deer-Cry Hall" near the Imperial Palace in Hibiya, which was commissioned by Foreign Minister Inoue Kaoru to house and entertain foreign visitors, and to allow them to meet Japanese guests, as a form of cultural exchange. Many of his students, such as Sone Tatsuzo, Satachi Shichijiro, Shimoda Kikutaro, Tatsuno Kingo and Katayama Tokuma, then went on to have distinguished and influential careers of their own. Conder encouraged Kingo, who graduated from the Imperial College in 1879, to further his studies at London University and arranged for him to apprentice with William Burgess while he was there. After Burgess's death in 1881, Kingo travelled throughout France and Italy, before returning to Japan in 1882. He was then instrumental in founding The Architectural Institute of Japan, based on the Royal Institute of British Architects. His overtly neo-classical Bank of Japan, completed in 1896, is one of the first European-style buildings in the nation to be designed by a Japanese architect.[6]

The Tokyo Train Station, in the Maranouchi District of the capital, is unquestionably Kingo's most prominent building (Figure 4.2).

Original construction of the monumental edifice was delayed because of the first Sino-Japanese War, but four platforms were opened on December 18, 1914, and it has served as the largest railway station in the nation ever since, with several intermediate repairs being carried out over the years. It was completely restored in 2013, to serve 14 rail lines, including a majority of the complex Shinkansen network that branches out from here to all parts of the country. The banded brick style that Kingo used quickly proliferated, appearing in virtually indistinguishable form in his Dai-Ichi-Kangyo Bank in Kyoto in 1906, the Fukuoka Cultural Center by Tokoma Katayama in 1909, and the Nakanoshima Central Public Auditorium in Osaka, by Shin'ichiro Okada and Tatsuno Kingo in 1918 (Figure 4.3). These variegated, red brick and white stone facades are reminiscent of a similar kind of sequencing used by Richard Norman Shaw in public buildings such as 1–2 St. James Street, which was under construction during Kingo's stay in London, and completed in 1882. Shaw used the same alternating pattern of stone on brick at New Scotland Yard in 1890, which was converted into Parliamentary Offices in 1979, including the capped corner towers used on the Tokyo Train Station.

A second phase of retrenchment: 1890–1930

This first helter-skelter period of change then shifted to a second phase of retrenchment, introduced by the Satsuma Rebellion in 1877, based on a general feeling that change was taking place too quickly and that cultural values were in grave danger of being lost. This resounding shift was cemented by the drafting of a Constitution which was deliberately released in 1889 on the anniversary of the founding of the Yamoto state given in the *Nihon Shoki*, and re-affirmed Shintoism as the state religion and the divinity of the Emperor.[7]

This second phase of qualified modernization, tempered by a collective soul-searching about the wisdom of wholesale borrowing from foreign sources, prompted Meiji to commission Motoda Eifu to draft the *Kyogaku Taishi*, or Main Points of Education in 1878, formalized as the Imperial Rescript on Education in 1890. By doing so, he hoped to reverse what he perceived to be the liberalizing effects of the Charter Oath of 1868, which encouraged "searching the world for knowledge" and to replace "the vain emulation of Western manners" with Confucian values of loyalty and filial piety.[8]

Nationalism, and the power of the military, continued to soar after victories in both the Sino-Japanese War, concluded by the Treaty of Shimonoseki in 1895, and the Russo-Japanese War, which ended in the Portsmouth Treaty in 1905. These military milestones, as indicators of Japan's systemic economic and technological strength, finally provided it with the international recognition, stability and freedom from foreign incursion it had been seeking since the Meiji era began. In spite of these successes on the battlefield, and the

regional respect that came from being the only Asian power to defeat a Western nation, however, internal political turmoil was rife. One instance of this was the High Treason Incident of 1910, involving a plot to assassinate the Emperor, leading to suppression of the left wing.

In a parallel condition of social upheaval during the Industrial Revolution, which had started a century earlier in Britain, and then spread to other Western countries such as the United States, there was also a belated, but ultimately enduring reflexive reaction to the rapid changes resulting from mass migration from rural to urban areas, and the accompanying social problems of poverty, homelessness, disease and crime that accompanied modernization.

Advocates for a measured retreat from modernization

It should not be surprising, then, that a reflexive theoretical *leitmotif* similar to that of the Arts and Crafts movement in Britain should begin to appear in Japan. A group of apologists, who were the equivalent of the Arts and Crafts leaders calling for a return to traditional values, started to emerge, trying to come to grips with the need to modernize in order to survive.

These advocates of a measured return to the past had a powerful role model in the increasingly popular folk hero Ryoma Sakamoto, who was a Samurai during the last gasp of the Tokugawa regime. He also played an important role in initiating the Meiji Restoration, by uniting the antagonistic Choshu and Satsuma clans against the Tokugawa government. He belonged to the Tosa Loyalist, or Kinnoto Party, whose motto was "Sonno-joi," or, "Revere the Emperor, Expel the Foreigner," before striking out, as a ronin, or lone Samurai, on his own. In spite of his deeply held belief in traditional values, he was a realist and understood the need for Japan to modernize. He took the first steps helping engineer Katsu Kaishu establish a navy to oppose the Tokugawa Shogunate as well as a fleet for the Kameyama Shachu Trading Company in Nagasaki, and also drew up an eight-point plan that provided the Shogun Tokugawa Yoshinobu with a face-saving way to abdicate. Sakamoto was assassinated in the Omiya, now the Teradaya, Ryokan, in Kyoto, on December 10, 1867 and has now achieved the status of a martyr among many in Japan who admire the courage and foresight he showed in balancing past values with the insistent demands of contemporary life.

As the bold Meijii experiment that started the year after Sakamoto's death played itself out, several intellectuals also voiced similar concerns about the breakneck speed of Western-style modernization, using equally quotable aphorisms. In his essay "History as it Is and History Ignored," the novelist-turned-historian Mori Ogai also questioned the policy of *wakon yosai*, or openness to the West. He extolled the virtues of the pre-Meiji period, and introduced the catch phrases "Rich country, strong army" and "Japanese spirit, Western learning." Fellow novelist Natsume Soseki also wrote about the conflicting ideals of duty and individual freedom. Like Ryoma Sakamoto, he also struck at the heart of the paradox that modernism presented, both then and now, in a country in which the opinion of the family and the group outweigh personal needs. In his popular novel *Sore Kara*, or "And Then," written in 1909, his protagonist, Daisuke, personifies what Soseki characterizes as the dangers of industrialization and Western culture, such as detachment and separation from traditional mores. Western philosophy was not spared, coming under scrutiny from both Nishi Amane and Kitaro Nishida. Amane cautioned against it as a potential cause of a loss of what he called "Japanese character," in spite of having introduced it into Japan, while Nishida took a more nuanced position, in trying to challenge external traditions with Zen counterpoints. His "Logic of Basho," which became the basis for the Kyoto School of Philosophy, refutes the dualism of Western concepts such as dialectical synthesis by substituting a decidedly Japanese alternative of a preference for a state of perpetual tension instead.[9]

Kakuzo Okakura was another writer and poet who resisted Western intrusion and championed the preservation of Japanese culture at this time. He was part of the Imperial Art Commission sent to study American and European aesthetic tastes in 1904, which convinced him of what he believed to be the superiority of his own culture, instead. He was subsequently appointed to direct the New Art School in Ueno, but resigned in 1897 to protest its European curriculum. He then started a new school at the *Nippon Bijitsuin*, or Hall of Fine Arts in Yanaka, focusing on Japanese decorative arts, such as earthenware, porcelain, lacquer-ware and metal-working, which soon attracted a large following. As one of his nation's first art historians and critics, he is credited with initiating "aesthetic nationalism" which he portrayed as culturally authentic, and extrapolated traditional values, which he characterized as being superior and ideal.[10] In his *The Ideals of the East*, Okakura famously maintained that Asian culture is unified and superior to that of the West, because it has evolved over a much longer period of time. He also argued that Japan should be the one to both preserve and promote this superior culture, because it had never been occupied, up to that point, and had an unbroken Imperial line. In *Awakening of the East*, which was published in 1939, after his death, he goes much further in advocating these chauvinistic views, which were used to support the establishment of a Japanese-controlled Greater East Asia Co-Prosperity Sphere.

A Japanese William Morris, or a British Yanagi Soetsu?

Because he established the *Nippon Bijitsuin*, Kakuzo Okakura is also frequently compared to William Morris, but Yanagi Soetsu, who is an equally vehement advocate of protecting Japanese cultural values, is surely a more likely analogue for the British intellectual omnivore. He is also foremost among those who converted from believing in the value of Westernization at the turn of the century, to being an ultra-nationalistic supporter of ethnic purity the mid-1930s, and as such he tracks a similar shift in national opinion. As a young, urbane, well-educated man from an upper-middle class background, he embodied metropolitan sophistication, and in 1910, he founded the *Shirakabe* group to promote the modernization of Japan. As he became increasingly aware of a need to establish and maintain ethnic cultural identity in the face of the onslaught of foreign values, however, he eventually changed his mind. After a decade-long period of extensive research into mysticism, Sufism and Zen Buddhism, he started to investigate the ideas of moral and religious purity inherent in medievalism, Gothic art and architecture, as put forward by Pugin, Ruskin and Morris.[11] The British potter Bernard Leach, who lived in Japan from 1909 until 1920, introduced Soetsu to the work of

Morris, and, inspired by his advocacy of a rediscovery of the honest beauty of handmade, utilitarian objects, Soetsu started to search out, study and collect similar items throughout rural Japan and Korea. In 1925 he developed the concept of minshū-teki-na kōgei or "the crafts, or arts of the people," shortened to Mingei, as a dignified, original source of Japanese ethnic identity. In that same year, he also wrote and published *Kogei no Michi*, or *The Unknown Craftsman*, which Leach translated into English.[12] In it, he proposed his "nihon ni okeru bi no hyōjun," or "criterion of beauty in Japan" based on the qualities of honesty, purity and harmony with nature, and found in getemoto, or everyday objects that were functional, inexpensive, unselfconscious, handmade, deliberately anonymous, and ideally made by a group and representative of their region.

The Japanese Guild of Crafts

In 1927, Soetsu founded the Japanese Guild of Crafts, based on Morris, Marshall, Faulkner & Co,

and designed the Mikunisō or Mikuni Villa, initially intended to be a Folk Craft Pavilion for an exhibition in Tokyo in 1928. It was purchased after the exhibition closed and moved to the grounds of a private residence in Osaka. A heated debate, swirling around Yanagi Sōetsu and his theory of Mingei today, pits those who point to his positive contribution in providing a model for a new proto-modern, middle-class lifestyle that synthesizes pride in Japanese design and Western sensibilities against others who claim that his views simply conform to the heightened nationalism and militarism of the time. In response to what has been termed Soetsu's "Oriental Orientalism" supporters point to his promotion of minorities within Japan, such as the Ainu and Taiwanese, as well as Korean and Chinese crafts, as being very courageous at the time, and uncharacteristic of a colonial mentality. In addition to Yanagi Soetsu and Bernard Leach, the *Mingei* movement eventually included the potters Kenkichi Tomimoto, Shoji Hamada, Kanjiro Kawai, textile artist Keisuke Serizawa, woodblock-print artist

Figure 4.4 Kawai House
Source: Miki Fujiwara

Figure 4.5 Kawai, Kiln
Source: Miki Fujiwara

Shiko Munakata, lacquer artist Kuroda Tatsuaki, and the painter Munakata Shikō. The Kyoto house of Kanijiro Kawai remains an important center of this movement today and his kiln evokes the resolve of this movement to retain ancient methods of firing pottery.[13] (See Figures 4.4 and 4.5.)

An innocent abroad

The paradigmatic Midwestern American and confirmed Arts and Crafts advocate Frank Lloyd Wright first visited Japan in 1905, just as the Russo-Japanese war was concluding, nationalism was intensifying and Yanagi Soetsu was coming of age. He was 37 years old when he and his wife Catherine and another couple disembarked and their ambitious itinerary included a trip from Nikko to Takamatsu. Wright first became aware of traditional Japanese architecture when he visited the *Ho-o-den* Temple, a miniaturized version of *Byodo-in*, in Uji, at the World's Columbian Exposition in Chicago in 1893, with his mentor, Louis Sullivan. This was a life-changing encounter, which not only inspired him to re-invent his design approach, but also led him to become one of the leading advocates of Japanese culture in the United States.

He later received the commission to design the Imperial Hotel in 1916, and returned to Japan again and subsequently opened an office in Tokyo (Figure 4.6).

He eventually designed 14 buildings during his stay, of which six were actually built. These are the Imperial Hotel and Annex, the Jiyu Gakuen School, the Aisaku Hayashi House, the Arinobu Fukuhara House and the Tazaemon Yamamura House. The Jiyu Gakuen School, completed in 1922, in Toshiya-ku, near Tokyo and designed in collaboration with Arata Endo, is a rare instance of Wright allowing someone else to share credit with him. Endo, who had visited Wright at his Taliesin Studio in Wisconsin, also assisted him on the Imperial Hotel, and directed six other local architects on the project. The Yamamura House was built in Ashiya-shi, Hyogo-ken, in 1924. His un-built projects are a United States embassy, a residence for Aisaku Hayashi in Tokyo, a hotel in Odawara, a motion picture theater in Ginza, the Mihara House in Tokyo, the Arinobu Fukuhara House in Hakone, the Tadashiro Inoue House in Tokyo, the Shimpei Goto House, a prime minister's residence and the Hibiya and Triangle Building.[14]

When Wright left Japan in 1922 he left behind a group of young followers, who, in addition to Arata Endo, included Kameki Tsuchiura, Yoshiya Tanoue, Makoto Minami, Takehiko Okami, Muraji Shimomoto, Teizo Sugawara, Taro Amano and Raku Endo. Arata Endo's designs afterward, such as his Kondo House in Fujisawa in 1925, and the Koshien Hotel, now Koshien Hall as part of Mukogawa Women's University in Nishinomiya in 1930, as well as the Kubo Auditorium in Mooka City in 1938, strictly conform to Wright's aesthetic. Kameki Tsuchiura, who had been introduced to Wright by Endo, and had worked on the Imperial Hotel, visited the master in the United States in 1924, in both Los Angeles and Taliesin and worked on several projects while he was there.

Figure 4.6 F.L. Wright, Imperial Hotel
Source: Miki Fujiwara

After returning to Japan in 1926, Kameki's design sensibility slowly shifted toward International-style modernism, but his exposure to Wright's standardized "textile block" methodology inspired him to attempt a similar system in wood, in an attempt to make more efficient, low-cost housing available to everyone. The house that he and his wife Nobu designed for themselves in Shinagawa in 1935, however, is strictly based on functionalist Bauhaus principles.[15]

The part that Wright played in the gradual integration of Western modernism into Japan at this early stage in its development, however, is debatable. Arata Isozaki, for one, categorically discounts his influence, saying that his approach to both form and space in the Imperial Hotel, in Tokyo, which Wright worked on between 1912 and 1923 and which was subsequently demolished, failed to resonate with Japanese sensibilities because it lacks a requisite sense of "flatness" and internal fluidity.[16]

Antonin Raymond as Wright's real legacy in Japan

The subsequent activities of most of those who assisted Wright on his architectural projects, such as Arata Endo, still await more clarification, but those of Antonin Raymond are so well known and integral to the subsequent growth of modernism in Japan that he may ironically be considered Wright's most lasting legacy. Raymond was born in Kladno, Bohemia, which is now in the Czech Republic. He worked with Wright at Taliesin, in Spring Green, Wisconsin and then joined him in Tokyo to help with the Imperial Hotel. He had also worked with Cass Gilbert in the United States, and this experience, along with his interest in Czech modernism and the reinforced concrete structures of Auguste Perret, put him at odds with Wright, who disliked exposed concrete and covered the frame of the Imperial Hotel with carved *Oya* stone, to avoid seeing it. Feeling that Wright did not really

Figure 4.7 Raymond, Reader's Digest
Source: Antonin Raymond Office

understand Japanese sensibilities, Raymond decided to go out on his own and set up the American Architectural and Engineering Company in Tokyo in 1921, which became Antonin Raymond, Architect and then the Raymond Architectural Design Office in 1937. Raymond's Reader's Digest Building of 1949, followed by the 1954 Church of St. Anselm, and Gunma Music Center in 1955, are clear testimony to the raw power of his use of concrete, which has had a lasting influence on contemporary Japanese architects (Figures 4.7, 4.8, 4.9).

True to his Arts and Crafts principles, Wright felt that by allowing Japanese laborers relative freedom in the carving of the *Oya* stone surface of the Imperial Hotel, he was encouraging both their natural talent and the Japanese craft tradition. But, in spite of his own sensitivity to the innate qualities of natural materials, and his obvious respect for Japanese culture, he seemed unable to translate that into receptivity to local context. Raymond, on the other hand, was paradoxically successful in doing that with concrete, by emphasizing

Figure 4.8 Raymond, St. Anselm
Source: Antonin Raymond Office

Figure 4.9
Raymond, Gunma Music
Source: Antonin Raymond
Office

the wood grain of the form-work, as well as having the workers expose the stone aggregate after the forms were stripped. These techniques, along with his awareness of light and shadow, and his straightforward treatment of post and beam configurations, won him the respect that has eluded his famous mentor. After being filtered through Raymond's distinguished apprentice, Kunio Maekawa, they later surfaced most overtly in the work of Kenzo Tange and Tadao Ando, among others.[17]

Notes

1 Andre Sorensen, *The Making of Urban Japan: Cities and Planning from Edo to the Twenty-First Century*, Nissan Institute, Routledge Japanese Studies Series, 2005.

2 Patrick Smith, *Japan: A Reinterpretation*, New York: Vintage, 1997, p. 52.

3 Naofumi Nakamura, "Meiji-Era Industrialization and Provincial Vitality: The Significance of the First Enterprise Boom of the 1880s," *Social Science Japan Journal*, Vol. 1, No. 2, pp. 187–200.

4   William De Bary, Carol Gluck, and Arthur Tiedemann (Eds.), *Sources of Japanese Tradition, Vol. II: 1600 to 2000*, New York: Columbia University Press, 2005, p. 163.

5   Botand Bognar, *NIKKEN SEKKEI: Building Future Japan 1900–2000*. New York: Rizzoli International, 2000, p. 123.

6   David B. Stewart, *The Making of a Modern Japanese Architecture, 1868 to the Present*, Tokyo: Kodansha International, 1987, p. 37.

7   Michael F. Marra, *Essays on Japan: Between Aesthetics and Literature*, E.J. Brill, 2010, p. 45.

8   William H. Coaldrake, *Architecture and Authority in Japan*, London: Nissan Institute, Routledge, 1996, p. 231.

9   Dallas Finn, *Meiji Revisited, the Sites of Victorian Japan*, Tokyo: Weatherhill, 1998.

10 Thomas Schneider, "Traditionalism and Modernization: The Case for Mori Ogai," *Comparative Civilizations Review*, Boston College, 2012, p. 59.

11 John Clark, "Okakura Tenshin and Aesthetic Nationalism," *East Asian History*, No. 29, Institute of Advanced Studies, Australian National University, Editor Geremie R. Barme, June 2005, p. 1.

12 Yuko Kikuchi, *Japanese Modernization and Mingei Theory, Cultural Nationalism and Orientalism*, London: Routledge Curzon, 2004, p. 43.

13 Ibid., p. 44.

14 Yuko Kikuchi, "The Myth of Yanagi's Originality: The Formation of *Mingei* Theory in its Social and Historical Context," *Journal of Design History*, Vol. 17, No. 4, 1994, pp. 247–266.

15 Karen Severns and Koichi Mori, *Magnificent Obsession: Frank Lloyd Wright's Buildings and Legacy in Japan*, 2005. Documentary.

16 Ibid.

17 Arata Isozaki, *Japan-ness in Architecture*, Cambridge, MA: MIT Press, 2006, p. 243.

CHAPTER 5

Modernism sidetracked on the road to war: 1930–1940

The third and final phase of the development of Japanese modernism opened with a series of shocking events in the early 1930s, euphemistically called "incidents." These included coup attempts and actual and attempted assassinations of prime ministers and the Emperor, as well as invasions of neighboring countries, and these occurred in rapid succession, against a harsh background of economic hardship. They started in November 1930, with an assassination attempt against Prime Minister Osachi Hamaguchi because he agreed to limitations on the size of the Japanese fleet in the London Naval Treaty. Then, an attempted coup d'état by the Sakurakai, a secret society inside the Imperial army, assisted by external ultranationalist groups, was thwarted in March 1931. In September 1931, following a staged incident which made it appear as if Chinese troops had sabotaged the South Manchurian Railway near Mukden, Japanese troops invaded and occupied the entire region, which they renamed Manchoukuo. A Protocol, signed on September 15, 1932 in Siking, China, declared that "in accordance with the free will of its inhabitants," Manchoukuo "has organized and established itself as an independent State".[1] In February 1933, the League of Nations ordered Japan to leave Manchuria, which it refused to do, leaving the League in protest instead. By 1931, the internal economic situation had worsened to the extent that rural areas were in the grip of famine, causing widespread discontent that was directed against the government and the corporate superstructure.

Having failed to replace the government in March 1931, Lieutenant Colonel Kingoro Hashimoto of the Sakurakai secret society tried again in October 1931. This time, in what is known as the "Imperial Colors Incident" the leaders were jailed and the Sakurakai was disbanded, but the Emperor did not impose heavy sentences, which encouraged further military interference in government affairs. In 1932, Japanese forces attacked Shanghai and occupied the city for several months before the Shanghai Ceasefire Agreement was brokered by the League of Nations. This was a prelude to the Battle of Shanghai at the beginning of the Second Sino-Japanese War in 1937. On May 15, 1932, Prime Minister Inukai Tsuyoshi was assassinated by a group of military officers and cadets. This also emboldened dissent, leading to the February 26 Incident in 1936, when a group of young Imperial Army officers sought to restore "kokutai" or national identity and harmony between the people and emperor, which they believed was being thwarted by the rich, upper classes, including politicians, high ranking officers in the military, government officials and the zaibatsu. They called their plan the "Showa Restoration," echoing the Meiji restoration 64 years earlier.

These "incidents," during what has been referred to as a decade of "government by assassination," add up to a concerted effort by the military to take power, and had their origin in the instrumental role that ex-Samurai played in the formation of the Meiji government. They concluded with a belief in the possibility of Pan-Asian unity, under Japanese control, following the "Asia is one" theory put forward by Tenshin Okakura.[2] This theory was realized as "the Greater East Asia Co-prosperity Sphere," later elaborated in a classified document with limited circulation entitled "An Investi-gation of Global Policy with the Yamoto Race as Nucleus" in 1943, which clearly enunciates the original ideological intentions of the "Sphere" as being a hierarchy, determined by Japanese superiority. From this vantage point, Japan was not invading other sovereign nations in Asia, but was liberating them from colonial occupation and exploitation by the West. Shinto became the state religion and the Emperor was accorded divine status, as a descendant of the goddess Amaterasu, reinforcing the idea of Hakkō ichiu, or "the entire world under one roof."[3]

A fateful coincidence

By historical accident, Japan and Germany each attained nationhood in 1871, which was relatively late on the worldwide timeline. They faced the same challenges of trying to unify a fractious collection of sovereign entities, mollify powerful martial factions and match the economic and technological status of other nation states, while also dealing with the consequences of rapid urbanization. Each fledgling nation also believed that military strength was an important part of achieving their goals. During this process, theorists on both sides started a dialogue and Karl Haushofer, who was an Army General and Professor at Munich University, was part of that. He was the founder of the "Munich School" which refined the concept of geopolitik as an inter-relationship between geography, warfare, imperial aspirations, and lebens-raum, and visited Japan frequently.[4] Japanese counter-parts, such as Shumei Okawa, Kingoro Hashimoto and Ishiwara Kanji, also envisioned a Eurasian entity shared between Germany and Japan. This led to a process from 1933 onward in which liberal voices were drowned out by cries for a Japanese-led Pan-Asian entity.

Negotiating treacherous crosscurrents

Because of their intimate connection with social expectations, cultural identity, and national aspirations,

Japanese architects were in an increasingly tenuous and potentially dangerous position as this treacherous and eventually tragic drama played itself out. In spite of sharing many overlapping ideological visions, Japan, Germany and Italy, as partners in the Anti-Communist Pact of 1936–1937, which led to the Three-Power Pact signed on September 27, 1940, obviously represented varied cultural backgrounds and each took a different position relative to modern architecture during this decade. These subtly variegated responses, which may be described as the repression of modernism in Germany, reduction to typologies in Italy and a more modulated response in Japan, provide an important insight into conditions for Japanese architects in both this critical conclusion of the pre-war period and its post-war aftermath.

Modernism in Japan

In Japan, the official position about modernism conformed to the National Socialist view in Germany, that it was left-wing conspiracy to be systematically eradicated. But there are several important qualifications. Arata Isozaki, for example, has categorically said that: "because of its internationalist associations, modern architecture was oppressed and persecuted in Japan during the 1930s" because of "the association of modernism with the socialist revolutionary movement" and "modernism had a strong adversary in the revived eclecticism based on imperialist ideology".[5] The eclecticism he is referring to is the officially sanctioned teikan yoshiki, or Imperial Crown style. Kikutaro Shimoda coined the name in 1920 in reference to the competition for the Diet, which was won by Takeuchi Shinshichi, who balanced Eastern and Western influences, rather than overtly choosing sides as others did.[6] It is not to be mistaken for earlier giyofu, or pseudo-Western style buildings constructed using traditional methods. The Imperial Crown style is most clearly evident in the Nagoya City Hall of 1933, the Gunjin Kaikan Building in Tokyo (1934), the Tokyo Imperial Museum by Jin Watanabe (Figure 5.1) (1937), the Tsukiji Hongan-ji by Itō Chūta completed in 1934 (Figure 5.2), the Aichi Prefectural Government Office (1938), which is also in Nagoya, and the 1939 Kana-gawa Prefectural Government Building in Yokohama. With the exception of the Tsukiji Hongan-ji, which

Figure 5.1 Tokyo Imperial Museum by Jin Watanabe
Source: James Steele

Figure 5.2 Tsukiji Hongan-ji by Itō Chūta
Source: James Steele

is inspired by Indian Buddhist cave temples, all of these share a traditional temple roof above a stripped-down, rectilinear, partly rusticated, colossally ordered, vaguely Rinascimento wrapper, with a steel and concrete structure.

In spite of the supposedly oppressive conditions and strictures that Isozaki describes, however, as well as the official requirement to use teikan yoshiki, the militarists were more circumspect than their German counterparts and modernist buildings kept appearing. This raises the question of how and why this was possible, and how extensive the exceptions to the rule were.

A lingering deference to foreign opinion

Several tantalizing hints begin to explain the question of how and why modernist buildings kept getting built. The first is an invitation offered to Bruno Taut by the Japan International Architectural Association to visit Japan in 1933, which the modernist theorist, Bauhaus affiliate, Glass Chain founder and Weissenhofseidlung participant readily accepted. Soon after his arrival, Association members Isaburo Ueno and Shotaro Shimomura took him to see Katsura Rikyū, which was difficult to access at that time, and not open to the public.[7] Far from simply being an act of random kindness to a foreign tourist, this visit was carefully choreographed as part of a concerted strategy of resistance against government control. The organizers of Taut's itinerary, which also included the Ise Shrine and the Tosho-gu Shrine at Nikko, where Tokugawa Ieyasu is buried, anticipated his positive reaction to the Imperial Villa in Kyoto, based on the attributes of transparency, modularity, prefabrication, free flow of space, honest use of materials and structural clarity that it has in common with modernist theory. The organizers were not disappointed, and their stratagem succeeded far beyond their expectations. Taut stayed in Japan until 1936, and during that time wrote *Houses and People of Japan,* published by the Sanseido Company in Tokyo a year after he left. It is essentially a paean to the beauty of Katsura, and a condemnation of the vulgarity of Tosho-gu, inadvertently re-affirming the rise of Imperial power and eclipse of the Shogunate, which played well with his local audience at the time. Arata Isozaki further explains that this confluence was perfectly timed, since Japanese architects felt "compelled to search for a valid conjuncture, if not an actual compromise, between modernism and nationalism" at that time, and now looked to the Imperial Villa as offering that possibility, so that "Taut's vision of Katsura became the corner-stone of a new paradigmatic shift."[8]

One possible answer, then, to the question of how modernists kept building, in spite of ultra-national repression, is that in spite of the extreme retreat from Westernization that had taken place by this point, after progressing through the Meiji Restoration the abbreviated Taisho period of Emperor Yoshihito, and then the Showa period of Emperor Hirohito up to and through World War II, some residual deference to the opinion of European experts, such as Taut, still remained. The Japanese practitioners that stage-managed his itinerary obviously felt that his opinion was still effective enough to provide an ideological space for freedom for architects who followed in his wake. This subliminal deference to foreign authority may also explain the sustained effectiveness of three other modernists, who chose to leave Japan before the war and apprentice with Le Corbusier in Paris for various periods of time. Architect Arata Isozaki has eloquently described the overlap as being a common commitment to "simplicity, humility, purity, lightness and shibusa or sophisticated austerity."[9]

The Ministry of Communication: a disseminator of Modernism

Tetsuro Yoshida, whose considerable talent has somehow been mysteriously overlooked by historians to date, also provides a second possible answer to the question of how modern architects managed to keep building during this time. They concentrated on designing structures that were seen as being essential engineering projects by the government, and so were beneath official radar, or were sources of pride as symbols of progress. In his book *Vers Une Architecture,* which was written in 1922, Le Corbusier praised common utilitarian structures, such as the grain silos in the American Midwest, and the engineering of airplanes, ocean liners, automobiles and trains, as being most representative of the modern spirit. This was also the case in Japan during this early stage of the introduction of the principles of the modern movement. The reflexive reaction that it received, and the resistance from hard-line traditionalists, was more muted when it came to the design of new infrastructure. Many of these projects are among the most forward looking, and skillfully designed and meticulously detailed buildings of the pre-war period. As Jonathan Reynolds has observed, the task that the Ministry of Communication set for itself was

> to promote and disseminate new technology . . . and the Ministry relied increasingly on modernist architectural forms to project a fittingly progressive image . . . [it] became the most important patron of modernist architecture and completed some of the best pre World War II modernist designs in Japan.[10]

Tetsuro Yoshida's vaguely Richardsonian 1926 Central Telephone Office, in Kyoto, (Figure 5.3) is a less

stellar example of this mission than his 1931 Tokyo Central Post Office (Figure 5.4).

Architects typically find sites at intersections, with their inherently challenging requirement of "turning the corner" in a graceful yet commanding way, to be among the most difficult design conundrums they face. Rather than being intimidated by this problem, however, Yoshida turned it into a civic attribute of the highest order. One of his most impressive accomplishments, however, which might normally go unnoticed by pedestrians, is the way he terminates this sweeping curve. There is a tree-lined, residential street at a right angle to the highway on the western side of the Post Office, so Yoshida effortlessly shifted gears to a residential scale, making the end of the building appear to be the final house in the residential row on that side (Figure 5.5).

This remarkable level of civil sensitivity is sorely missing among architects and urban planners today, who can learn a great deal from the modesty of this

Figure 5.3 Central Telephone Office, in Kyoto
Source: Miki Fujiwara

Figure 5.4
Tokyo Central Post Office
Source: James Steele

Figure 5.5
Tokyo Central Post Office
Source: James Steele

effort. A second Post Office, built in Osaka at the same time as the Central branch in Tokyo, is also sited at an intersection, but in this instance, Yoshida faces the corner with a tall, flat segment which announces the main entrance, and by pulling the vertical pilasters, which carry the floors and the lid-like roof in front of the spandrels, in a technique also used by Louis Sullivan on his Wainwright Building in St. Louis, in 1891, Guaranty Building in Buffalo in 1896, and Carson Pirie Scott Building in Chicago in 1899, Yoshida achieves the same effect of making the structure appear to be what Sullivan, in his article "The Tall Office Building Artistically Considered" referred to as "every inch a proud and soaring thing, rising in sheer exultation from bottom to top."[11]

His monumental 1939 design for a City Hall in Beppu, in the south, near Fukuoka, in Miyazaki Prefecture, facing the Inland Sea, turns this technique on its side, using streamlined horizontal banding to offset the otherwise massive bulk of the rectilinear building. In the same year he designed a Research Laboratory for the Nippon Electric (now NEC Corporation) Tamagawa plant, which became the first Japanese

company to successfully test microwave multiplex communications systems. It was immediately placed under military control, however, and is not well documented.

Other architects, such as Takeo Yasui, Bunzo Yamaguchi and Yoshiro Taniguchi also made significant contributions to this utilitarian genre. Tanaguchi, for example, who is the father of famed contemporary Modernist Yoshio, graduated from Tokyo University in 1928, and designed the Hydraulics laboratory at the Tokyo Institute of Technology in 1932. Yasui was also presented with a corner site for his Gas Company Headquarters Building in Osaka in 1933, as a right angle rather than the gentle curve provided to Yoshida for his Tokyo Central Post Office. Yasui's solution, which is once again reminiscent of Sullivan's Carson Pirie Scott Department Store, was to use a drum-like tower, which is higher than the uniform roof-line used elsewhere to soften the angle (Figure 5.6). Like Yoshida, he has also chosen a simple, utilitarian white tile as the skin, but has accentuated the cornice line of each floor to streamline the elevations, and emphasize the idea of speed in recognition of the movement of cars

Figure 5.6
T. Yasui Gas Company Headquarters Building in Osaka
Source: Rokkaku Kijo

along the street. One façade of the building, which has now also been converted into commercial use, runs along an entire city block, and Yasui has used a higher, black plinth base here in response to the increased number of pedestrians along this side.

A power station in Toyama-ken, built by Bunzo Yamaguchi in 1936, also typifies the no-nonsense, straightforward elegance of modern architecture deliberately masquerading as civil engineering to escape censure just prior to the beginning of World War II in Japan. All of the familiar benchmarks, such as functionalism, the honest use of industrial materials and a reinforced concrete post and beam grid structure that allowed for a non-loadbearing curtain wall and increased natural light, are evident here, but are the result of answering the demands of efficiency and productivity, rather than making an ideological statement.

In addition to a residual deference to foreign experts, and the willing promotion of progressive infrastructure, Japanese modernists also survived by networking and finding strength in numbers. Organizations, such as the Bunriha Kenchiku Kai, or Association of Secessionist Architects, in 1920, the Sousha, or Creation of the Universe Society in 1923, and the Shinokenchikukarenmei or New Architects League in 1930, served as an invaluable means of communication and mutual support.[12]

"We rise up . . ."

The Bunriha Kenchiku Kai, or Secessionist Architecture group, which was the first of these, had six members, who had been students of Josiah Conder. These are: Yamada Mamoru, Horiguchi Mamoru, Kikuji Ishimoto, Mayumi Takizawa, Shigeru Yada and Keiichi Morita. Unlike Josef Maria Olbrich's Vienna Secession movement, however, their intention was to irrevocably break with tradition, rather than academia. To underscore this, they published a manifesto, and held several exhibitions, unequivocally declaring their allegiance with early twentieth-century German modernism. The manifesto reads:

> *We rise up,*
> *we part from the architecture of the past so as to create a new school which gives true meaning to all construction.*

> *We rise up*
> *so as to awaken all those sleeping in the architectural sphere of the past, so as to rescue all of those on the point of drowning.*

> *We rise up*
> *to realize this ideal of ours and we offer with joy all we possess, even at the risk of falling, even at the risk of dying.*

> *We all swear this to the world.*[13]

Among this group, Horiguchi Sutemi (1895–1984) Yamada Mamoru (1894–1966), and Kikuji Ishimoto (1894–1963) were the most prominent and produced the most overtly Modernist buildings. In 1922, two years after he graduated from Tokyo University, Horiguchi designed the Tokyo Peace Exhibition and Memorial Tower in Ueno, which affirms the initial Expressionist proclivities of the group, because it is so obviously inspired by the Wedding Tower or Hochzeitsturm on the Mathildenhöhe in Darmstadt by Joseph Maria Olbrich. The wedding tower was designed as part of the exhibition halls of the artists colony established by the Grand Duke of Hesse, Ernst Ludwig, to commemorate his marriage to Princess Eleonore Solms-Hohensolms-Lich, on February 2, 1905. The tower, which was completed in 1908, is located at the highest part of the city, and has five curved spires that crown the main red brick shaft, as well as two horizontal bands of windows that run two-thirds of the way across its surface.

Horiguchi's tower, by comparison, surmounts a pair of long ramps on either side, and is far less monumental than its German predecessor, with three curved bell towers instead of five, turned against the axial sight line, instead of being seen frontally as in Darmstadt. Horiguchi visited the Bauhaus in 1922 in the same year that Wassily Kandinsky started teaching there. Kandinsky had been instrumental in starting Der Blaue Reiter, or Blue Rider movement in 1911, named after his painting based on this dream-like image, along with Franz Marc, Paul Klee, Auguste Macke, Alexei von Jawlensky, Marianne von Werefkin, Gabriele Munter, Lyonel Feinger and Albert Bloch. As a refinement of German Expressionism, it was based on what its practitioners considered to be eternal spiritual truths, also expressed in subjective, symbolic ways. In architecture, this translated into the rejection of the familiar forms and techniques of the past, which were replaced with curvilinear, concrete structures and an emphasis on the use of glass. Horiguchi's Meteorological Station on Ō Island, which he completed after he returned to Japan, shows the impact that this trip had on him. He also designed several noteworthy residential projects prior to the war, in a decidedly more International Style manner, such as the Kikkukawa House (1930), Okada House (1934), Nakanishi House (1936), and Wakasa House (1939). The Wakasa House, in particular, with its flat roof and ramp system, shows a keen understanding of Le Corbusier's Citrohan prototype, but rather than prominently using a reinforced concrete columnar grid, he retains punched window openings in the flat white walls.

Mamoru Yamada, on the other hand, represents the more subjective, Expressionistic side of European Modernism. His Central Telegraph office, built in Tokyo in 1925, with its emphatically vertical series of multi-storied, arched windows, is in the best tradition of Erich Mendelsohn and Bruno Taut. By the time the Shinokenchikukarenmei or New Architects League was formed, in 1930 however, the government was on high alert to shut down what they considered to be left-wing organizations, and the League was forced to disband. This is considered a watershed example of government suppression of Modernism, and afterward the incentive to find ways in which to integrate contemporary and sukiya sensibilities was even stronger.

Kikuji Ishimoto is the third of the most prominent of the six members of the Bunriha group. He admired Erich Mendelsohn, Bruno Taut and Peter Behrens, because of what he saw as the consistency of their rejection of tradition, due to their common experience of World War I, which Japan had not endured. He railed against the emphasis on Classicism as taught by rote at the Faculty of the Engineering of the Department at Tokyo Imperial University, and cited it as the primary reason for establishing the new movement. In July 1920 he helped organize an Exhibition of the Bunriha group at the Hakuboya Department Store and the publication of the "First Selection of Architecture Works by the Secessionist Group" including the manifesto published by Iwanami Shoten. Nine more exhibitions and three books followed over the next eight years.

After graduation, Ishimoto joined the Planning Section of Takenaka Komuten, and then went to Germany in 1922 to study at the Bauhaus under Walter Gropius. He used the difference between the Papiermark and the Yen to best advantage to buy books on architecture to take back with him to Japan, where they were difficult to find, establishing a private library for like-minded friends. He returned to the disaster of the Great Kanto Earthquake of 1923, and the opportunity to design the Tokyo Branch of Yamaguchi Bank (1923), the Kyoto Gion Branch of Nomura Bank (1924), and the Nishinoda and Kobe branches of the Osaka Saving Bank (1925). He became a lecturer at Kyoto University in 1927 and designed the Tokyo Asahi Shinbun, which allowed him to disseminate his views on modernism more effectively and helped him receive a commission to design the Shirokiya department store. This, along with the newspaper office, is his best-known work. A chance meeting with Yasushi Kataoka at this time resulted in the formation of the Kataoka-Ishimoto Architectural Studio in 1927, and a more International Style direction, which is evident in the Hiroshima Branch of Fukutoku Insurance (1929), the Kure Branch of the Yamaguchi Bank (1929), the Asahi Newspaper Employee's Club (1929) the home of the artist Seiji Togo (1930) and the Yokohama branch of the Tokyo Asahi Newspaper Company (1931). After Kataoka retired the office became the Ishimoto Architectural Studio, with a similar direction seen in the Nagoya Branch of the Sanjuyon Bank (1934), the Hakata Stock Exchange (1934), the headquarters of Nippon Typewriter (1936), the Fukuoka branch of the Mitsui Bank (1937) and the Oita City Hall (1937).

Synthesis as a fourth approach

In addition to appeals to foreign authority, or claims of progressive design for the good of the nation, or intensive lobbying by forming Modernist organizations and networks, to co-exist and build within government structures, a fourth approach, personified by Togo Murano, was to deny association with modernism altogether, and profess sukiya as a methodology, instead. Murano is now paradoxically recognized as one of the first modernists in Japan in spite of his professed attempt to rise above style. He was born in 1891, and entered the Department of Electrical Engineering at Waseda University in 1913. He then transferred to the Architecture Department two years later and graduated in 1918. He then moved from Tokyo to Osaka to work at the Kansai office of Setsu Watanabe, spending 11 years there. During that time he designed and supervised the construction of a wide variety of building types. He left Japan in 1920 to travel to America and Europe, to widen his architectural horizons, and became especially interested in Scandinavian architecture during that time. After his return in 1929, he opened his own office in Tokyo. His work from that point until his death in 1984, which is not very well known outside Japan, offers an excellent example of the cultural cross currents that were affecting architects at this time, as they were trying to negotiate the treacherous ideological shoals of appearing to be progressive while still respecting nationalism and traditional expression. Protestations aside, Murano both embraced the Modernist ethos and rejected its claim of cultural anonymity. He adopted parts of its formal, functionalist language but also managed to translate it into a clearly identifiable Japanese character, person-

ifying an inherent paradox that continues to evolve from this point forward, of an obvious affinity toward foreign influence and a rejection of it, as well as a respect for technological determinism and an attempt to subvert or deny it.[14]

His Morigo Office Building, in the Nihonbashi district of Tokyo, was the first project he realized after he established his own office in 1931 (Figure 5.7).

Even though he did travel abroad he did not serve an apprenticeship, as Maekawa, Sakakura and Yoshizaka did, but he channeled the Miesian axiom of "less is more" in this stunningly restrained, early example of an instinctively pure, Japanese translation of that minimalist ideology. The building occupies a corner site, at the intersection of a main street and a smaller service alley. At first glance, it appears to be a box-like shaft, with a very thin, hat-like roof, and a façade that appears to be exceptionally flat, due to windows that are flush with the exterior wall. After moving closer, however, it becomes clear that it has a rectangular footprint, is raised up on a massive, plinth-like base, and each elevation is treated differently. Murano has intentionally not made the windows in the

Figure 5.7 Morigo Office Building
Source: James Steele

Figure 5.8 Japanese Wing or Kasuien, Westin Hotel, Kyoto
Source: James Steele

wall above the plinth flush with the exterior wall, to make a thoughtful point about frugality. To reinforce it, he has deliberately contrasted the more luxurious grey granite that he has sparingly used for the columns of the plinth and the wide frames around the inset windows at street level, as well as the thinner granite frames around the windows above, and the less expensive and more utilitarian glazed beige tile skin. On the alley-side elevation, just the slightest inset, of less than a foot, announces an interior plan change at this point, and is obviously also meant to send that message, since it required great effort to achieve it, with no obvious functional effect.

This carefully crafted, exquisitely detailed building, which may now be seen to be the predecessor of so many others in the dense urban landscape of Tokyo and other major cities in Japan, announces the debut of one of the most talented, and arguably least appreciated proto-Modernists to emerge at this early stage. He remarkably also managed to realize several other distinctively modernist projects prior to the war, such as the Hokkoku Bank in Kanazawa in 1932, the Osaka Pantheon in 1933, the Institute of German Civilization

in Kyoto in 1935, the Nakayama House Ashiya in Kobe in 1934, the Sogo Department Store in Osaka in 1936 and the Ube City Public Hall in 1937.

After the war, the Japanese Wing or Kasuien, that Togo Murano designed for the Westin Miyako Hotel in Kyoto in 1959, offers a useful insight into one essential aspect of the debate between Traditionalists and Modernists in the late 1920s and early 30s (Figure 5.8).

This project shows that Murano was able to design a more than passable version of a traditional Shoin, in spite of being equally capable of producing the most eloquent examples of a Modernist aesthetic of anyone practicing during the pre-war period. Taking advantage of the steep slope at this part of the hotel property, he prefaced his cluster of rooms, which are treated as individual houses, with a solid side on the common, inward-facing sitting area that acts like a wall in front of the compound. A small gateway offers tempting glimpses into a central, karasansui style, raked stone Zen garden, as well as a steep, planted rock wall with a dramatic waterfall on the right side. The house-like rooms, which are affectionately designated as "Yuki" at the lower level of the slope, and "Tsuki" above, have the

Figure 5.9 "Tsuki", Westin Hotel, Kyoto
Source: James Steele

feeling of being a small village and sweep upward in an arc from the bottom of the slope to the top of the high rock wall (Figure 5.9). Each of these have tatami mats on the floor, no Western furniture, futon beds, and hinoki wood soaking tubs in the bathrooms, with wide sliding windows overlooking the courtyard and gardens below.

The significance of this skillful rendition is that it was produced by the most talented modernist of his generation, showing that traditionalism resides not far beneath the surface of even the most avant-garde architect in Japan.

Overcoming modernity

A symposium that included prominent writers, philosophers, artists, cinematographers, musicians, historians and scientists was held in Tokyo in the summer of 1942, soon after a critical defeat at the Battle of Midway that is considered to be the beginning of the end of Japanese hopes for victory in World War II. The intention of the organizers, at this critical point in the war, was to take stock of the tremendous sociological

changes that had taken place in Japan since the beginning of the Meiji Restoration. The Proceedings have recently been translated and edited and convey a deep sense of anxiety about the loss of cultural identity that had resulted from a headlong rush to modernize and embrace new technologies. During the Symposium, some argued that modernity had to be overcome because the failures of capitalism, democracy, and liberalism had led inevitably to the war, seemingly oblivious to the fact that it was the perversion of those institutions that had caused it.[15]

Benito Mussolini was executed on April 28, 1945, and Adolf Hitler committed suicide two days later. On May 7, German Chief of Staff General Alfred Jodl unconditionally surrendered, leaving Japan to face the Allied forces alone. In spite of an attempted military coup to prevent him from doing so, Emperor Hirohito capitulated in an unprecedented radio broadcast on August 15, 1945, which was the first time his subjects had heard his voice. The war had lasted for three years and eight months, resulting in the nuclear destruction of two cities and the complete devastation, by firebombing, of almost every other. Occupation started soon afterward, and lasted near seven years, until April 1952. With the stated aim of demilitarizing and democratizing Japan, Supreme Commander for the Allied Powers, and essentially new Shogun Douglas MacArthur, dictated that there be no travel outside the country, no major political, administrative or economic decisions, no public criticism, and certainly no autonomy or sovereignty.[16]

The unthinkable prospect of foreign intrusion that had instigated the Meiji Restoration had finally occurred. During the turbulent metamorphosis that took place during this formative period, from the Mejii Restoration to the beginning of World War II, Japanese architects managed to prevail by co-existing with the political, economic and technological changes that were taking place, in a variety of ingenious ways. This transformative experience, as well as the war and its aftermath, prepared them to take on the challenges of a new world order.

Notes

1 John W. Dower, *War Without Mercy: Race and Power in the Pacific War*, New York: Pantheon, 1986, pp. 6–8.

2 Piers Brendon, *The Dark Valley: A Panorama of the 1930s*, New York: Vintage, 2002, p. 66.

3 Ibid., p. 74.

4 Andreas Dorpalen, *The World of General Haushofer*, New York: Farrar and Rinehart, 1984; Cemil Aydin, "Japan's Pan-Asianism and the Legitimacy of Imperial World Order," *Asia-Pacific Journal: Japan Focus*, Issue 11, 2008, p. 5.

5 Arata Isozaki, *Japan-ness in Architecture*, 2006, p. 256.

6 Ibid., p. 260.

7 Hiroshi Watanabe, *The Architecture of Tokyo*, Editions Axel Menges, 2001, p. 59.

8 Ibid., p. 59.

9 Arata Isozaki, *Japan-ness*, p. 257.

10 Jonathan Reynolds, *Maekawa Kunio and the Emergence of Japanese Modernist Architecture*, Los Angeles: University of California Press, 2001, p. 67.

11 Louis Sullivan, *Kindergarten Chats and Other Writings*, New York: Dover, 2012, p. 34.

12 Amanai Daiki, "The Founding of Bunriha Kenchiku Kai: 'Art' and 'Expression' in Early Japanese Architecture Circle, 1888–1920," *Aesthetics*, The Japanese Society for Aesthetics, No. 13, 2009, p. 235.

13 Ibid., p. 237.

14 Botand Bognar, *Togo Murano: Master Architect of Japan*, New York: Rizzoli.

15 Richard F. Calichman, *Overcoming Modernity: Cultural Identity in Wartime Japan*, New York: Columbia University Press, 2008.

16 John W. Dower, *Embracing Defeat: Japan in the Wake of World War II*, New York: Norton, 1999, p. 48.

PART III

From re-birth to economic collapse

CHAPTER 6

Post-war reconstruction, from survival to recovery: 1945–1950

In an unintentional, yet deliciously ironic victory for pre-war modernists, one of the first acts of General Douglas MacArthur, as Supreme Commander of the Allied Powers, was to establish his Tokyo office in the 1933 Dai-Ichi Seimei Building, designed by the Corbusian disciple Yoshikazu Uchida (Figure 6.1). After settling in, in the fall of 1945, he then embarked on what may now be seen as a three-stage sequence of strategies intended to both pacify Japan and transform it into a mirror image of its conquerors.

Stage one: punitive edicts and a new constitution

During the first, overtly punitive stage of this process from 1945 to 1947, a war crimes trial was convened, the army was disbanded, military officers were barred from political office and a directive was issued in December 1945 entitled the "Abolition of the Governmental Sponsorship, Support, Perpetuation, Control and Dissemination of State Shinto." The timing and context of this edict indicates the importance that the Allied command attached to the dismantling of what they considered to be the ideological fulcrum of "State Shinto" that they believed the militarists had forged between their indigenous animistic religion and Imperial expansion. The upshot of this edict was that Shinto was then equated to other religions, its shrines and administrators were no longer

supported by government funds, and strict guidelines were issued regarding official and educational visits, especially to shrines honoring members of the military who had died in the war.

This edict was accompanied by further far-reaching reforms contained in a new Constitution drafted by General MacArthur and his staff and presented to the Japanese government after it seemed reluctant to replace the former Meiji document of 1889. In addition to the secularization of the divine status that the Japanese had previously accorded to the Emperor, an attempt to break up large corporate conglomerates called *zaibatsu*, expanding women's rights, and constricting a much-reduced military force to a defensive role, one of the most important of these was the *Nochi Kaiho*, or Emancipation of Farm Land clause, which was a corollary to the Allied perception that wealthy landowners were among the strongest supporters of military expansion. It resulted in 38 percent of cultivated land initially being purchased by the government from landlords and re-sold at low prices to tenant farmers and the re-allocation of nearly 90 percent of large tracts of this land by 1950.[1]

As far as the socio-political and legal legacy of war is concerned, the American Occupation (which lasted from General Douglas MacArthur's arrival in Tokyo on August 30, 1045 until the Treaty of San Francisco finally took effect on April 28, 1952) was also fresh in the minds of all of those present. It had only ended eight years before the World Conference opened. Ownership of land has historically been an especially controversial issue in Japan because of its hierarchical social strata and the fact that there isn't much of it on this small archipelago. Of all of the policies dictated by SCAP that became part of the new Postwar Constitution passed by the Diet in 1947, those that were related to property rights seemed to be the most resented by architects at the time. Article 29 reads: "The right to hold property is inviolable. Property rights shall be defined by law, in conformity with the public welfare, Private property may be taken for public use upon just compensation therefore."[2]

The Land Reform law that Article 29 refers to drastically altered the social structure of rural Japan, and the relationship between landlords and the tenant farmers they controlled in a dictate that actually extended back to the Taika reforms of 646 AD. At that time, land was redistributed and new taxes were imposed as a result of a newly adopted Sino-centric legal system, and peasants were forced to sell their land and work as tenant farmers for landlords. So, the Land Reform law replaced a hierarchical class system that remained relatively unchanged since long before the Tokugawa Shogunate with a re-distribution system based on equal assets and income.[3]

Before the war, landlords owned about half of all arable land and about 30 percent of that was tilled by tenant farmers who paid their rent with half the crops they produced, which was usually in rice (kosaku). This left the tenants with barely enough for survival and in the event of a poor harvest they could possibly either be evicted or face starvation. In any case this arrangement kept the farmers in a chronic state of poverty, a harsh equation that was the legacy of the Tokugawa Shogunate. During that time, the daimyo, or nobles, relied on this stipend of rice (the kokudaka) for their income, which effectively made tenant farmers indentured servants. A World Bank report on pre-war Japan describes this relationship as one of dependency, in which "the political and military power of each daimyo was measured by the kokudaka" and "in principle, peasants were directly attached to their daimyo and bound to the land."[4]

The stated objective of the Meiji government that replaced the Tokugawa regime was to transform Japan from a rural, agrarian economy to an urban, indus-

trialized nation state. But, a decade after the Restoration started in 1868, there were still 15 million farmers working on 5 million hectares of land. More than half of that was allocated for wet paddy field rice production, on farms that averaged less than one acre in size. The technology that the Meiji government embraced ironically also made smaller farms possible, because of more intense cultivation using better seeds and fertilizer, and so while the nation industrialized its rural landscape continued to retain its rigid feudal structure.[5]

Attempts at land reform did not just suddenly appear out of nowhere after the war. The Land Tax Revision Act of 1873 set the stage for change by enforcing a Doomsday Book type of survey that took nine years to complete, recording the ownership of each property, the number of tenants and livestock on it, and the amount and type of the crops that were produced. Land titles were then issued to landlords, which essentially legalized their rights to each property and the tenants that worked on it, creating an accurate record of land ownership that facilitated future reform. Just before the war, the Land Revision Act was augmented by the Farmland Adjustment Act, which allowed local governments to acquire uncultivated land by compulsory purchase. It also mitigated the power of the landlords somewhat by recognizing the property rights of tenant farmers, even if the land they tilled was sold. Toward the end of the war and immediately thereafter, agriculture virtually came to a standstill in Japan, imported foods were unavailable and starvation was rampant. To address this crisis, and rapidly increase productivity, the government itself made another attempt to revise property rights in a Land Reform bill introduced on December 4, 1945. It called for the transfer of all property owned by absentee landlords and untenanted land to the government as well as the replacement of all land rent in kind or crops, to cash and the reorganization of the Farmland Committee to implement these changes.[6]

The bill was hotly debated and on December 9, 1945, before it could be passed, MacArthur put forward even more far reaching proposals of his own. He considered land reform to be of the highest priority, for obvious humanitarian reasons, as well as being a political bulwark against Communist inspired social unrest as well as an effective means of replacing an

Figure 6.1 Dai-Ichi Seimei Building
Source: Miki Fujiwara

entrenched hierarchical class structure with what he believed would be a more egalitarian, democratic system.

These reforms were facilitated by agrarian economist Wolf Ladejinsky and Japanese Minister of Agriculture Hiro Wada. The Land Reform bill that they devised once again completely reorganized the social framework of rural Japan, and by extension, the nation as well. Rather than settling for land transfer, it sought the complete elimination of the landlord system, replacing it with owner farmers and an equal distribution of assets and income. Any landowner who did not live on his or her property, or in the village or town it was located in, was designated as "absentee" and fallow tenanted land over one acre, except in Hokkaido, where the area was increased to four hectares, was subject to

compulsory purchase by the government. If the land was cultivated, but exceeded three hectares (12 hectares in Hokkaido) it was also to be sold, if deemed unproductive. The sale price was calculated by applying a fixed multiplier to the rental value, which had already been established for taxation, in 1938. The multiplier was a factor of the ratio of the value of the land to the rent, based on prices in 1945. Due to post-war inflation, however, these prices were very low. Tenants who had been farming the land were given preference in resale.[7]

Stage two: "the reverse course"

MacArthur supported labor unions as a way of weakening the Zaibatsu, but, by early 1948, this had a substantially negative effect on the economy, and threatened to destabilize the new government. By late 1947 and early 1948, the emergence of an economic crisis in Japan alongside concerns about the spread of communism sparked a reconsideration of occupation policies in America, ushering in a period sometimes called the "reverse course." In this stage of the occupation, which lasted until 1950, the economic rehabilitation of Japan took center stage. SCAP became concerned that a weak Japanese economy would increase the influence of the domestic Communist movement, and with a Communist victory in China's civil war increasingly likely, the future of East Asia appeared to be at stake. Occupation policies to address the weakening economy ranged from tax reforms to measures aimed at controlling inflation. However, the most serious problem was the shortage of raw materials required to feed Japanese industries and markets for finished goods.

Stage three

On June 25, 1950, 75,000 North Korean soldiers crossed the 38th parallel, which was and still remains the boundary between the Democratic People's Republic of Korea in the north and the Republic of Korea to the south. On June 27, the United Nations Security Council adopted a Resolution entitled "A Complaint of Aggression Upon the Republic of Korea" and in July sent troops to the peninsula, made up mostly of American forces. After several advances and reversals on both sides, including a successful flanking maneuver by General MacArthur at Inchon in September 1950, the United Nations forces followed the retreating North Korean troops toward their capital, P'yongyang. MacArthur also sent the First Marine Battalion, X Corps, to Korea's east coast, and they moved inland from there. On October 25, 1950, an end to the conflict seemed at hand when Communist Chinese forces staged human wave attacks across the border, culminating in the Battle of Chosin Reservoir, and retreat back across the 38th parallel. Finally, in July 1953, the Korean War came to an end.

The Korean War in 1950 provided Japan with an economic windfall because it became the principal production and supply depot for the UN effort there. The conflict also placed Japan firmly within the confines of the US defense perimeter in Asia, assuring its people that no one could threaten it. As the Cold War intensified, the United States started to turn its attention toward other parts of Asia and on September 8, 1951, 48 nations signed the San Francisco Peace Treaty officially ending the military occupation of Japan.

An economic miracle

While the Occupation was over, the United States need for a presence in Japan was not, since it felt it had to counteract Communist expansion in Asia, both with a military presence and by helping to raise the Japanese standard of living, and five years after the occupation ended, the gross national product nearly doubled, from $24 billion in 1955 to $43 billion in 1960. In addition to a dedicated work ethic, this can also be attributed to the absence of a large defense budget due to Article 9 in the new Constitution banning military, cost reductions and technology sharing by the United States which boosted industrial growth, and the pro-active regulatory and protectionist policies of the Ministries of Finance and International Trade and Industry. Its Policy Concerning Industrial Rationalization fostered cooperation between the Japanese government and private industries, as well as keiretsu, or manufacturers, suppliers, distributors, and banks. Strengthening the policy of shushin koyo, or lifetime job security, also boosted morale and productivity.

Hero and anti-hero: Kenzo Tange and Togo Murano

Among all of the architects who contributed to the reconstruction effort, Kenzo Tange and Togo Murano stand out as representatives of the antithetical public attitude about the desirability of change immediately following the war, because they each emphasized either tradition or technology in their projects. Kenzo Tange, who was selected by the War Damage Rehabilitation Board in 1946 to assist with the planning of cities that had been devastated by the war, quickly became the internationally recognized face of this remarkable transformation. He was then an assistant professor at Tokyo University and had just opened his highly influential Tange Laboratory, which subsequently included such illustrious participants as Fumihiko Maki, Arata Isozaki, Kisho Kurokawa and Sachio Otani.

The Hiroshima Peace Memorial

In 1949 Tange won an international competition for the design of the Hiroshima Peace Memorial Park, including a museum dedicated to documenting the tragic aftermath of the dropping of an atomic bomb there on August 6, 1945. His axial design, which was built in 1955, includes the museum itself, at ground zero, anchored by an auditorium, gallery, hotel, library, conference and office complex on its western end and a 2,500-seat theater to the east, spanning across the park. The exposed concrete museum, which rests on six-meter high piloti and is accessible by a freestanding stair, filters views through its columns toward the Atomic Bomb Dome, beside the Motoyasu River to the north. The Dome was one of the few buildings to withstand the attack, and has been left in disrepair as a symbol its severity (Figure 6.2).

Tange, who was a member of Le Corbusier's Congrès International d'Architecture Moderne, presented several projects at their meeting in Otterlo in 1959, which underscores the obvious influence behind the design of the museum. This conference is also notable as the end of CIAM and beginning of Team 10, as well as the keynote address by Louis Kahn that had an enormous impact on Metabolist philosophy. The government's selection of Tange, as a well-known modernist, to design the park and the final selection

Figure 6.2 Hiroshima Peace Memorial Park
Source: Miki Fujiwara

of a concept inspired by its French-Swiss rather than German variant, must certainly not be coincidental. It demonstrates a desire to distance a newly democratic Japan from pre-war resistance to the movement by ultra-nationalists already documented here, and the negative associations that the Axis alliance had afterward. There are other, equally nuanced aspects of the design that harken back to Japan's distant past, such the large arch in Peace Plaza, which distinctly resembles a Kofun tomb.

The Kagawa Prefectural Government Hall

The Kagawa Prefectural Office, which was completed in 1958, was one of the projects that Kenzo Tange presented at Otterlo. It was sharply criticized by Team 10 leader Peter Smithson for being too overtly inspired by a historical typology, highlighting the importance of the dialogue about the extent to which

tradition should continue to be a factor in contemporary Japanese architecture at this time. Tange framed the elegantly minimal office building with a rationalized, abstract version of the dou-kung bracketing used in temples such as Todai-ji, in Nara, making them more rectilinear than they normally are (Figure 6.3).

A distinguished alter ego

Undeterred, Tange designed another City Hall in Kurashiki two years later, which he characterized as the heavier, Jomon-like alternative to the elevated Yayoi aesthetic he adopted at Kagawa (Figure 6.4). This delicate balance between cool, cerebral Rationalism and less restrained Expressionism can be also found in the work of Togo Murano, who offers a pragmatic counterpoint to Tange's urbane sophistication. In contrast to the City Halls at Kagawa and Kurashiki, his Yonago City Public Hall reverts to pure Modernist Functionalism, with the slope of the floor of its audi-

Figure 6.3 Kagawa Prefectural Office
Source: Miki Fujiwara

Figure 6.4 City Hall in Kurashiki
Source: Miki Fujiwara

Figure 6.5 Yonago City Auditorium
Source: Miki Fujiwara

torium clearly expressed by the concrete structure used to elevate it, without Eastern overtones (Figure 6.5).

Murano, who was 22 years older than Kenzo Tange, was a grizzled veteran of the heated aesthetic dialectic, between Modernism and tradition that Tange was enduring, having arrived in a sukiya-style compromise in his youth. This is best seen in his Kasuien Annex to the Miyako Hotel in Kyoto and was intended to protect him and his dedication to modernism from criticism by ultra-nationalists just before World War II. He originally trained as an Electrical Engineer at Waseda University before changing his major to architecture in 1915. Unlike Tange, he practiced in Osaka, and Kansai, rather than Tokyo and also travelled extensively throughout the United States and Europe to further his education, so was he was arguably more worldly. During his travels, he was especially impressed by the mosaics by Puhl and Wagner in the Gyllene Salen in Ragnar Ostberg's Stockholm City Hall. This icon of Swedish National Romanticism inspired his use of

mother-of-pearl tiles in the subaquatic, dream-like interior of his Nissei Theatre in Tokyo, completed in 1961, which contrasts sharply with the monumentality of the exterior (Figures 6.6 and 6.7).

The Memorial Cathedral for World Peace

The Memorial Cathedral for World Peace, by Togo Murano, is his complement to Tange's Peace Memorial at Hiroshima. It replaces a Catholic Church on the same site that was destroyed by the atomic bomb in 1945. He also won a competition that included Tange, to design this Cathedral, which is reminiscent of Auguste Perret's L'Eglise Notre-Dame du Raincy, in his use of an exposed concrete frame with brick infill. The bricks were made with clay and ashes from the site, raising questions about residual radioactivity that may not have been fully understood at the time of construction in 1954 (Figure 6.8).

Figure 6.6 Nissei Theatre in Tokyo
Source: Miki Fujiwara

Figure 6.7 Nissei Theatre in Tokyo, Detail
Source: James Steele

Figure 6.8 Memorial Cathedral
for World Peace
Source: Miki Fujiwara

Tange Olympic Stadium

The Yoyogi National Gymnasium and Swimming Pool, designed by Tange for the 1964 Tokyo Olympics, provides a fitting closure to this remarkable period of post-war recovery, since it sent an unmistakable message to the world that Japan had survived this time of extreme hardship, and was once again a nation to be reckoned with (Figure 6.9).

This was not the first sinuous departure from rectilinear Modernist orthodoxy, since illustrious paragons of the movement had already contributed their own radical departures from the rectilinear norm. In his Philips Pavilion, designed with Iannis Xenakis for the Brussels World's Fair in 1958, Tange's mentor Le Corbusier had already developed a tensile structure of steel cables strung from three rakish steel posts supporting concrete hyperbolic paraboloids. Eero Saarinen also used a decidedly Expressionist vocabulary in his designs for both the Ingalls Hockey Rink at Yale University and Dulles Airport Terminal, completed between 1958 and 1962. The double curved structure of the Ingalls stadium, which includes a gently

arched 290-foot long reinforced concrete spine, supporting a cable net roof that is hung from it to edge beams around the building, especially predicts Tange's triumph.

The Yoyogi ensemble combines a large gymnasium and a smaller swimming pool, sited in a graceful pirouette atop an 80-meter square raised platform that recalls the gently curving plinth base of a Japanese castle. Echoing Saarinen, the gymnasium is also covered by a suspension structure, but in this case there are two cables stretched between concrete masts at each end of the hall. Secondary cables are then attached at right angles to this tensile bridge, sloping down to a curving set of elevated ring beams, shaped like interlocking "C"s. The entire roof was then covered in copper sheeting. The result is a dynamic interplay of forms and surfaces that may owe a debt to Western precedents but is unmistakably Japanese in feeling, and so becomes yet another perfect metaphor of creative assimilation.

At the same time as this stunning global success, Tange also designed a modest sports arena for Takamatsu in Kagawa Prefecture between 1962 and 1964, using the same vocabulary. Unlike the Yoyogi Gym-

Figure 6.9 Tokyo Olympic Stadium
Source: James Steele

Figure 6.10 Takamatsu Gymnasium
Source: Miki Fujiwara

nasium, however, this boat-like hall is raised above the ground to allow public access under it, and then up into it, using the sloping sides for seating. Unlike the Olympic venue, which has been renovated several times because of its historical value and continued usefulness, the Kagawa Gymnasium is in less wealthy circumstances and has unfortunately fallen on hard times (Figure 6.10).

Notes

1   Rem Koolhaas and Hans Ulrich Obrist, with Kayoko Ota and James Westcott (Eds.), *Project Japan Metabolist Talks*, Taschen, 2013, p. 21.
2   Shinenori Matsui, *The Constitution of Japan: A Contextual Analysis*, London: Hart, 2011.
3   Toshihiko Kawagoe, "Agricultural Land Reform in Post-War Japan: Experiences and Issues," World Bank Policy Research Working Paper 2111, May 1999.
4   Ibid., p. 13.
5   Ibid., p. 16.
6   Wolf Ladjinsky, *Agrarian Reforms as Unfinished Business, The Selected Papers of Wolf Ladjinsky*, World Bank Research Publications, Oxford University Press, 1977.
7   R.P. Dore, *Land Reform in Japan*, Oxford: Oxford University Press, 1959.
8   Mitsuaki Adachi (Ed.), *Kunio Maekawa: Sources of Modern Japanese Architecture*, Tokyo: Process Architecture, 1984.

CHAPTER 7

The Le Corbusier syndrome

For a number of subliminal reasons that have yet to be fully explored, the French-Swiss architect Charles-Edouard Jeanneret-Gris, or Le Corbusier, has had an inordinate influence on successive generations of Japanese architects. His architectural genealogy in Japan starts with three major followers, beginning with Kunio Maekawa, who was born into a distinguished samurai family in Niigata in 1905. His father was a civil engineer, but later worked in the Japanese Home Ministry. Kunio graduated from what was then Tokyo Imperial University in 1928 and with the help of his uncle, Naotake Sato, who worked for the Japanese Foreign Service in Paris, he obtained an unpaid position with the Swiss-French architect, at 35 Rue de Sevres. Maekawa lived with his uncle's family during his two-year apprenticeship, primarily working with Le Corbusier's brother Pierre Jeanneret, as well as head interior designer Charlotte Perriand, and Alfred Roth, who had helped Le Corbusier and Jeanneret design House 13 and Double House 14–15 at the Weissenhofseidlung in Stuttgart, under the supervision of Ludwig Mies van der Rohe (Figure 7.1).

While in Le Corbusier's Paris Atelier, Maekawa worked on the Cité Mondiale, or Mundaneum, which was intended to be attached to and to augment the peaceful mission of the League of Nations in Geneva. It was to hold Paul Otlet's Universal Decimal Classification Collection, then housed at the Musée du Cinquantenaire, in Brussels, as a new "City of Knowledge." Le Corbusier responded with a monumental, spiraling shaft, as the antithesis of the Tower of Babel, which also implied the human quest for knowledge, from its labyrinthine square base upward toward understanding at the top. Although never built, his Mundaneum drew a negative reaction from Czech critic Karel Teige, who characterized it as an emotional, and teleological departure from strictly scientific rationalism. This critique was later amplified in Teige's *The Minimum Dwelling*, in 1932, in which he also pointedly criticized the residential designs of Le Corbusier, among other Modernists.[1]

The intensity of this debate, and the impressive cast of characters involved in it hint at the high level of Maekawa's involvement in the Modern Movement in Paris, and after working for Le Corbusier for two formative years, he returned to Japan in 1930. He then amplified that initial engagement by joining the office of Antonin Raymond, whose expressively powerful use of reinforced concrete later echoed the Brutalist style initiated by Maekawa's first mentor. His early work shows how completely Maekawa had absorbed Le Corbusier's principles overlaid with Raymond's penchant for large expanses of exposed cast in place of reinforced concrete, steel and glass. By the time he was able to open his own office in 1935, nationalism was at a fever pitch in the run up to World War II and the teikan yoshiki, or Imperial Crown style, was being promoted as the design method of choice to be used throughout the "Greater East Asia Co-Prosperity sphere" that the government envisioned as its future Empire.

Figure 7.1 Portrait of Kunio Maekawa
Source: Maekawa Office

His championing of Le-Corbusian modernism put Maekawa at odds with those who were advocating a return to a more historicist direction, to the extent that he was labeled as being unpatriotic.

In 1937, the Imperial Household sponsored a competition for the design of a new National Museum in Ueno Koen to replace one that had been leveled by the Kanto earthquake of 1926. It was also intended to honor the beginning of the Showa age and brought the debate between traditionalists and modernists to a head, because competitors were requested to "express the Japanese spirit through the use of the teikan yoshiki," or Imperial style.[2] In an obvious attempt to reconcile East and West, competition winner Jin Watanabe used a narrow, extended, horizontal row of square generic windows above a ground level row

of elegantly vertical, classical pilasters as the supporting cast for a traditional Japanese roof. By contrast, Kunio Maekawa's submission, of three parallel rectilinear, unadorned concrete boxes, made no concessions at all to historical precedents, and was obviously intended as an act of defiance against government restrictions.

The Maekawa House, 1942

Three years before the conflict ended, Maekawa found respite by designing his own house, which has since been relocated to the Edo-Tokyo Open Air Architectural Museum in Tokyo Musashi-Koganei (Figure 7.2). Due to lack of building materials at the time it is very modest, but with the addition of a loft space it is much larger than its 100-square-meter footprint would suggest so that when his own office was firebombed, it served as his architectural headquarters as well. It must have been inspired by his own family residence in Nigata, which he remembered fondly, and, with its triangular profile, external shinbashira columns supporting each gable end, deeply recessed windows and traditionally derived grid, it is among the best modern examples of the overlapping of Japanese and Western sensibilities in the nation.

Tokyo Bunka Kaikan: the Metropolitan Festival Hall, 1961

After the war, however, Maekawa came into his own by becoming one of the most formidable and prolific proponents of Corbusian Modernism in Japan. One of the largest of his lengthy list of distinguished projects is the Tokyo Bunka Kaikan, or Metropolitan Festival Hall in Ueno Park, which was built in 1961 and renovated in 1998–1999 (Figure 7.3).

In this massive project for the Tokyo Metropolitan Foundation for History and Culture, which is sited in the most visible and heavily travelled portions of the park, Maekawa managed to seamlessly combine a large, 2,303-seat concert hall and a smaller 649-seat theater by encompassing both of them within a slightly curving, horizontal roof supported by a recessed peristyle of columns. This unobtrusive vertical structure

Figure 7.2 Maekawa House, Tokyo Musashi-Koganei
Source: Maekawa Office

Figure 7.3 Metropolitan Festival Hall in Ueno Park
Source: Maekawa Office

Figure 7.4 Metropolitan Festival Hall in Ueno Park
Source: Maekawa Office

Figure 7.5 Metropolitan Festival Hall in Ueno Park, Interior
Source: Maekawa Office

then penetrates through an elegantly detailed masonry plinth base, which sweeps up to meet it, serving as a sensitively scaled ensemble, of stone base and mildly Brutalist concrete column and roof, that syncopates the movement of the thousands of pedestrians that walk by it each day. The base, which echoes the foundation of a Japanese castle, projects out past the cornice line at certain parts of the perimeter, to accommodate gardens and cafés, adding a particularly civil note to what might otherwise have been a coldly monumental building, providing a lesson in how modernism can be humanized.

This lesson continues with the massing, which accommodates different elevations, rather than the uniform, acontextual wrapper favored by the International Style (Figure 7.4). The fly-towers for the two halls are unobtrusively located at the back of the entire ensemble, but nonetheless provide a monumental sculptural surprise for those who venture around to that side of the complex. The interior of the main hall, with its free form, organic acoustic baffles, is a time capsule of the 1960s aesthetic (Figure 7.5).

Tokyo Marine Tower

In the mid 1970s Maekawa designed two other notable Tokyo landmarks. The first of these, built in 1974, is a 30-story tower above a high arcaded base in the Maranouchi District, between the Tokyo Train Station and Imperial residence, as the headquarters for Tokyo Marine Holdings, which is a multinational holding company and the oldest and largest property-casualty insurance group in Japan (Figure 7.6). It is sturdy and safely conservative and blends in, as a good neighbor

Figure 7.6 Tokyo Marine Holdings, Tower
Source: Maekawa Office

Figure 7.7 Tokyo Marine Holdings Tower
Source: James Steele

to the other office towers around it today, but was quite a sensation when first constructed, given the difficulty of building vertically in earthquake-prone Japan. By using the technique introduced as the "colossal order" by Michelangelo at the Campidoglio, and later popularized by Louis Sullivan, of accentuating the vertical surface of the columns and suppressing the windows, the tower is made to seem higher than it is. Its surface, which is clad in terracotta colored tiles, shows its age, but is a reminder of Maekawa's continuous experimental attempts to introduce ceramics into the Corbusian palette, in order to soften his Brutalist surfaces (Figure 7.7).

Surprisingly, it wasn't until 1984 that the editor of *Process Architecture* was finally able to convince Maekawa to publish a monograph on his work, and the book tellingly emphasizes the tiling and concrete techniques and details he used in his work, rather than going into extensive descriptions of the projects themselves, illustrating that, even at this rather late date, these were of utmost concern to him. He also relates how excited people in Tokyo were when his Kinokuniya Bookstore was being built right after the war ended in

1946, because it provided a beacon of hope amidst the devastation surrounding it, and came to symbolize a modern future.[3]

Tokyo Metropolitan Art Museum, Ueno, 1975

Ceramic also dominates the palette Maekawa used for his 1975 design for the Tokyo Metropolitan Art Museum, located a short distance away from the Festival Hall, to the north-west (Figure 7.8). Maekawa once again puts people first in this design, by using a staggered rank of four tile-clad rectilinear blocks, which each end with projecting black steel-framed bay windows, and progressively move inward to create an increasingly intimate internal courtyard. The main entrance to its six galleries is below grade in the middle of this central courtyard, and they include display space for painting, sculpture, ceramics and calligraphy, and include the work of both contemporary Japanese and foreign artists (Figure 7.9).

Figure 7.8 Tokyo Metropolitan Art Museum, Ueno
Source: Maekawa Office

Figure 7.9
Tokyo Metropolitan
Art Museum, Ueno
Source: Maekawa
Office

Two more pilgrims travel to Paris

Junzo Sakakura and Takamasa Yoshizaka followed Maekawa to Le Corbusier's Paris office, but both the timing and duration of their respective apprenticeships had an important impact on their subsequent career paths. Sakakura arrived in Paris in 1930, just as Maekawa returned to Tokyo, at the beginning of the chaotic decade that was to re-define the meaning of nationalism in Japan. Le Corbusier required that he study architectural construction for several months before starting in the office, and once he did, he attained a position of some authority before he left in 1937. Takamasa Yoshizaka did not work for Le Corbusier until after the war, arriving in Paris in 1950 and only remaining for two years.

Junzo Sakakura

In 1936 Tokyo University professor Kishida Hideto was asked to organize a limited competition for the design of the Japanese Pavilion at the Exposition Internationale des Arts et Techniques dans la Vie Moderne to be held the following year in Paris. An entry by Kunio Maekawa was dismissed as being too modern, and a more traditional scheme by Maeda Kenjiro was selected instead. However, it was subsequently discovered that French regulations required the use of local materials and labor and since Sakakura had just returned from Paris, he seemed to be the most logical candidate to submit and oversee the construction of a new design that would comply with Exposition codes.

Figure 7.10 Kamakura Museum of Modern Art
Source: Hartmut Poeling

He had been involved in the Swiss Pavilion project while in Le Corbusier's office, and his design for the Japanese Pavilion, which unfortunately has not been well documented, reflects it.

The dramatic siting and emphasis on soaring piloti-like columns of his Japanese pavilion is recalled, however, in his Institute of France-Japan in Tokyo, which he designed in 1951, the same year he produced his much admired Kamakura Museum of Modern Art, which is the first public art museum in Japan, located near the Tsurugaoka Hachiman Shrine there (Figure 7.10). It is a more sedate two-story rectilinear structure, which echoes the Kinkaku-ji Pavilion in its elegant simplicity and lakeside reflection. It is sheathed in white stone and elevated on thin steel pipe columns.

In 1955, Sakakura also collaborated with Kunio Maekawa and Junzō Yoshimura on the International House of Japan in the Roppongi district of Tokyo, intended to foster cultural exchange. One of the most notable achievements of this Center is that it is an oasis of calm, in spite of being located in the midst of one of the busiest districts in Tokyo, and as such it underscores the ability of Japanese architects to integrate their buildings with nature to an extent that Western Modernists have been unable to do. It has a beautiful garden that seems much larger than it actually is because of a skillful use of the principle of Shakkai, or borrowed scenery and seems to go on forever when viewed from the main dining room. Its actual size only becomes apparent when walking through it (Figure 7.11).

West plaza of Shinjuku Station, Tokyo, 1967

In addition to these more well-known projects, Junzo Sakakura made a less recognized but much more substantial contribution to the urban context of postwar Tokyo, especially in his planning in the early 1950s of the West Plaza of Shinjuku Station, and the Shibuya Bus Terminal and Plaza, which is now one of the busiest pedestrian intersections in the world, and has come to symbolize the frenetic character of this contemporary global city. While the Metabolists were conjuring utopian dreams, Sakakura was in the proverbial trenches, shaping the future of the city block by block. Shibuya Crossing later served as a staging

Figure 7.11 International House of Japan in Roppongi
Source: Maekawa Office

ground for the student protests of the 1960s, and must be included in any meaningful discussion about the difference between the Western and Asian attitudes about urban space.

A third important disciple

Takamasa Yoshizaka was the third of this first, most influential group of Corbusian disciples. He graduated from the Waseda University Department of Architecture in 1943, and served in the army during the war, before receiving a grant from the French Government in 1950 to work at 35 Rue de Sevres.

Because of this, his experience in Paris was far different than that of Maekawa and Sakakura, starting with his opportunity to visit the Unite d'Habitation and experience this Brutalist prototype, created out of necessity due to a lack of proper materials and formwork, which defined the style. While in Le Corbusier's office he worked on site supervision of this project

in Marseilles, as well as the design of another Unite in Nantes-Reze, completed in 1955 and a law school in the city center of Chandigargh, which came into the office at that time, as part of the Maxwell Fry and Jane Drew Master Plan for the new capital city in the Punjab.

After he left Paris, he travelled extensively throughout both France and India, and eventually opened his own office, called Atelier U, in Tokyo in 1964. Unlike Maekawa, or Sakakura, his own style did not adhere as closely to the strict rationalism of Le Corbusier's early work, but because of his later exposure to the Unite de Habitation, and other examples of the French master's more humane beton brut "Monol" phase, when he returned home.

After returning to Japan, Yoshizaka translated many of Le Corbusier's books into Japanese, introducing the idea of the Modular to a new audience, and started a movement called Discontinuous Unity, which involved the integration of natural laws and environmental

Figure 7.12 Yoshizaka Inter-University Seminar House, Tokyo
Source: Miki Fujiwara

forces into architecture. He established a studio at Waseda University and during the late 1960s and early 1970s his students combined several of their offices into Team Zoo, and substituted traditional wood construction, earthen walls and rough concrete for glass and steel.[4]

In 1965, Yoshizaka designed the Inter-University Seminar House, in Hachioji, Tokyo, which clearly demonstrates his singular, Brutalist approach, using Le Corbusier's later more monumental vocabulary. It backs into a slight rise, and is accessible from a bridge on its upper floor, and its massive, relatively unfenestrated concrete walls, which angle steeply upward from a relatively small, square footprint, are abruptly capped by a thick flat roof, definitely presenting a different approach to form than that used by the other members of this pioneering trio (Figure 7.12).

The rebirth of the museum of unlimited growth

As often happens with unrealized designs, the Mudaneum that mired Maekawa in controversy in Paris found new life at a much smaller scale as the National Museum of Western Art in Tokyo. In 1959 he, along with Sakakura and Takamasa, helped Le Corbusier realize what was to become his only building in Japan, and Maekawa's Festival Hall, built two years later, was obviously intended to frame and act as a visual foil for it. The Museum was built to house the collection of Kojiro Matsukata, which was returned to Japan by the French government in 1959. As with the Mudaneum, it was based on the concept of a rectangular spiral and has a double height atrium, with overlooks strategically placed to emphasize the view into the sky-lit central space (Figure 7.13).

Figure 7.13 National Museum of Western Art in Ueno
Source: James Steele

Notes

1   Karel Teige, *The Minimal Dwelling*, trans. Eric Dluhosch, Cambridge, MA: MIT Press, 2002.

2   Jonathan M. Reynolds, *Maekawa Kunio and the Emergence of Japanese Modernist Architecture*, Berkeley and Los Angeles: University of California Press, 2001, p. 246.

3   *Kunio Maekawa: Sources of Modern Japanese Architecture*, Process Architecture, 1984.

4   Hiroki Onobayashi, "A Profile of the Versatile Takamasa Yoshizaka," *Japan Architect*, August 1966, p. 32.

CHAPTER 8

Metabolism revisited

Japanese Metabolism is still something of a mystery, in spite of the extensive analysis it has generated since it debuted in Tokyo in 1960. The intention here is to try to dispel a bit of that mystique and to position the movement within the narrative of its effect on Japanese architecture today.

What is known for certain is that Japanese representatives to the 1956 International Design Conference in Aspen, Colorado convinced the organizers that they should hold the next event in Tokyo. After they agreed, a planning Committee was formed, headed by Junzo Sakakura, Kunio Maekawa and Kenzo Tange. Sakakura was appointed Chair, and Tange was asked to organize the conference, because he was the youngest of the three and had previously worked for Kunio Maekawa.[1]

Tange was subsequently invited to teach at MIT and asked Takashi Asada, who had been his student in the formative years of the Tange Laboratory at Tokyo University to replace him. Asada then turned to fellow Tange Lab student Kisho Kurokawa as well as magazine editor Noboru Kawazoe for assistance, and they, in turn, recruited Masato Otaka, Kiyonori Kikutake, Kenji Ekuan and Kiyoshi Awazu to join them. Kikutake is credited with using the name Metabolism for the first time in reference to his Marine City project in 1958, which actually translates as shinchintaisha, meaning "renewal" or "replacement."

From this point on, facts and recollections begin to blur. The backgrounds, interests, personal agendas and areas of expertise of this group, which presented a united front to a select audience of more than 200 local and international participants at the World Design Conference when it opened on May 11, 1960, were very diverse, united only by their experience with Kenzo Tange, who initiated it. Although the numbers and names of the initial signatories vary from one reference to another, the brochure that they distributed at the event entitled *Metabolism: The Proposals for a New Urbanism*, is the definitive source, and lists Noboru Kawazoe, Kiyonori Kikutake, Kisho Kurokawa, Fumihiko Maki, Masato Otake and Kiyoshi Awazu as founding members. In addition to a manifesto, the brochure also contained four essays, illustrated with selected projects, which, in the order they appear, are: "Ocean City" by Kikutake, "Space City" by Kurokawa, "On Group Form" by Maki and Otaka and "Material and Man" by Kawazoe. Using fissionable metaphors, the group said that they "regard human society as a vital process – a continuous development from atom to nebula" and chose the name because "we believe design and technology should be a denotation of human society."

Extensive preparation preceded this deceptively thin volume, however. It included study sessions, invited lectures and presentations that were held at Maekawa's International House in Roppongi, which became the unofficial headquarters for the group before their debut, concentrating on the search for a coherent theory to make their effort congruent with past manifestos.[2]

Theory today is often the stepchild of invention, fabricated after the fact to justify a frenzied and mysterious creative process that has just occurred. The mystical meta-language that the Metabolists used, including terms such as "consciousness only," "symbiosis," "regeneration" and "impermanence" initially seems to conform to this trend, but they actually did construct a cohesive philosophy that has not yet been sufficiently explored. It consists of a central philosophical core, wrapped with several related strands that create a fairly comprehensible whole.

The spindle and various strands of an unexplored theory

As the cryptic terms they used in press releases indicate, the essence, or core, of their theory revolves around the essential reality that Asia in general and Japan specifically did not have first-hand experience with the European Enlightenment and the Positivism that followed. Its own philosophical traditions, of Shinto, Buddhism, Confucianism and Daoism all pointed in the opposite direction, teaching a profound respect for the unpredictability of life, as well as trust in intuition, the acceptance of ambivalence, learning through experience and a natural, hierarchical order rather than an abstract constructed one. They sought to integrate or create a synthesis of the Japanese interpretation of Zen Buddhism explored earlier here and Edmund Husserl's insight into the relationship between consciousness and "the phenomena" we observe. The link between these seemingly disparate ideas is the Zen concept of shoshin, or "beginner's mind" on the one hand, as a unified, non-dualistic discipline of regenerative empathy and Husserl's definition of phenomenology as the "cognition of essences" and the "eidetic reduction" of reality in opposition to facts that are derived empirically.[3] Each of these favor concentrated intuition over the use of empirically derived, preconceived axioms as a way of finding meaning in the world. The Metabolists wanted to arrive at a transformation, on their own terms, of the age-old Western dichotomy between Apollonian rationality and Dionysian spontaneity, an entirely new point of view about the difference between science and an empathy with nature.

Kisho Kurokawa's reference to iconic precedents such as Ise and Katsura as "pretexts" provides an additional first theoretical strand, of using iconic examples from Japanese history to literally clarify this central idea. Each of these structures are in a constant state of indeterminate flux, with either the periodic re-building process at Ise, or with architectural elements, such as a modular structural system and sliding shoji screens that allow the configuration of Katsura Rikyū to be changed at will. Each building also has multi-valent codes that can be interpreted in many different ways depending on one's location in time or space.[4]

Another recognizable, second theoretical thread of the Metabolist philosophy, behind the public pronouncements, relates to the traditional Japanese concept of Katachi, which is best defined as art, but also means form, shape or design. The catalyst behind interest in it was a visit by the atomic physicist Mitsuo Taketani, who spoke to the Metabolist group during its formative stage. He wrote *The Doctrine of the Three Stages of Development* in 1936, based on Hegel's three-part philosophy of Entwicklung or evolution of ideas, from "dinge an-sich" or "the thing in itself", through "anderssein" or "other-ness," and ending in "an-und-für-sich" or "on the whole."

Taketani, on the other hand, inspired Kiyonori Kikutake to develop his own three stage theory, beginning with "ka", which has many meanings depending on context, but the closest is making, "kata" as formation and "katachi" as the final form, as an explanation of his own design process.[5] Taketani's introduction of Hegel, and his *Science of Logic* also prompted debate about the ideas of his disciples, such as Friedrich Engels and his *Dialectics of Nature*, in which he tried to establish a connection between phase change in nature and social transformation, which would have obvious interest for this group.

A third part of Metabolist discussions about alternative belief systems specifically related to their own history and culture also included Watsuii Tetsuro's concept of "fudo," or climate, which he expands to include the singular seasonal conditions in Japan and the way these have shaped the character and world view of its people, on the macrocosmic level, and their perception of the social space between an individual and a group, the concept of a social self on the other. The kanji character of "ma" that Tetsuro used for this space is the same as the ideogram for "door" or "gate" and "sun," which has such a profound relevance for Japanese architecture as well. In direct opposition to the Western, and particularly American need for independence, Watsuji stressed an individual can only really find meaning in life within this "in between" state negotiated with social obligations.[6]

A fourth strand in the Metabolists' comparison of Eastern and Western philosophies is Ernst Cassirer, who attempted to bridge the gap between them. He originally questioned the idea that concepts about reality should be derived by abstracting experience through an inductive process of empirical investigation, before amplifying his beliefs through research into cultural history at the *Kulturwissenschaftliche Bibliothek Warburg* in Hamburg, which prompted a conversion. His *Philosophy of Symbolic Forms* reiterates the Hegelian idea that phenomenology is the basis of all philosophical knowledge. Phenomenology, for Cassier was "the ladder from immediate consciousness to pure knowledge."[7] His appeal lay in his opposition to Positivism as a scientific world-view that dictates that all sensory experience can be reduced to quantitative systems that can be proven by the rules of logic or mathematics, derived through an empirical methodology. Metabolists rejected the reductivism inherent in the Positivist mindset, which views science as an unvariegated unity based on the unquestioning acceptance of what are assumed to be a cumulative, fixed set of axioms, in spite of cultural differences, and an insistence that teleological and metaphysical phenomena can and should be tested by empirical means. The search for a unifying theory paled however, in the face of the very real challenges faced by the Metabolists in their search for a solution to the dangers that the onset of globalization and Western influence presented to Japan. They were attracted to those ideas that would allow them to create a new social order to do so, not based on a formal style, but on a philosophy deeply rooted in their own ethnic background and shared vivid memories of the disastrous war that had just devastated their country. They also had strong opinions about the lasting socio-political and legal implications of policies enacted during the humiliating occupation that followed it such as land reform. Their intense national pride was heightened by post-war repression and a common desire for a new identity for post-war Japan.

Gunter Nitschke, who has been a life-long observer of Japanese culture, provides a fifth strand. He believes that these various philosophical doctrines have been able to be synthesized, because they share the operative idea of mujokan, or transience, which pervades every concept of "form, space and place in Japan, whether traditional or modern," and reflects its "impermanent quality of life, nature, and human artifacts" which also explains the mutually reinforcing compatibility between the Shinto appreciation of the transience and renewal in nature and the Buddhist doctrine of the transience of the human body and mind.

Mujokan, from mujo, as well as dukka, or suffering and emptiness, or anitya, are the tilakkhana or three basic Buddhist conditions of existence. It also relates to the concept of "mono no aware" or an empathy for, and sadness about the ephemeral essence of life, and things, that heightens appreciation for both, related to the qualities of wabi and sabi discussed earlier in reference to the ritual of the tea ceremony.[8]

The ruinous legacy of war

The Japanese experience with mujokan, and the impermanence of life in the face of recurring earthquakes, fires, and ceaseless conflict certainly escalated during and after World War II. While the nuclear devastation of mid-August 1945 has been well documented, the destruction caused by the firebombing of other Japanese cities that preceded it has not. Raids that started in June 1944 and continued until Hiroshima and Nagasaki culminated in "Operation Meetinghouse" which killed almost 100,000 people, made more than a million homeless, and burned nearly 16 square miles of Tokyo.[9]

Their personal experience with such apocalyptic destruction certainly explains the darker side of the Metabolists' optimism, or what Arata Isozaki has referred to as its "linear thinking without a cultural context" that presumably included being in denial about this repetitive pattern of epic paroxysm and change.[10]

They also deeply resented certain parts of the new post-war Constitution, such as its revised definition of property rights, in spite of the fact that it simply formalized ideas that the Japanese government had already initiated. Their anger stemmed from a collective sense of national pride, repressed during the occupation that ended on April 28, 1952, and a belief that these reforms not only violated tradition, but also exacerbated the lack of space available to build the new society that they envisioned.[11]

Recent literature specifically addresses the negative consequences of the war and the Occupation within the Metabolist group, identifying a collective form of post-traumatic stress disorder, which qualifies the myth of utopian idealism they promoted and tempers it with evidence of "cultural nihilism" and the desire to find new meaning within "the erasure of memory and loss of identity." There are hints of this attitude, of hoping for the best, but expecting the worst, in the nuclear metaphors they nervously used in their manifesto, and their belief that "design and technology" representing both creation and destruction, should be a "denotation of human society."[12]

Four degrees of separation

Despite the unified face that Metabolism presented to the West, its initial membership was a constellation of distinct personalities that revolved in four distinct orbits around a vacuum that should have been occupied by Kenzo Tange. The motives of its members were quite different, and have been aptly described as having "a contradictory voice, historical consciousness and political orientation" and were generally divided between one more vocal faction that advocated larger utopian and scientifically based solutions to city growth and another that promoted a smaller scale, uncontrolled, aggregated approach to urban planning.[13] Tange, who was certainly the most illustrious and widely recognized member of the group, was displaced simply because of his international fame and his association with Western modernism and the establishment. So he, and his disciple Arata Isozaki, were relegated to fighting for space outside the clusters already occupied by Mega-structuralists Kinoyori Kikutake, Kisho Kurokawa and Noboru Kawazoe, the Collective Form group of Fumohiko Maki and Takahasi Asada, and the neutral territory occupied by graphic artists Kenji Ekuan and Kiyoshi Awazu.

A new utopia

Kinoyori Kikutake, Kisho Noriaki Kurokawa, and Noboru Kawazoe sought to transform Japan into a technological paradise and Kikutake, who was the elder statesman of the group, had already made impressive strides in that direction. His essay in the Manifesto included his "Tower-shaped City" and "Marine City," which bears a striking resemblance to Bertrand Goldberg's Marina City in Chicago built in 1959, as well as his "Ocean City," intended for 500,000 residents that he envisioned would grow biologically and eventually die and sink into the sea at the end of its lifecycle. The symbolic implications of these projects, of building vertically in response to less land being available because of new legal restrictions and a growing post-war population, as well as a floating city in neutral, international waters that would be less likely to be destroyed by war, are clearly indicative of the ideological motives of his faction within the group.

In a lecture given on November 10, 2012, at the Harvard Graduate School of Design following Kiku-take's death on December 26, 2011, his disciple Toyo Ito somewhat surprisingly characterized his contribution to the Metabolism initiative as that of being the strongest advocate for tradition in the group, and pushing back against those whom he described as just representing "Japan for Japan's sake." He then used that differential as a mechanism for a comparison between Kikutake and Kenzo Tange, as the external figurehead of the movement, trying to corroborate his claim of Kikutake's existential traditionalism by pitting his "Jomon" sensibilities against Tange's more sophisticated "Yayoi" tendencies, which Kikutake described as being evil.

To prove his point, Ito began by juxtaposing Kikutake's Sky House, with its pitch-roofed Minka profile, with Kenzo Tange's Tokyo residence, as an aloof columnar evocation of the Yayoi ideal embodied by Katsura Rikyū (Figure 8.1). The Sky House, completed in 1958, derives its name from its four vertical supports, located at the midpoints of each of the sides of its square plan, which elevate it off the ground. Its completely open interior is also surrounded by a Katsura-like interstitial space, similar to an engawa, which was intended to be filled with moveable, plug-in, prefabricated kitchen and bathroom modules as necessary, making it a paragon of Metabolism's mantra of combining permanence and change and the substitution of parts at a much smaller scale.[14]

Figure 8.1 Kikutake Sky House, Skyhouse
Source: Iwan Baan

Ito's point about the pitched roof is inspired, because Kikutake used the same device on his Tokoen Hotel in Tottori, and so obviously intended to contravene the International Style ideal of historical anonymity in each instance, as well as to conjure up the earliest, indigenous Jomon origins of Japanese architecture. So, in this juxtaposition of symbols, he is underscoring Metabolism's opposition to Modernism on the one hand, and his own passionate support of Japanese tradition on the other.

Ito emphasized that this same juxtaposition, of technology and tradition, is most powerfully expressed in Kikutake's 1963 Izumo Shrine Administrative Building in Shimane (Figure 8.2). He manages this delicate balance with a symbolic synthesis of sophisticated construction techniques, such as the use of large pre-cast concrete beams spanning the entire 40-meter length of the building, between triangular frames that recall the racks used by rice farmers to dry their freshly harvested crop. Sachio Otano also used this metaphor, of the triangular rice-drying frame, in his Kyoto International Conference Center, in 1966 (Figure 8.3). Continuing the natural metaphor, Kikutake also allows water to flow down and over the louvers between the secondary vertical, diagonal columns when it rains. Kikutake has once again seamlessly blended the systemic approach favored by his faction of the Metabolist movement with references to the most ancient aspects of Japanese history.

In spite of being only 26 years old when the World Conference opened in 1960, Kisho Kurokawa had already designed his radical Agricultural City project, followed by his own version of a Floating City two years later. Both of these were never realized, but his Nakagin Capsule Tower, which was completed in 1972, and Sony Building in Osaka have now become potent symbols of the movement, because they conform to the ideal of fixed infrastructure and prefabricated replaceable parts.

Figure 8.2 Izumo Shrine Administrative Building
Source: Kikutake Office

The Nakagin building has two towers and each of the 140 capsules attached to them measures 2.3 meters by 3.8 meters by 2.1 meters (Figure 8.4). Although never implemented, each capsule was intended to be replaceable, connected to one of the two main shafts only by four high-tension bolts. Construction was divided between the two towers and their energy-supply systems and equipment, built on site, while the capsules were built and fitted out elsewhere and shipped to the site, and craned into place. Each capsule is a welded lightweight steel-truss box clad in galvanized, rib-reinforced steel panels, coated with rust-preventative paint and finished with glossy Kenitex spray (Figure 8.5). They are attached independently and cantilevered from each shaft, so that they can be easily removed. Since it was intended for short-term use by salary men who had stayed too long in Tokyo after work and missed their trains Nakagin also symbolizes the beginning of this culture in post-war Japan (Figure 8.6).

The Sony Tower, which was built at the same time as the Nakagin project, using capsules that are the same size as those at Nagakin, is sheathed in stainless steel instead of Kenitex-coated panels. It was designed as an "information tree" connected electronically to Sony showrooms in other major cities (Figure 8.7).

A more humane alternative

While they shared the general concern about the impact of post-war changes on traditional Japanese culture and the urban chaos that ensued, the Collective Form cluster, represented by Fumihiko Maki and Masato Otaka were exploring a softer approach. When he was recruited to join the Metabolist group, Maki was teaching at Washington University in St. Louis and was in Tokyo on his way back to the United States after travelling in Southeast Asia and the Middle East. He was struck by the simplicity, cohesive-

Figure 8.3
(left) Kyoto International Conference Center
Source: Hartmut Poeling

Figure 8.4
(below) Nakagin Capsule Tower
Source: Tomio Ohashi

Figure 8.5 Nakagin Capsule Tower
Source: Tomio Ohashi

Figure 8.6 Nakagin Capsule Tower, Interior
Source: Tomio Ohashi

Figure 8.7 Sony Tower
Source: Tomio Ohashi

ness and uniformity of the villages he had seen during his trip, as well as the total lack of any coherent theory about this phenomenon, in contrast to the overwhelming concentration of research on single buildings. He recognized that the accumulated forms of the villages he had studied were the tangible expression of regional, vernacular wisdom refined over many generations, and thought about how one designer could achieve the same result in a single lifetime, or at least within one project.

In a subsequent article entitled "Collective Form" he identified "compositional" (or arranged), "group" (or sequential) and "mega" (or structural) form as three variations of collective expression. He sought a "master program" that would help him derive a physio-spatial language that would more accurately reflect social values while still fulfilling structural and functional requirements.[15]

The Collective form group was also able to eventually realize its alternative viewpoint in the Hillside Terrace project, by Maki and the Sakaide Artificial Ground development by Masato Otaka. Hillside Terrace, in the Daikanyama district of Tokyo, started in 1969 when the Asakura family asked Maki to design apartments and shops on a 250-meter-long strip of land along the main road. The traditional private residence of politician Torajiro Asakura, built in 1919, hidden within Maki's Modernist context, testifies to the origins of what must certainly be the most remarkable extant example of an architect's endurance, evolving in six distinct phases until 1992 (Figure 8.8).

While far more subdued, Otaka's Sakaide project, which was also begun in 1968–1969 but completed in 1983, also played out over an extended period of time, but was part of government search for a solution to seismic destruction and overpopulation. The Artificial Land Sub-Committee, established in 1963, thought that creating a second elevated datum might solve these problems and commissioned Otaka to design prefabricated worker housing units on a concrete slab raised nine meters above grade, with shops and parking below (Figure 8.9).

The parallel universe of Kenzo Tange

In spite of the fact that Kenzo Tange had instigated the organization of the World Design Conference where Metabolism was introduced, and that his efforts to bring recognition to the young architects who debuted there started a year earlier at the final meeting of the Congrès International d'Architecture Moderne in Otterlo in 1959 (where he introduced Kinonori Kikutake's Tower City and Sky House), he was marginalized by younger members of the group because he was absent during its formative phase, and the fact they also felt that he represented the establishment. He started teaching a semester-long studio at the Massachusetts Institute of Technology right after the Otterlo Conference, designing a residential community of 25,000 inhabitants to be constructed on the water of Boston Harbor, and after it ended, he immediately launched another "Lab" at Tokyo University. Frustrated by the legal tangle of property restrictions discouraging new growth, he implemented ideas gleaned from the Boston study and produced a prototypical plan for Tokyo Bay as a solution to the lack of housing and affordable land in the capital to cope with the doubling of the population in Tokyo in one decade, from 5.4 million in 1950 to 10 million at the start of the World Design Conference in 1960.

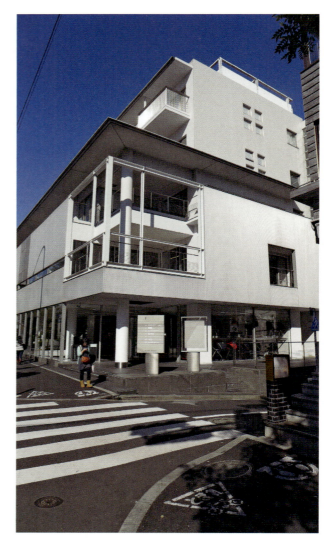

Figure 8.8 Hillside Terrace
Source: James Steele

Conforming to the paradigm of the technological contingent of the Metabolist group, of using fixed and movable parts, his dendritic mega-structure was based on a set of large three level parallel highways, 40 meters above the water, spanning 80 kilometers across the entire bay, from Ikebukuro in the north-west to Kisarazu, in Chiba Prefecture, in the south-east. This network was intersected at right angles by secondary service streets, providing access to modules containing residential and commercial uses, offices and transportation hubs, which could be added to as growth increased.

Tange presented his radical Tokyo Bay Plan during an entire 45-minute segment on NHK TV, broadcast

Figure 8.9 Otaka Sakaide Artificial Ground
Source: Miki Fujiwara

Figure 8.10 Yamanashi Broadcasting and Press Centre
Source: Hartmut Poeling

Figure 8.11 Shizuoka Press and Broadcasting
Source: James Steele

on January 1, 1961. Although never built, it was an international sensation that upstaged his Metabolist colleagues, and provided both Kikutake and Kurokawa with fodder for their own versions, which followed.

First out of the gate with his own interpretation of the utopian set of Metabolist principles, Tange continued his productive streak with the Yamanashi Broadcasting and Press Centre in Kōfu, designed in 1966 to accommodate the "movable" components, of a newspaper printing plant on the ground floor, and a radio station and television studio in private compartments above, clustered around 16 "fixed" concrete columns, containing services such as stairs, lifts, sanitary

facilities and mechanical equipment (Figure 8.10). Yamanashi was followed by the Shizuoka Press and Broadcasting center, in 1967, in the Ginza district of Tokyo. In this instance, there is only one 7.7-meter diameter, 57-meter-high core, servicing box-like, glass and steel office modules that are cantilevered from it (Figure 8.11).

A complex, prescient legacy

What, then, can be said for certain about this movement, which seems to be as maddeningly amorphous as its name? There are several consistent threads. The first of these is that it did not emerge overnight, but was a long time in the making, rising out of the suppressed rage and resentment of the post-war period. Its primary agenda was to address the desperate shortage of housing resulting from the massive destruction

Figure 8.12 Harumi Housing
Source: Kunio Maekawa Office

of the war, as well as the limited land area available to do that. Up to that point the Harumi Housing project by Kunio Makawa was the most advanced attempt to answer this pressing problem and was held up as an example by the Metabolists of what could be achieved (Figure 8.12).

Perhaps the most important, and least appreciated motive behind the movement, was its thinly veiled nationalism, and the felt need to express a collective pride that had been repressed by both political necessity and legal decree. America had conquered Japan physically but not spiritually, and while the material hardware it had used to do so was begrudgingly admired, Americans were considered to be brutish and not respected as equals, in either historical longevity or cultural refinement, and Metabolism was ultimately a riposte to the Western-style Modernism they were importing, all over the world.

Notes

1   Zhongjie Lin, *Kenzo Tange and the Metabolist Movement: Urban Utopias of Modern Japan*, London: Routledge, 2010.
2   Rem Koolhaas, Hans Ulrick Obrist, *Project Japan: Metabolism Talks*, Taschen, 2011, p. 235.
3   Edmund Husserl, *Ideas Pertaining to a Pure Phenomenology and to a Phenomenological Philosophy*, Book 1, F. Kersten, Trans. Martinus Nishoff, The Hague, 1983, p. 3.
4   Kisho Kurokawa, "New Wave Japanese Architecture", originally the transcript of his lecture at the Academy Forum, 1992, and subsequently published as *Kisho Kurokawa: from Metabolism to Symbiosis*, London and New York: Academy Editions/St. Martin's Press, 1992. No pagination.
5   Mitsuo Taketani, "The Doctrine of the Three Stages of Development," in Soshichi Uchii, "Is the Philosophy of Science Alive in the East? A Report from Japan," Lecture given at Kyoto University, March 14, 2002. And author interview with Chiaki Arai, Tokyo, December 15, 2015.
6   Watsujii Tetsuro, *Fudo Ningegaku-tek Kosatsu (Climate and Culture)*, Trans. Geoffrey Bownas. The Hokuseido Press; Watsujii Tetsuro, *Climate and Culture: A Philosophical Study*, Trans. from Fūdo, by Geoffrey Bownas, Westport, CT: Greenwood Press, 1961.
7   Ernst Cassier, *The Philosophy of Symbolic Forms*, Vol. IV, Ed. John Michael Krois and Donald Phillip Verene, Trans. John Michael Krois, New Haven: Yale University Press, 1996, pp. xv–xviii.
8   Gunter Nitschke, "Rock Flower: Transience and Renewal in Japanese Form," *Kyoto Journal*, 50, Transience Perspectives on Asia, June 2002, pp. 2–12.
9   Robert M. Rodden, Floyd John, Richard Laurino, *Exploratory Analysis of Firestorms*, Stanford Research Institute, Office of Civil Defense, Department of the Army, Washington, D.C., May 1965, pp. 39, 40, 53–54.
10 Arata Isozaki, quoted in Koolhaas and Obrist, op. cit., p. 43.
11 Koolhaas and Obrist, op. cit., p. 309.
12 Cherie Wendelken, "Putting Metabolism Back in Place: The Making of a Radically Decontextualized Architecture in Japan," lecture given at "Anxious Modernisms: Postwar Architectural Culture, 1943–1968," presented at the Canadian Centre for Architecture, Montréal, April 30 and May 1, 1999, in collaboration with the Harvard Graduate School of Design. Disc. #4: Recorded and produced by the Centre Canadien d'Architecture/ Canadian Centre for Architecture.
13 Koolhaas and Obrist, op. cit., p. 309.
14 Lecture by Toyo Ito, "What Was Metabolism? Reflections on the Life of Kiyonori Kikutake," November 10, 2012. Graduate School of Design, Harvard University, Cambridge, MA.
15 Fumihiko Maki, *Investigations in Collective Form*, Washington University School of Architecture, St. Louis, June, 1964, p. 7.

CHAPTER 9

Expo '70
A joyful vision of a new world

Four years after the Metabolists introduced their manifesto at the World Conference in Tokyo, the Ministry of International Trade and Industry within the government of Eisaku Sato, which was in office from November 9, 1964 until July 7, 1972, announced that Japan would host the first international exposition to be held in Asia. After deciding on an opening date of March 15, 1970, they set up a study committee, which operated as a quango, under the political and financial control of the Ministry, but run by a newly established Japanese Association for the World Exposition. This was chaired by Seiji Kaya, and was responsible for the master planning, design, construction and operation of the Exhibition, as well as its final dismantling. Also guided by the International Exposition Bureau, (BIE) a "Thematic" subcommittee was established under this overarching structure, whose first self-appointed task was to visit previous post-war exhibitions, such as the 1958 Brussels World's Fair, The New York Exposition of 1964, planned by Robert Moses, and the Montreal Expo, set to open in 1967.

The recent determination of the Occupation forces to democratize the hierarchical state structure in Japan prompted the planning committee to adopt a decentralized administrative model, but the central government still controlled the finances, determined the ideological direction of the event and decided who would participate. Recognizing that the majority of those attending the exhibition would be Japanese, the organizers sought to allay public fears about the pace of change, to replace defeatist resignation with progressive optimism, and exchange a perception of the inferior quality of Japanese products and goods with one of technological excellence. They also wanted to convey to a wider global audience that Japan had abandoned aggressive expansionism and was now on the path to peace and prosperity, so Progress and Harmony for Mankind was chosen as the theme for the Expo.[1]

At yet another level, the government wanted to finally implement the utopian concepts put forward by the Metabolists and use the exhibition as a testing ground for new urban planning ideas, so this was to be the realization of their agenda. Although some earlier international events, such as the World's Columbian Exposition of 1893, had also adopted a somewhat ambitious agenda, none had been intended as a prototype for social engineering on such a large scale, in attempting to deal with the unprecedented urban growth that was essentially choking Tokyo at the time. Several initiatives, such as the Kinki Regional Plan, had already been launched, but Expo '70 was seen as a means of focusing attention on the need for a much larger concerted planning effort and presenting it to both a national and international audience. Osaka was a prime location for such a study because of the growth of the corridor between that city and

Kyoto, and so 330 hectares in the Senri Hills were chosen as the site.

The Association made a deliberate decision to appoint design professionals who would be more amenable to Western planning methods to guide this effort, placing Takeo Kuwabara and Sakyo Komatsu on the Theme Committee, and putting Uzo Nishiyama and Kenzo Tange in charge of the master plan. Komatsu, in particular, was able to strike a delicate cautionary balance between the dual roles of tradition and technology in constructing a new Japanese society.

Tange envisioned this as an opportunity to design a self-perpetuating urban system in microcosm that would serve as a prototype for actual cities to follow, and used Metabolist analogies to describe his concept for the master plan. He introduced the idea of a central climate-controlled Festival Plaza-Symbol Zone as a meeting place for people from all over the world, with electronic connections symbolizing the interaction between the public and the technology that served them. He described this Plaza as the trunk of a tree with four moving walkways or branches that extended out to each of the four gateways into the Expo grounds.

He also described the 30 private domestic and foreign pavilions and plazas attached to them as buds, or the conceptually interchangeable, less permanent part of the Metabolist system adapted for use at the exposition.[2]

The central Plaza was directly accessible by a new monorail station stop on a track from Osaka that still runs to the site, as a main point of entry. Unlike the glass and steel enclosure designed by Joseph Paxton for the Crystal Palace Exposition of 1851, in London, which was the first of its kind and set the pattern for others that have followed, Tange conceived the roof of the Festival Plaza as free-floating and assigned Tomoo Fukuda and Koji Kamiya the task of engineering it. They responded with a 108-meter by 291.6-meter space truss roof, hovering 30 meters above the Plaza, supported by six large columns. The space frame grid was 10.8 meters square and 7.637 meters deep, covered by a transparent membrane to protect visitors from sun and rain. A fragment of the original roof still stands on the site, demonstrating just how huge it was (Figure 9.1). The entire 4,800-ton roof was built on the ground and lifted by pneumatic jacks located on each of the six columns.

Figure 9.1 Space Frame Fragment
Source: James Steele

Figure 9.2
Capsule
Source: Tomio Ohashi

The opening and closing ceremonies were held here, as were special events to showcase the idea of a world community, such as the celebration of the national days of each of the participating nations, accompanied by music and dancing and light shows by Gutai, an avant garde group of artists based in Osaka known for their support of globalism and utopian views and music especially composed for the Expo by Takemitsu Toru and Takahashi Yuji. The Crown Prince was the Honorary President of the Japan World Exposition, and so he and the other members of the Imperial family attended the opening, which also included a parade of representatives of all of the nations that participated.[3]

In addition to Fukuda and Kamiya, Nishiyama and Tange commissioned 10 other architects to design various parts of the Exposition. Kinoyore Kikutake contributed a "Landmark" or "Expo Tower," which has also unfortunately been demolished. This was intended to be a reference point for visitors to avoid getting lost on the enormous site. Kikutake also used a space frame structure of three tall masts connected by a glass-enclosed elevator to a cluster of octagonal pods containing an observation room, lounge and communication facilities to create it. The 127-meter-high tower has been likened to a launching tower for a spaceship, recalling that the United States' Apollo 11 mission, and the first astronauts landing on the Moon, took place on July 20, 1969. This had an enormous impact on the collective consciousness of Japan, as well as the technological approach to each of the domestic pavilions at the Expo (Figure 9.2).[4]

Arata Isozaki was responsible for the lighting and audio-visual equipment, as well as the mechanical, electrical and electronic installations throughout the

Figure 9.3 Toshiba
Source: Tomio Ohashi

Festival Plaza, to illuminate and synchronize musical performances and electronic presentations. This was an enormous responsibility, since the space could be rearranged to accommodate audiences ranging from 1,500 to 10,000 people. Isozaki also designed two 20-meter-high robots, Demi, or RM, the performer and Deku, or RK, the controller who greeted visitors as they entered the Symbol Zone. They introduced a noticeably random factor into Tange's rational ordered technologically perfect world.[5]

Kisho Kurokawa designed two pavilions and used a serrated tetrahedral steel structure to support a hydraulically controlled circular "Global Vision" theater for the first of these, for Toshiba (Figures 9.3 and 9.4).

The second, Takara pavilion, perfectly expresses Metabolist principles, with a prefabricated steel exoskeleton, which supported metal capsules that could be inserted into or out of it (Figures 9.5, 9.6 and 9.7). Junzo Sakakura and Sachio Otani also made notable contributions to the Expo. Sakakura died before his

Figure 9.4 Toshiba
Source: Tomio Ohashi

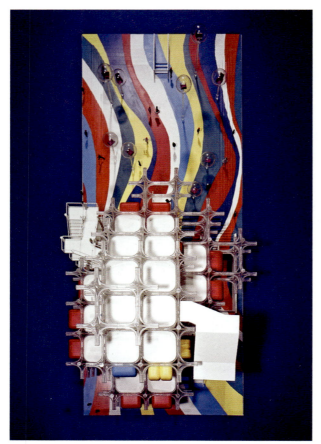

1,200-ton Electrium pavilion supported by four huge columns was completed. It also featured a circular auditorium that was pre-assembled and lifted into place by jacks. This, in turn, had a jauntily angled exhibition room suspended from it by steel cables. Sachio Otani, who designed the Kyoto International Conference Hall in 1963, won the commission in Japan's first national architecture competition and had previously worked in Kenzo Tange studio on the Hiroshima Peace Memorial Museum. He designed the "Fairy Tale" pavilion for the Sumitomo Group using nine disc-shaped domes on a moving belt.

Figure 9.5 *(left)* Takara Pavilion
Source: Tomio Ohashi

Figure 9.6 *(below)* Takara Pavilion
Source: Tomio Ohashi

Figure 9.7
Takara Pavilion
Source: Tomio Ohashi

The Tower of the Sun

Taro Okamoto was perhaps the most controversial architect-artist selected by Nishiyama and Tange. His father, Ippei, was a famous cartoonist, and his mother, Kanoko, was a writer. He continued the family tradition by studying art at the Sorbonne in Paris from 1930 until 1940. He also studied ethnology with Marcel Mauss while he was there concentrating on the tribes of Oceania, as well as attending the Collège de Sociologie Sacré organized by George Bataille. While in Paris, he also met and frequented the studios of Picasso, and Surrealists Man Ray, Andre Breton and Kurt Seligmann. After returning home, he wrote *Shinpi Nihon* or *Mysteries in Japan* describing the Jomon pottery at the Tokyo National Museum and *Nihon*

Sai-hakke: Geijutsu Fudoki; A Rediscovery of the Japan: Topography of Art.

He was commissioned to design the Theme Space and responded by attempting to tell the entire story of the evolution of the human race, and to predict its future. His "Tower of the Sun," which still stands on the site, rose up through a circular opening in the membrane roof, recalling a Shinto himorogi, or divine fence, with a Sakaki tree in the center as the yorishiro of the kami, or deity (Figure 9.8). The sanctity of this tree was described earlier here as being mentioned in the Nihon Shoki or "Chronicles of Japan", which recounts how the deities decided to dig up a Sakaki tree from Mt. Kagu and hang a string of Yasaka jewels on the upper branches, a mirror in the middle and blue and white colored offerings below to entice Amaterasu out of the rock cave of heaven. These objects, as well as a dance by Ame-no-Uzume-mikoto, in a moss belt and Sasaki-leaf headdress, finally lured her out, returning sunlight to the world.[6]

The cryptic, Janus-like face on the tower pales in comparison to the phantasmagorical interior that clearly conveys Okamoto's fascination with mysticism (Figure 9.9). It was closed to the public soon after the Expo ended, but has been re-opened in 2016 and depicts the progress of human evolution represented by figures climbing up on the branches of an enormous tree. Okamoto carried this same idea of evolution into the levels of the Theme Space, conceiving of the underground level as the origin of humanity in the past, the present as grade, and the space frame roof as the integration of humanity and technology in the future.

Okamoto and Tange had entirely different personalities, making it unclear why he was selected, and in several presentations that they made together, Tange jokingly referred to them as the Jomon and Yayoi sides of the Japanese personality.

A glimmering dream, a harsh reality

The Expo, which ran from March 14 to September 2, 1970, fulfilled its goal of attracting a wide audience, but the balance between international and local visitors

Figure 9.8 Tower of the Sun
Source: James Steele

was not even. Almost 98 percent of the 64 million people who attended were Japanese, representing about 50 percent of the population of the country at that time, so the organizers did correctly anticipate the potential of transmitting an upbeat image of the future to their fellow citizens, against heavy odds.[7]

By the end of what was referred to as the "Izamami period" from 1966 to 1969, because it rivaled the creation of the island nation, Japan surpassed Germany by having the second largest gross national product in the world, but was also experiencing all the upheavals plaguing other developed nations at that time, such as disillusionment with materialism and the general feeling of a loss of meaning in life, chronic inflation, trade surpluses, environmental degradation and pollution, and social unrest. The end of the Occupation had also unleashed the specter of Marxism once again, and in October 1966, the Labor Movement joined the International Anti-Vietnam War Coalition, creating the Beheiren, or Peace in Vietnam initiative. The Japan-United States Mutual Cooperation and Security Treaty, which had substantially contributed to recovery by eliminating the need for a defense budget, turned out to be a mixed blessing during the Cold War, because it forced Japan to share the nuclear threat, and allowed American troops to be stationed there, giving them a staging area for military activity in Southeast Asia.

The Zengakuren, or All National Student Federation, organized demonstrations when the American involvement in Vietnam escalated in 1964. These accelerated, and soon spilled over into academia, for the first time in Japan's history, forcing the government to cancel the University Entrance Examinations in 1969, causing national chaos.[8]

Several of the Metabolists, but most notably Arata Isozaki, were involved with the Marxist faction behind these protests, underscoring his radically dystopian opposition to the optimistic, progressive aspect of that movement, and his negative view of mass production and systematic urban planning. His reservations coincided with an unsettling consensus that the Expo conformed to Pierre Bourdieu's concept of a spectacle and its inherent "metamorphosis of taste" as a controlled attempt to define a technological aesthetic by the organizers who are "the producers of culture."[9]

As such it effectively stultified the creative energy of the Metabolist revolution it intended to physically validate, and fatally diffused it, through its descent into superficiality and "kanki bunka," or the stasis of suburban mediocrity instead. Three years after it closed, the oil crisis brought the Metabolists' dream to an abrupt end.[10]

Notes

1   Pieter van Wesemael, *An Architecture of Instruction and Delight: A Socio-Historical Analysis of World Exhibitions as a Didactic Phenomenon, 1798–1851–1970*, Rotterdam: 010 Publishers, p. 570.

2   Kenzo Tange, "Towards Urban Design," *The Japan Architect*, September–October 1971, Vol. 46, No. 9–10/176, p. 34.

3   Ming Tiampo, *Gutai: Decentering Modernism*, Chicago: University of Chicago Press, 2010.

4   Peter Eckersall, *Performativity and Event in 1960s Japan: City, Body, Memory*, Basingstoke: Palgrave Macmillan, p. 126.

5   Marcus Shaffer, "Incongruity, Bizarreness and Transcendence: Ritual Machine vs. Technocratic Rationalism at Expo '70," in *Globalizing Architecture Machine Traditions*, p. 48–51. Conference Proceedings of the 102nd Annual Meeting of the Associated Collegiate Schools of Architecture (ACSA), April 10–12, 2014, Florida International University, Miami.

6   See Part I: An enduring cultural framework. Chapter 1: The land and its people, and Arata Isozaki, *Japan-ness in Architecture*, Cambridge, MA: MIT Press, 2006, p. 73.

7   Peter Eckersall, *Performativity and Event in 1960s Japan: City, Body, Memory*, Palgrave Macmillan, p. 115.

8   Koichi Hamada, "Japan 1968: A Reflection Point During the Era of the Economic Miracle," Economic Growth Center, Yale University, Discussion Paper #764, 1966, p. 2–6.

9   Peter Eckersall, op. cit., p. 117.

10 Hajime Yatsuka, "Architecture in the Urban Desert: A Critical Introduction to Japanese Architecture after Modernism," *Oppositions Reader: Selected Readings from a Journal for Ideas and Criticism in Architecture, 1973–1984*, Ed. Kay Micheal Hayes, Princeton Architectural Press, 1998, p. 257.

CHAPTER 10

The Shinohara School

After the utopian promises of Metabolism as distilled in the Osaka Exposition in 1970 remained unrealized, Kazuo Shinohara stepped into the void with an alternative worldview that appealed to many of his contemporaries and a devoted following of younger architects and students. That legacy, of this master of several carefully constructed yet seemingly impenetrable contradictions is still legible today, in the latest generation of Japanese architects.

Shinohara was born in Shizuoka in 1925 and graduated from the Tokyo Institute of Physics, now the Tokyo University of Science in 1947. He received his second degree in Architecture from the Tokyo Institute of Technology, in the Seike Kiyoshi Lab in 1953, and opened his own architectural office the following year. He eventually became a Professor at his Alma Mater in 1970 and taught there until he retired in 1986. He concentrated mainly on residential design in his practice, setting a personal goal of producing one house each year and managed to build about 55 of them before his death in 2006.[1]

As a dedicated academic and theorist who was also engaged in practice, he had a broad impact that crested during the 1980s, and has arguably been as influential among younger architects in its own way as the Tange Lab was at Tokyo University. The "Shinohara School" is clearly legible today in the work of Toyo Ito, Itsuko Hasagawa, and Kazunari Sakamoto, and so by extension to Kazuo Sejima, Ryue Nishizawa, and Kengo Kuma as well as their disciples, such as Atelier Bow Wow.

The 2011 Memu Meadows Experimental House, in Hokkaido, by Kengo Kuma, is an especially overt testimonial to Shinohara's influence. It is elegantly simple, recalling the earth houses of the Ainu, and uses a double skin membrane and heat recovery system from an indoor fireplace to keep indoor temperatures within the comfort zone during the extremely cold winters in this northern region.

An equally referential, simply rectilinear house in Takaya, Hiroshima completed by the Suppose Design Office of Makaoto Tanijiri and Ai Yoshida in 2012, recalls the two distinct levels or zones that Shinohara used in several of his houses, with a wooden floor and a traditional irori hearth, raised above a compacted earth floor, or doma. Like Shinohara, they have also used sliding screens to evoke those in a traditional Japanese residence.

Four phases

Shinohara, who approached his houses as works of art, associated with creative people in all disciplines and divided his projects into phases or periods in the way that painters do. He identified four of these in his own work, which retrospectively track larger social changes taking place in Japan over the course of his career.

The first phase, arising out of what he has described as his "emotional encounter" with and extensive knowledge of Japanese history, is expressed in a unity of all of the elements of a program into a single space with a unified theme, involving only a minimal number of "operations" or interventions to satisfy programmatic requirements. These first houses are ephemeral, with thin structural frames, and often have shoji-like partitions. This period is clearly bracketed by his first decidedly archetypal House in Kugayama, in 1953, up through his minimal House in White in 1966, inspired by the seventeenth-century Jito-in Shoin in Nara. This has one main floor area divided by a screen wall into public and private zones, supported by an umbrella-like roof framing structure that branches out from a Shinbashira, or central column like that of the Izumo shrine. He has written extensively about the Western concept of space, lyrically expanding on a theme covered extensively here, that there is no similar concept in Japanese traditional architecture. He identifies Western space as dynamic, related to the ever-present impetus of time, unlike the Japanese recognition of the absence of continuity, as part of a

"culture that avoids dealing with substantial entities." This is expressed as a transparent expanse, or void, and the nonexistence of space.[2]

His second, more rectilinear phase is heavier, and more segmented, mirroring the cumulative social impact of the student demonstrations of the late 1960s, and his Cubic Forest House in Kawasaki, Japan, of 1971 with its square footprint and alternately modular grid, creating "fissures," signals the beginning of this period.

His third phase is best represented by his 1982 House Under High Voltage Lines, in which he deliberately embraces a conflicting set of regulations controlling construction near the power lines that run across the site, leading him to create a concave roof that delineates their path. Throughout this process he can be seen as evolving toward an inextricable interrelationship between image and meaning, attempt-

Figure 10.1 Centennial Hall, Tokyo Institute of Technology
Source: Tomio Ohashi

Figure 10.2 Centennial Hall
Source: Tomio Ohashi

ing to cut the "simple rectilinear relationship between form and function" in his belief that this simplistic Modernist equation has now been superceded by technological advances that have rendered it ineffectual.[3]

This is the theme of his fourth and final phase best understood in his largest project for the Tokyo Institute of Technology.

A zero degree machine

Shinohara's Centennial Hall, which is located at the Okayamama Station entrance to the Tokyo Institute of Technology campus, contains a museum, social facilities, and meeting rooms, within a four-story cube and a restaurant bar and lounge in a half-cylinder that bisects the roof and cantilevers out beyond the edge of this rectilinear base (Figure 10.1). The half-cylinder deflects in the middle, with one end pointing to the train station to the east and the other toward a park in the middle of the campus on the west. Both the cube and the cylinder are sheathed in a glistening metal wrapper. To offset any possibility of structural failure in an earthquake, Shinohara's engineer, Toshihiko

Kimura, conceived of the cylinder as a horizontal box beam fused to the vertical corners of the cube. On the third floor, the half cylinder slices diagonally across the ceiling of a lobby, reception room, and a small conference room, deliberately creating confusion between form and function, and recalling the internal concave roof caused by the invisible electrical current House Under High Voltage Lines, at a much larger scale (Figure 10.2).

Shinohara has cited the Apollo lunar landing module and the F-14 jetfighter as inspirations, but rather than being literally adopted here, they are each metaphors for unselfconsciously designed machines engineered purely to function well, without any aesthetic considerations at all. He has described this as a search for "optimistic synchronization of fact and function in a period of social revolution" in which "relative value can be achieved from elements that have lost meaning and have been reduced to a zero degree."[4]

Photographer Tomio Ohashi, whose images of Centennial Hall appear here, has sensitively understood Shinohara's intention of making the building an integral part of the industrial landscape of the railway station

Figure 10.3 Centennial Hall
Source: Tomio Ohashi

Figure 10.4 Centennial Hall, Tokyo Institute of Technology, Interior
Source: Tomio Ohashi

nearby, and by extension, making it a commentary on what he referred to as the "random noise" of the city (Figure 10.3), the juxtaposition of random fragments, in a constant process of impermanence, demolition and re-building, in which transformation rather than creation is key, that makes Japanese cities different from their Western counterparts (Figure 10.4).

Kazuo Shinohara seems to continue to resist meaningful interpretation, and yet, as his quest for a "degree zero" indicates and the next chapter about Postmodernism in Japan will explain, he does anticipate a critically important trajectory in architecture, which is its symbiotic tracking of economic cycles, and concomitant dependency upon the technological advances that each of these periods create. By searching for this final condition he shows that he intuitively understood this process, and as a rational scientist, simply wanted to circumvent all the steps leading to it.

He has often been categorized as being critical of the various manifestations of Modernism in Japan, such as those devoted to Le Corbusier, or the Metabolists, who were mostly dedicated to technological solutions to overcrowding, which they described as urban disorder.

This view is overly simplistic because he believed they simply didn't go far enough in developing production systems that truly reflect the post-industrial age. Modernism, for him, was an early "first act" of this cycle, involving an enchantment with the structural possibilities made possible by new industrial materials, followed by the "comic relief" or Postmodernism, before the second act of Modernism began. He was trying to fast-forward to that second act, which is why Centennial Hall so closely resembles the context-free object buildings being produced by parametric advocates today.[5]

The mathematical city and the beauty of chaos

In 1967, Shinohara also put forward the idea of the "mathematical city," anticipating the Deconstructive discovery of Chaos Theory over a decade later. Unlike the Metabolists, who wanted to create a tabula rasa and proposed formal, unified, large-scale solutions to the urban problems facing Japan after the war, Shinohara proposed informal disunity, but one based on the disorderly order of chaos, stressing that large-scale urban solutions were not possible without understanding how informal composition works and can be systemically, mathematically applied. His houses, in this sense, were individual explorations into the possibility of new types of order, moving from the part to the whole, which could combine to create a city, and he enthusiastically promoted the messiness of Tokyo, as proof of life.

A hidden order

In 1989, two years after Shinohara's Centennial hall appeared, Ishihara Yoshinobu was also promoting the idea of Chaos Theory as a way of understanding Japanese cities in his cult classic *A Hidden Order*, which is an attempt to make sense of the seeming irrationality of Tokyo. Like Shinohara, he also begins by exploring the traditional Japanese house, and makes some important points that help to elucidate Shinohara's earlier work. Yoshinobu starts with the floor, and explains that before the Meiji Period, residences were all made out of wood, with raised floors to offset the effects of hot, humid summers and cold, dry winters. He makes the key point that Japan used to be, and in many cases still is, a "floor culture," in which manners and customs evolved to accommodate this way of life, lowering the line of vision of those sitting down by 30 centimeters. Shoji screens were always opened or closed from a kneeling position, and the line of vision was downward, because the tatami covered floor was the brightest surface in the room. There was no furniture and ceilings were very low by Western standards. This is especially important when evaluating Japanese garden design. This differs significantly from Chinese gardens, which were viewed from a chair.[6]

Yoshinobu's discussion of the difference between a traditional Japanese "floor" culture and its antithetical "chair" culture equivalent in ancient China, raises an interesting question about Shinohara's early house designs, which were predicated on historical typologies, yet also had furniture that he designed as part of an obvious gesamtskunstwerk or total work of art intentionality that seems to be at odds with his reputation for an anti-Western bias.

Much of Shinohara's reputation for indecipherability, then, can simply be put down to his being far ahead of his time, as a scientist who intuitively understood that the trajectory of contemporary architecture was becoming inexorably tied to that of global capitalism. But a bit of the sheer strangeness of his forms to Western sensibilities, like those of other Japanese architects such as Shin Takamatsu, can now be safely ascribed to cultural difference.

Post-structuralists will be especially heartened to hear that, as research progresses on this touchy topic, findings indicate that people of different cultures simply think differently. Researchers Dr. Richard Nisbett and Dr. Kaiping Peng at the University of Michigan have found that the way people perceive and assimilate memories, and the logical categories they use and rules they apply to cope with a myriad of life situations, are far more pliable than psychologists once assumed. Their studies indicate that this difference extends to conflict resolution, in which Asian subjects were less likely to support only one side in an argument, and Shinohara's theories substantiate this difference.[7]

Notes

1   Yasumitsu Matsunaga and Kazuo Shinohara, *Kazuo Shinohara*, IAUS 17, Rizzoli, and the Institute for Art and Urban Studies, 1982, p. 11. For a complete listing of his most important houses, *Kazuo Shinohara: Complete Works in Original Publications*, JA 93 Spring 2014. Some of the most notable are: Tanikawa House, House in Kugayama No. 2, House in Komae, House in Chigasaki, Umbrella House, House with a Big Roof, House with an Earthen Floor, House in White, House of Earth, Yamashiro House, Suzusho House, North House in Hanayama, South House in Hanayama, The Uncompleted House, Shino House, Cubic Forest, Repeating Crevice, Sea Stairway, Sky Rectangle, House in Seijo, House in Higashi-Tamagawa, House in Kugahara, Prism House, Tanikawa House, House in Uehara,

House in Hanayama No. 3, House in Ashitaka, House on a Curved Road, House in Karuizawa, House in Itoshima, House in Hanayama No. 4, House under High-Voltage Lines, House in Yokohama, Tenmei House.

2   Kazuo Shinohara: "Anthology: 1958–1978," in Yasumitsu Matsunaga, *Kazuo Shinohara*, Institute for Architecture and Urban Studies and Rizzoli International NY, 1982, p. 11.

3   Kazuo Shinohara, Gustavo Gili Ediciones ARQ 2GN. 58/59, p. 16.

4   Yasumitsu Matsunaga and Kazuo Shinohara, op. cit., p. 12.

5   Ibid., p. 13.

6   Ishihara Yoshinobu, *A Hidden Order: Tokyo Through the Twentieth Century*, Kodansha, Tokyo, 1989, p. 63.

7   Erica Goode, "How Culture Molds Habits of Thought," *The New York Times*, August 8, 2000.

CHAPTER 11

Postmodernism
Apostasy or prophesy?

After post-industrial angst was first made manifest in the arts, as an aesthetic symptom of an underlying revolutionary blurring of class boundaries in the late 1950s and early 1960s, a rapidly expanding field of architectural critics scrambled to make sense of it all.

But before they did, Philadelphia architect Robert Venturi was one of the first to openly express dissatisfaction with what he termed "the puritanically moral language of orthodox Modern Architecture" in his landmark 1966 book *Complexity and Contradiction in Architecture*, making a plea for richness rather than clarity of meaning, implicit rather than explicit function, as a "both-and" rather than "either-or" approach to form.[1]

He had already proven that this was more than mere rhetoric in his design of a house for his mother Vanna, in Chestnut Hill in 1964. It is widely considered the first built expression of Postmodernism because he substituted a patented Modernist form-follows-function approach with coded, semiotic messages hidden within what he has referred to as "a child's drawing of a house" representing the fundamental aspects of shelter, such as a gable roof, chimney, door and windows.[2]

But Venturi went further than merely suggesting child-like forms, charting unknown territory by treating the front façade as a message board, rather than a Modernist form-follows-function exercise of describing the uses within. It is much larger than it needs to be, for a start, introducing his concept of the façade as a "decorated shed" detached from the enclosure that conveys an image, rather than a Modernist "duck" with a skin that exactly conforms to its purpose. Venturi was inspired by British Arts and Crafts architect Edwin Lutyens, who treated the skin of his houses as a changeable surface on which openings seemed to be able to be moved at will, and organized the windows of his mother's house along a horizontal band, implying that they were moving across it like letters on a neon sign.

The datum itself recalls a dado, or chair rail, used inside a house to prevent damage to a wall, which further confuses assumptions about inside and outside and where the skin stops. The gable is the most significant message of all, however, since the child-like pediment, signifying shelter is cleft in two, just as many American families were starting to be at that time, and the chimney behind it, which is an equally powerful symbol of security, turns out to be a light monitor, when seen from the side.

And then, three years after *Complexity and Contradiction in Architecture* appeared, Michael Graves, who was part of the New York Five, along with Peter Eisenman, Charles Gwathmey, John Hedjuk and Richard Meier, started to demonstrate dissatisfaction with their common veneration of Le Corbusier. Graves did so in his Hanselmann house, in Fort Wayne,

Indiana (1968), Benacerraf house in Princeton, New Jersey (1969) and Synderman House, also in Fort Wayne (1972), in which he increasingly challenged the "Five Points" dogma of the grid, free elevation, free plan, strip window and roof garden put forward by his French-Swiss guide, and like Venturi, he started to use them as a semaphore, instead. In the Hanselmann house, for example, a steep stair leading from the parking lot to a self-styled piano nobile is formally exaggerated beyond functional purpose, and then, in an overtly Cubist maneuver, its angular edge is visually flipped 90 degrees and repeated as a flat panel on the façade. At the Benacerraf house, which is really just a children's playroom added to an existing bungalow, the scale of a stairway is also emphasized to simply imply ascent, and a steel pipe column is rotated 90 degrees to become a railing. By the time Graves designed the Snyderman house he had exhausted his Corbusian vocabulary and the layering of surfaces in front of the demising wall that he explored in the first two projects begins to explode. This led him to attempt his first built paean in his Plocek House in Warren, New Jersey, in 1977. He defended his new embrace of what he called "figurative" classicism, based on anthropomorphic sources, as a desire to establish a more existential relationship with his clients, and this intention along with a more humorous motivation was also certainly a factor when Charles Moore designed his neon lined Piazza d'Italia in New Orleans in 1976. Graves soon followed with the first major public expression of the new style in his Portland building in 1980. If Venturi's adventures had raised concern among mainstream Modernists, and Graves's early explorations had heightened it, these final apostasies in New Orleans and Portland undoubtedly caused intellectual apoplexy.

This disdain turned to despair when a jury unanimously chose a design for an addition to the Alte Staatsgalerie in Stuttgart by James Stirling of Michael Wilford & Associates in London combined with the unveiling of Philip Johnson and John Burgee's AT&T Tower, at 550 Madison Avenue, in the heart of Manhattan, both completed in 1984. Stirling was considered to be a hardcore Hi-Tech advocate, and Johnson had been single-handedly responsible for importing High Modernism into the United States with the landmark International Style exhibition he and Henry-Russell Hitchcock curated at the Museum of Modern Art in 1932. His successful attempts in convincing both Walter Gropius and Ludwig Mies van der Rohe to relocate to America before the war had also essentially ensured the spread of the German variant of Modernism through the educational institutions that each of them led. This high-profile reversal by such major proponents of Modernism in the past raised the significance of Postmodernism to a new level, making it clear that it had arrived on the world stage. While architects in the developing world held on to Modernist conventions because they symbolized progress, many others in the developed equivalent then rushed to board this stylish new train.

Theoretical scaffolding

Whether by intuition or intent, their use of architectural elements, such as the roof, chimney, stairs, columns, windows and doors in a semiotic rather than purely functional way inserted the first three pioneers of Postmodernism squarely into the debate about the relatively new field of structural linguistics, introduced by Ferdinand de Saussure, and best described in his *Course in General Linguistics* which was released posthumously in 1915.[3] Saussure argued that language is a structured social system, subject to both fixed conventions and changes over time. He was concerned about the ways in which it constructs meaning, rather than analyzing content, and viewed objects as "texts" which have shared "codes and conventions" rather than universally accepted meanings. He saw language as a "signifying system" that creates meaning rather than simply expressing it.[4]

As such, Saussure was a Structuralist who believed that language is a quasi-mutable but deeply engrained part of a universal framework of human culture. His linguistic theory was then applied to anthropology by Claude Lévi-Strauss, best described in his book *The Elementary Structures of Kinship* in 1949, in which he held that families should not just be studied as individuals but as an interactive unit in which identity is formed in relation to others.[5]

Structuralism subsequently engaged a cadre of philosophers such as Gilles Deleuze, Francois Lyotard, Michael Foucault, Jacques Derrida and Jacques Lacan, until it was eventually dismantled in the nihilistic sequel of Deconstructivism. Of these, Lyotard specifically concentrated on Postmodernism, in ways that were directly applicable to architecture, calling into question the entire "grand narrative" of modernism, based on a belief in a chronological, historical trajectory of progress, and the infallibility of science.

Instead, Lyotard intriguingly posited that Postmodernism actually preceded Modernism as a historical tendency, and rather than describing it as disjunctive, as others were at the time, Fredric Jameson describes him in his foreword to Lyotard's book as "seeing Postmodernism as a discontent with this or that modernist style – a moment in the perpetual 'revolution' and innovation of high modernism to be succeeded by a burst of fresh invention," only being labeled Postmodernism for convenience's sake until a new Modernism came along.[6]

A stunningly useful insight

Jameson subsequently provided his own defining take on the architectural aspect of the condition in his own landmark book *Postmodernism, or, The Cultural Logic of Late Capitalism*, in 1991, which provides an essential insight into the Japanese variant of the style as well as contemporary work. Because it came at the end of a veritable deluge of other attempts at analyzing the phenomenon, Jameson did have the benefit of 20/20 hindsight, but he managed to finally provide an inspired, economically informed, teleological explanation for it.

Jameson pushes back against later theorists who were opposed to periodization, in their belief that it constitutes a "grand narrative" and also rejects the contention that it represents a fundamental rupture from Modernism because its ideological tenets were exhausted. Among all other theorists analyzing it, he is also one of the few to appreciate that architecture is the medium in which aesthetic changes and theoretical propositions are most physically apparent.

Rather than simply approaching Postmodernism as yet another float in a long, colorful parade of discrete styles, Jameson insists that it must be examined as "an implicitly or explicitly political stance on the nature of multinational capitalism today."[7] He cites the cyclical economic theory of Ernest Mandel to support this claim, who in turn refined Nikolai Kondratiev's belief that each of the five identifiable phases of capitalism

since "the financial agricultural revolution" of 1600–1780, move through three phases of expansion, stagnation and recession.[8]

In addition to Mandel, Kondratieff's five phases of capitalism were subsequently also fine tuned by Joseph Schumpeter in 1939, and then most recently by Daniel Smihula, who added five more "revolutions" to the monetary component of agrarianism in the eighteenth century, captured so well by Raymond Williams in *The Country and the City*. These are: Industrial (1780–1880), Technical (1880–1940), Scientific (1940–1985), Information and Telecommunications (1985–2015) and Post-Information and Technology (2015–2035).[9]

Further refinements

By tying Postmodernism to one of the economic cycles of late capitalism, Jameson moves it into the category of what he terms "a cultural dominant" and rather than denying periodization and critiquing historicism, he claims that it can only be understood in comparison to the "waves" that precede and follow it. As such, he assigns architecture to the status of a mere commodity, consistent with the intensified craving for novelty and reduction of the creative process to a crass economic exchange, described as the "Culture Industry" by Theodor Adorno and Max Horkheimer in *Dialectic of Enlightenment* in 1979.[10]

Beyond the lack of depth which this "culture of the image or the simulacrum" engenders, one of the most recognizable symptoms of this demand for increasingly faster gratification is the desensitization, total lack of opprobrium and ennui that has now replaced the high modern concept of shock.[11]

The Japanese view

Japan broke into the arcane world of Western sensibilities about Structuralism in architecture in 1977, when Charles Jencks selected the Nibani-kan, by Minoru Takeyama for the cover of the first edition of his book *The Language of Post-Modern Architecture*. This three-dimensional super-graphic, located in the Tokyo entertainment district of Kabuki-cho, along with the Ichiban-kan, which is its slightly more sedate, black and white companion piece, were both completed

Figure 11.1 Takeyama Niban-kan
Source: Hartmut Poeling

in 1969, shortly after the Venturi declaration of difference, and show that Takeyama shared his belief in architecture as a message board (Figures 11.1. and 11.2).

The Metabolists, however, have been cited as anticipating Postmodernism long before this because of their early critique of its high Modern antecedent, but this is too simplistic in light of Jameson's critical proviso. They did promote tradition, Japanese culture and history, and did attempt to marry it to the latest

technological developments available to them, but at the time the movement was launched, Japan was still a developing country, recovering from a disastrous war.[12]

Both Kisho Kurokawa and Arata Isozaki, who have each been shown to represent different factions of the Metabolist movement, have now also become closely associated with its Postmodern sequel in a critically different way. Because Kurokawa continued to embrace the Metabolist Manifesto throughout the remainder of his career, to the point of later claiming authorship of

Figure 11.2 Takeyama Ichiban-kan
Source: Hartmut Poeling

the entire movement, he may actually be identified as a proto-Postmodernist, since he was advocating that Western-style Modernism be replaced with a Japanese alternative, based on a mixture of tradition and technology.

Kisho Kurokawa

He explained his position in an extensive series of books, articles, lectures and portfolios, re-coded as his "Philosophy of Symbiosis" as a transition from "the Age of Machine to the Age of Life." Sounding very much like Venturi, he advocated a shift from "single-coded modernism" and "the avant-garde role of inarticulate architecture" to one that more closely adhered to the new economic reality of the transition period from an industrial to an information society as well as the "diachronicity and synchronicity" of Japanese tradition, which he characterized as more humane than Western materialism.

Figure 11.3 Kurokawa Wacoal
Kojimachi Building
Source: Tomio Ohashi

Specifically addressing Postmodernism, Kurokawa cited Charles Jenck's definitive 1984 book *The Language of Post-Modern Architecture*, and listed what he believed to be its essential aspects: double coding, or speaking to people on both a literal and figurative level, hybridity, or mixing opposing elements such as historical and modern styles, elite with popular culture, intentional schizophrenia, or contradictions, the use of multivalent semiotics, or language, and an architec-

ture that responds to the complex content and plurality of the city.[13]

These features permeate his later work, from the early 1980s until his death on October 12, 2007. The Saitama Museum, of 1979–1980, for example, has both contextual and semiotic aspects that were alien to high modernism. It is located in the middle of a park, and was built to accommodate rows of old growth trees. To allow more flexibility at the ground floor, the permanent collection is below grade, lit by a central atrium, and special exhibits are held on the first and second floors. A concrete lattice at the main entrance provides an open, but enclosed, engawa-type space, and also has obvious Structuralist allusions, as a mnemonic bridge back to the ancient chashitsu tradition of Japan.

His Wacoal Kojimachi Building in Tokyo, of 1984, on the other hand, uses far more literal coding. It is the Tokyo headquarters of a Japanese fashion giant, faced with horizontal synthetic marble and aluminum strips, in which Kurokawa incorporated Japanese, Chinese and Korean motifs into the interior decoration, and directed a large circular window, which looks like the hub of an enormous pencil sharpener, toward the Imperial Palace nearby (Figure 11.3).

Arata Isozaki

Arata Isozaki found it easier to detach himself from the Metabolist mindset because of his dissatisfaction with their optimistic vision of a brave new world made possible by technology and progress, and his considerably darker view of an apocalyptic alternative,

stemming from his memories of post-war destruction. Expo '70 caused him to have a breakdown, and after he recovered he decided to abandon the Modernist project entirely in favor of an apolitical, a-contextual direction best illustrated by his Tsukuba Civic Center, in Ibaraki, built from 1979 to 1983 (Figure 11.4).

As a symbol of apostasy by someone widely considered to be a true believer in the Metabolist vision, this project caused the same level of global consternation among modernists as Johnson's AT&T Building and James Stirling's Stuttgart Statsgallerie, but attracted even more pointed criticism because of his overt copying of parts of other Western Postmodern icons (Figure 11.5). Yet, in spite of the fact that it appears to be a sampler of bits and pieces borrowed intact from buildings by Robert Venturi, Michael Graves, and Charles Moore, as well as more historical models such as Michelangelo's Campidoglio and Ledoux's Salt Works at Chaux, Isozaki somewhat cryptically describes this as an attempt to "deconstruct" them "by means of Japanese elements." Eerily echoing Kurokawa's recitation of Post-modern attributes, he also says that he feels these literal references allowed him to

Figure 11.4 Isozaki Tsukuba Civic Center
Source: Tomio Ohashi

Figure 11.5 Isozaki Tsukuba Civic Center
Source: Tomio Ohashi

"eliminate all traces of a unifying system that might extend outward from the whole. Consequently, the elements quoted from heterogeneous sources overlap in a fragmented and non-continuous way. I refer to this ironically as schizophrenic eclectism."[14] Jun Aoki, who worked on this project while he was in Isozaki's office, recalls suggesting the Campidoglio, but placing it below grade as the perfect metaphor of this new city and the vacuity and the emptiness of the contemporary condition.[15]

The Toy Block series

Not all converts to the Postmodern direction were as morbid as Isozaki. By adopting Johan Huizinga's belief that play is part of our prehistoric make-up, for example, Takefumi Aida added some much needed levity to this period, in much the same way that Charles Moore did in the United States, by reminding us that while humor was noticeably absent from early Modernism, because of its high-minded convictions about saving society, it certainly is a central part of human behavior. Huizinga stressed that play is unstructured and free, and has no material agenda, and Aida likened his design of a series of 10 Toy Block houses to this childhood experience (Figure 11.6).

A sarcastic Ionian caricature in Setagaya

Kengo Kuma is as enthusiastic about writing about architecture as Kurokawa was, and has described the equally playful, exaggerated renditions of Classicism he produced during the first phase of his career as a deliberate critique of the American origins of Postmodernism, as what he believes is a rejection of the European roots of the modern movement. Once one understands his intent, this is obviously the motive behind his 1991 M2 Building in Setagaya (Figure 11.7). Its name is a shorthand version of "Mazda Too"

Figure 11.6 Takefumi Aida, Toy Block House
Source: Takefumi Aida Office

Figure 11.7 Kuma, M2, Setagaya
Source: Miki Fugiwara

Figure 11.8 Sou Fujimoto, Tokyo Apartments
Source: Sou Fujimoto

since it originally housed the research and design division of the Mazda Motor Corporation, but more appropriately perhaps has now found new life as a funeral parlor.

Kuma's contention, of Postmodernism as a denial rather than an evolutionary extension of Modernism, brings us back full circle to Jameson's invaluable clarification of that common misconception, as well as the lack of understanding about the economic trajectory that unites them both.[16]

The extent of that trajectory is legible within the youngest generation of Japanese architects as well, as indicated by the Tokyo Apartments project by Sou Fujimoto (Figure 11.8). It consists of four house-shaped units stacked on top of each other, and obviously owes an immediate debt to the Herzog & de Meuron, Vitra Haus completed in 2006. The intention of calling the entire preconceived notion of domesticity into question by manipulating its most sacred images, which is demonstrated by of each of these projects, however, was unmistakably pre-empted by Robert Venturi 40 years earlier, in a modest house near Philadelphia that opened the entire issue of imagery in architecture to global debate.

Notes

1 Robert Venturi, *Complexity and Contradiction in Architecture*, Museum of Modern Art, New York, 1966, p. 16.

2 Robert Venturi, "Diversity, Relevance and Representation in Historicism, or Plus ca Change," *Architectural Record*, June 1982, p. 114–119.

3 Ferdinand de Saussure, *Cours de Linguistique Générale*, Trans. Roy Harris as: *Course in General Linguistics*, Charles Bally and Albert Sechehaye, Eds., Open Court Press, 1915.

4 John E. Joseph, *Saussure*, Oxford: Oxford University Press, 2012, p. 72.

5 Claude Levi-Strauss, first published in French as: *Les Structures Elementaires de la Parente* in 1949, then as *The Elementary Structures of Kinship*, Ed. Rodney Needham, Trans. J.H. Bell, J.R. von Sturmer, and Rodney Needham, Traviston, 1970.

6 Fredric Jameson, Foreword, Jean-Francois Lyotard, *The Postmodern Condition: A Report on Knowledge*, Minneapolis, MN: University of Minnesota Press, 1979, p. xvi.

7 Fredric Jameson, *Postmodernism, or, The Cultural Logic of Late Capitalism*, Durham, NC: Duke University Press, 1991, p. 186.

8 Nikolai Kondratieff, *The Long Wave Cycle*, Trans. Guy Daniels, E.P. Dutton, 1984.

9 Daniel Smihula, *Long Waves of Technological Innovations*, Bratislava: Studia Politica Slovaca, 2011.

10 Theodor W. Adorno and Max Horkheimer, *Dialectic of Enlighenment*, Verso, 1979, p. 120.

11 Jameson, op. cit., p. 188.

12 Florian Urban, "Japanese 'Occidentalism' and the Emergence of Postmodern Architecture," *Journal of Architectural Education*, Vol. 65, No. 2, pp. 89–102, March, 2012.

13 Kisho Kurokawa, *Intercultural Architecture: The Architecture of Symbiosis*, American Institute of Architects Press, 1991.

14 Arata Isozaki, *Arata Isozaki: Works in Architecture*, RIBA Architecture Center, London, 1995, p. 6.

15 Jun Aoki, Interview with the Author, December 16, 2015.

16 Kengo Kuma, *Studies in Organic, Kuma & Associates*, Tokyo: Toto, 2009, p. 14.

CHAPTER 12

A decade of excess
Life inside the bubble

The Bubble Economy in Japan, which lasted from 1986 until 1991, had a number of systemic causes, primarily related to an ingrained tradition of interpersonal relationships, centered around the Keiretsu, reorganized from the Zaibatsu of the prewar period which were broken up during the Allied Occupation. Due to the political pressures caused by the Cold War, the Zaibatsu were allowed to restructure, using the same corporate names, and they clustered together around banks and shared each other's stock. This hidebound structure was compounded by the dominance of the Ministry of Finance that distorted the development of an effective financial market, which resulted in hugely inflated stock and real estate prices, guided by strict tax law, with high capital gains taxes to discourage speculation. This lack of liquidity meant that property values were artificially inflated, which was reflected in the artificial increase in land cost, and banks, which had grown wealthy on the prosperity created by an overheated manufacturing economy, made large loans using these properties as collateral.

By 1990 the aggregate value of all real estate in Japan was vastly inflated compared to prices elsewhere in the world. Interest rates on deposits were deregulated in 1985, initiating fierce competition among banks for deposits, and the interest payments they yielded.[1] Property development became a key contributor to the Japanese economy during this period, and this monster required constant feeding. As the government ran out of funds to carry out major projects it privatized the process, offering private businesses special concessions to carry them out.[2]

This inexorable mechanistic nexus, between a large government agency, the banks, the Keiretsu and the "big five" group of general contractors referred to earlier here, who each have their own sizable design departments, inevitably included, and still includes architects as part of the Doken Kokka, or construction state, who were also caught up in the demand for larger projects to keep the economy afloat.

A visual stroll through any of the major Japanese trade magazines that covered the over-heated construction market at this time, such as Japan Architect, A+U, Global Architecture (GA), or Shinkenshiku, among others, offer multiple built examples of this bloat. However well intentioned the architects involved may have been, they were affected by it. The few examples chosen here were designed by esteemed members of the group of architects who were born before the war, and lived through not only the extremism that caused it and its consequences, but also the rush of the economic miracle that followed defeat and they offer incontrovertible witness to that upward pressure.

A cathedral of data

Two buildings by Kenzo Tange provide the first useful examples. His Tokyo Metropolitan Government

Figure 12.1 Tokyo Metropolitan Government Building
Source: James Steele

Building in Shinjuku, as the first of these, was finished in December 1990, just before the bubble burst, replacing the Tokyo Metropolitan Government Building at Yūrakuchō, which Tange also designed in 1957. This was demolished and is now site of the Tokyo International Forum, by Rafael Vinoly, which has received equal attention because of its large scale (Figure 12.1).

The new Tokyo Metropolitan Government Building houses the offices of those who administer all 23 wards of the Tokyo Metropolitan area, within three buildings that occupy an entire city block, with three levels below grade. The most identifiable part of this gargantuan complex is the 48-story main building. It is divided into two cathedral-like towers at the 33rd floor, and anticipates Toyo Ito's more integral attempt to symbolize the information age at Sendai by a decade by being fenestrated to resemble a computer chip.

Among other issues related to the appropriateness of their scale, both this complex and the International Forum raise interesting questions about the historical use of public space in Japan, or Asia in general, in comparison to the piazzas and plazas of Europe and the United States. The temples and shrines, as well as commercial streets that have been investigated earlier here, were the most easily accessible, and officially sanctioned public spaces in Japan in the past, simply because of the governmental distrust of large gatherings. This history, combined with the private familial and residential focus within the culture that continues today, makes these Western models questionable and may explain why they remain largely unused today.

Boulee realized in Minato-ku

The new headquarters that Tange designed for Fuji Television, along the waterfront in Minato-ku, is also illustrative of a sustained tendency toward large scale (Figure 12.2). It cost 185 billion yen, was completed three years after the Tokyo Metropolitan Government Building, and became fully operational in 1997. It consists of two towers spread out to anchor each end of a rectilinear horizontal plinth that serves as a public plaza at the ground level, connected by three pairs of bridges spaced five stories apart. Tange and the engineers from the Kajima Corporation used four large steel "masts" representing the four companies

Figure 12.2 Fuji Television
Source: James Steele

that make up Fuji TV, as the main structural system of the 123.45-meter high, 25-story building, which also includes a spectacular, 32-meter diameter titanium observation sphere, the "hachitama" which is suspended from the uppermost set of bridges. It weighs 1,350 tons and was built on the roof of the seventh floor and then raised into place by hydraulic jacks.

Fuji TV, which was founded in 1957, but didn't start broadcasting until 1959, was originally located in Shinjuku, but moved to Odaiba as part of its campaign to become the "City of the Future." This new, high-tech headquarters, resembling a habitable erector set, certainly conforms to that now somewhat dated image.

Mega-scale representations of land and sky

Hiroshi Hara provides three additional projects of the hundreds by others that may be cited as reflecting the mindset of the bubble phase well into the decade after it ended, which are the Yamato International Headquarters in the Ota district of Tokyo, competed in 1987, the 1993 Umeda Sky Building in Osaka, and the Kyoto Station Complex in Kyoto of 1997.

Hara received his Bachelor of Architecture in 1959, as well as a master's degree in 1961 and a PhD in 1964 from the University of Tokyo and started collaborating with Atelier Φ in 1970. It became known as Hiroshi Hara + Atelier Φ in 1999. He then established the Hara Laboratory at the Institute of Industrial Science at Tokyo University, and between 1972 and 1978 he and his students visited more than 200 villages both in Japan and in over 40 other countries, throughout the Mediterranean region, Central and South America, Eastern Europe, the Middle East, Southeast Asia, and West Africa, interviewing the inhabitants and surveying and documenting their dwellings. They did this by systematically categorizing them into morphologies, in terms of form, spatial organization and material, relative to social and geographic factors.

Tomio Ohashi, whose work appears throughout this book, accompanied Hara to many of the villages within Japan that he and his students surveyed, and they jointly produced a limited edition portfolio of them, which includes Ohasi's extraordinary photographs.

These ethnographic studies, which are in the best tradition of Fumihiko Maki's *Collective Form* in the 1950s, sets Hara apart from others within Japan, who focused on urban growth during this period. His opposing views surfaced in his pointed criticism of his mentor Kenzo Tange, and his concept for Expo '70, which Hara characterized as being an overt corporate spectacle that celebrated capitalism and only served to reaffirm the stringent cult of personality imposed by Modernism.

The "Dwelling Group Domain Theory" or Jūkyo Shūgōron, that Hara and his students, who included Riken Yamamoto and Kengo Kuma, who are also discussed here, put forward was that Modernists failed to learn that people are inherently social beings who thrive in groups, and that the only way to recover an under-

standing of how important that is to architects and those they serve is by studying vernacular precedents.[3]

This extensive research informed his further interest in Martin Heidegger's concept of Ent-fernung or "removing" described in *Being and Time* as the essential part of an architecture that is "proximally ready-to-hand" rather than the concept of phenomenology, which he dismisses as being too abstract.[4]

In spite of its scale, both of these strands of Hara's investigation, of utilizing the lessons to be learned from studying human habitation and understanding the value of proximity, or engagement and a sensitivity to context, can be substantiated in his 1987 Yamoto International Office Building, in Tokyo (Figure 12.3). This headquarters of a company that produces upscale textiles is in a warehouse district on land reclaimed from Tokyo Bay, nearby, and is near a park that provides an unobstructed view of the front elevation (Figure 12.4). Echoing Fumihiko Maki's concept for the Spiral on Omotesando, Hara also envisioned this as an internal city, with the difference being a reflective aluminum facade that acts as both a mirror for the natural environment, and a substitute for the surrounding urban context that is missing here. It also recalls similar critiques of Modernism by other members of Hara's generation, in being based on the Japanese principle of mujo, or impermanence, rather than rigidity (Figure 12.5). This search for transience, or uncertainty carries over into the interior, in which each space and detail is treated differently, rather than being divided up into cubicles. These clusters are then connected by internal streets, grouped around an external court, in a pattern that can be found in his early design of the Keisho Kindergarten in 1968.

Fictional re-enactments of a complex world

These noble sensibilities, of respect for traditional precedents and sensitivity to earth and sky, become a bit more difficult to trace in subsequent projects, such as Hara's Umeda Sky Building completed in 1993, and Kyoto Station, inaugurated in 2002, primarily due to issues of scale.

The Umeda Sky Building, designed by Hara and built by the Takenaka Corporation, is situated to the north-west of the Japan Rail Station in Osaka. It was

Figure 12.3 Yamoto International Office Building
Source: Tomio Ohashi

Figure 12.4 Yamoto International Office Building
Source: Tomio Ohashi

Figure 12.5 Yamoto International Office Building
Source: Tomio Ohashi

Figure 12.6 Umeda Sky Building
Source: Hartmut Poeling

intended to be part of a City in the Air initiative in Osaka (Figure 12.6). It was also originally designed to have four towers, but was finally reduced to two 173-meter, or 40-story shafts connected by a bridge, or "floating garden" accessed by escalator, with a circular Observation deck cut out of the middle at the 39th floor, allowing for 360-degree views of Osaka and Awaji Island in the distance. This deck echoes a garden at street level, typically filled with vendor kiosks. There is keen structural logic in connecting the two towers with this bridge, since it helps to stabilize them during the earthquakes that frequently occur in Japan, as well as providing an escape route if there is a fire in one of the towers.

In addition to the idea of the suspended observation deck, the Umeda Sky Building also shares the same square erector set structural lexicon that Tange also used on the FujiTV towers, but Hara has sheathed his in mirrored glass, perhaps to reduce the impression of angularity. As with the FujiTV Observation Sphere, this bridge was also pre-assembled and lifted into place, with each of them perpetuating a technological shibboleth promoted by Metabolism, decades before.

Hara's Kyoto Station was inaugurated in 2002, to commemorate the 1,200th anniversary of the founding of this historic city, which has largely retained its traditional fabric because it escaped the firebombing that devastated other urban centers in World War II. This gargantuan, 470-meter long terminal, which occupies a 3.8-hectare site, is second only to Nagoya

Figure 12.7 Kyoto Station
Source: James Steele

station in size and includes the Hotel Granvia, Isetan Department store, the 100 stores and restaurants of the Porta shopping center, a movie theater, museum and transportation and government offices, under one, all-encompassing 15-story high roof (Figure 12.7). The terminal was exceptionally challenging to build because of the layers of subway tracks beneath the on-grade train lines involved, and engineer Toshihiko Kimura solved the puzzle with a massive 15.5-meter deep matrix that supports the entire complex. It is south of the historic core, including the Imperial Palace, as well as Nijo-jo and the Nishi Hongan-ji and Higashi Hongan-ji (temples established by Tokugawa Ieyasu in 1602), and effectively acts as a linear barrier between the center and the southern part of the city. As such it is reminiscent of the "Chinese Wall" or eight-block long viaduct designed for the Pennsylvania railroad in Philadelphia that was finally demolished in 1950 to improve accessibility and make way for redevelopment.

A crystalline screen in Roppongi

It is extremely difficult to reconcile this intrusion into the sensitive fabric of the most historical city in Japan with this architect's demonstrated commitment to humanizing the built environment, and so, the lingering effects of the bubble mentality might be a contributing factor in trying to rationalize this urban intervention. Given the relatively modest size of the 48,980 square meter National Art Center in Tokyo, by Kisho Kurokawa, which was of the last projects he completed before his death in 2007, this fever has now abated, but the seven 2,000-square-meter galleries of this museum, which make it the largest exhibition venue in Japan, indicate that the tendency toward monumentality remains (Figure 12.8).

Figure 12.8 National Art Center in Tokyo
Source: James Steele

Notes

1   J. Barkley Rosser, Jr. and Marina V. Rosser, *Comparative Economics in a Transforming World Economy*, Chicago: Irwin, 1996.

2   Christopher Wood, *The Bubble Economy: Japan's Extraordinary Speculative Boom of the '80s and the Dramatic Bust of the '90s*, The Atlantic Monthly Press, 1992, pp. 24–27.

3   Hiroshi Hara, *100 Lessons: Learning from Villages*, Tokyo: GA Architect, 1987.

4   Hiroshi Hara, "Architectural Environments for Tomorrow", in *Architectural Environments for Tomorrow*, Kazuyo Sejima and Ryue Nishizawa, Eds., Tokyo: Access, 2011, p. 9.

PART IV

Transitional figures

CHAPTER 13

Witness to war

Fumihiko Maki, Yoshio Tanaguchi and Arata Isozaki

There are three distinct overlapping waves, or layers of architects practicing simultaneously within the short period of time between the run up to World War II, and the economic funk of the early part of the twenty-first century in post-bubble era Japan, who have made a discernible impression on the latest generation of architects today.

The first of these came of age before that devastating global conflict and experienced the politically charged prelude to engagement, as well as living through both the war and its aftermath. They were a part of the first nation in the world to experience nuclear devastation, but also shared the pain of extensive firebombing, poverty, starvation and homelessness as well as occupation by a foreign power that several other nations have experienced. The architects in the second group were born just before the conflict ended, while those in the third group were born during the end of the Occupation, and so they grew up in the midst of its aftermath.

The nascent experience of each group has been profoundly different yet they have all shared several inescapable realities, such as an initial humiliation stemming from a loss of identity and autonomy, resurgent national pride, followed by the opportunity to ride the crest of the "economic miracle" to success. The first wave was especially fortunate in having had the advantage of 40 years of continuous economic growth, and the opportunity to fulfill the nation's need to replace architectural stock lost during the war as it rose again from the ashes.

After the passing of Kunio Maekawa, Junzo Sakakura, Takamasa Yoshizaka and Togo Murano, and especially of leading lights Kenzo Tange in 2005 and Kisho Kurokawa in 2007, Fumihiko Maki and Arata Isozaki became the surviving elder statesmen of this group.

Fumihiko Maki: a search for universality

In addition to his involvement as a self-described "associate member" of the Metabolist group, as well as his landmark *Investigations in Collective Form* and its elongated realization at Hillside Terrace, which has already been discussed in a previous chapter on Metabolism, Fumihiko Maki's essential dialectical engagement with Modernism still requires a bit more analysis (Figure 13.1).

Since he was born in the Yamanote district of Tokyo in 1928 he was a teenager when the Japanese involvement in World War II began, and he lived through and understood the architectural acrimony of the prewar period. And yet, he was drawn to early Modernist

Figure 13.1 Hillside Terrace
Source: James Steele

Modernist masterpieces such as the Isaku Nishimura and Nitto houses near his own neighborhood, the house of Frank Lloyd Wright apprentice Kameki Tsuchiura, the Sasaki house in Den'enchofu by Yoshiro Taniguchi and others by Sutemi Horiguchi and Antonin Raymond. He was attracted to them because they offered a shining, albescent alternative to the otherwise dark wooden houses surrounding him and he remembers that "there was something liberating and magical about them."[1]

An impeccable Modernist pedigree

Maki studied with Kenzo Tange at Tokyo University, and after graduating with a Bachelor of Architecture in 1952, received a Master of Architecture at the

Cranbrook Academy of Art in 1953, and a second Master of Architecture, at the Graduate School of Design, at Harvard University in 1954. He then apprenticed at Skidmore, Owings and Merrill, New York and Sert Jackson and Associates in Cambridge before becoming an assistant professor at Washington University in St. Louis, in 1956, and it was during this time that he wrote *Investigations in Collective Form* as a result of a Graham Foundation Fellowship he received in 1958, which involved research in Southeast Asia, the Middle East, and Europe. During these travels, he was recruited into the Metabolist ranks, during a stopover in Tokyo in 1959. After four years in St. Louis, he relocated to Harvard once again, teaching at the GSD from 1962 until 1965, when he returned to Japan to establish Maki and Associates, in Tokyo, just as the "economic miracle" was well underway.

In the course of little more than a decade, then, Maki had either been taught by, worked with or befriended an impressive pantheon of high Modernists, including Kenzo Tange at Tokyo University, Eliel Saarinen and Eero Saarinen at Cranbrook, and Walter Gropius and Marcel Breuer at Harvard, as well as Josep Luis Sert, among others. Gropius was appointed Chairman of what was then the Department of Architecture at Harvard, in 1938 and had retired in 1952, but his legacy of eliminating history from the curriculum and educating students in all aspects of the built environment, including landscape and planning, was still firmly in place when Maki arrived.

His 12-year experience in the United States, within the Bauhaus rather than the Corbusian tradition being perpetuated by Maekawa, Sakakura and Yoshizaka in Japan during the same time, also sets him apart, as both a paragon and champion of that more technological and less monumental ideological stance, when he returned home. This ahistorical, interdisciplinary and decidedly universal approach is evident throughout his work, which is undeniably, and understandably Modernist, with several caveats highlighted in this selection of several iconic buildings chosen from the multitude of projects Maki has realized in the course of his extraordinarily long career. They provide especially important insights into the ways in which he has modulated, or interrogated this position with each of them providing a didactic commentary on various aspects of its principles.

An orderly internal city

The Spiral, which is the first of these, was designed for the Wacoal Group on a 30-by-60-meter site in the Aoyama district in 1985, and typifies Maki's engagement with urban issues (Figure 13.2). Its form is both a response to the complex, irrational morphological chaos of Tokyo, and a novel brief that included a mix of uses, such as a restaurant, shops, offices, and a gallery type exhibition space. To reflect each of these, Maki decided to create a more orderly internalized city of his own, and adopted a decidedly fragmented, Constructivist approach for the exterior using a collage of bold forms. These fractured surfaces, which include a huge, square tilted shoji-like screen, and a giant cone, are intended to mirror the character of the context, and evoke urban memories as well as hinting at his hidden purpose of fabricating a more orderly alternative within.

Constructivism, which originated in post-revolutionary Russia and only lasted from the mid-1920s until Stalin turned toward a more traditional national style in the early 1930s, sought to invent typologies that were more appropriate to those needed in a Communist state, and Maki felt sympathetic to this variant of Modernism because he was also confronting new functional adjacencies in this case.

He concentrated on the time-honored Modernist device of procession to combine them, which is implied by ascending steps on the elevation, and used a stately internal street to lead people past several street-front shops and a lower ground-floor restaurant toward a large sky-lit exhibition space at the back of the building. This is encircled by the spiraling 15-meter diameter ramp to the upper level that gives the building its name, and in addition to its anticipated use as an art gallery this soaring space quickly became a favorite venue for fashion shows and receptions because of the filming and people-watching possibilities provided by the ascending surface.[2]

A three-dimensional, metallic Torii gate

A year after completing the Spiral, Maki designed the National Museum of Modern Art, in Kyoto, on the site of what had once been an Annex to the Kyoto Municipal Exhibition Hall for Industrial Affairs,

Figure 13.2 Spiral
Source: Tomio Ohashi

Figure 13.3 National Museum of Modern Art, in Kyoto
Source: Tomio Ohashi

that was demolished to provide space for his building (Figure 13.3). In addition to incorporating this precedent, as well as a canal along the periphery, Maki also responded to the nearly Heien-Jinju Shrine, which was built in 1895 to commemorate the 1,100th anniversary of the founding of Heian-kyo and is dedicated to the Emperors Kammu and Komei, the first and last Emperors to rule there. The Shrine includes a replica of the Imperial Palace, and an extensive garden, as well as a large Torii gate, which announces the complex.

Maki sketches extensively, and this gate figures prominently in all of his early drawings of the project, establishing its scale, as well as its foursquare front elevation, on which glazed corners echo the massive columns of the gate, nearby. This gesture to tradition is found, to some extent, in each of these projects, underscoring his belief that Modernism must be tempered with regional values.

Point, lines and planes

Tepia, a third example of Maki's Modernist catechism, was completed in 1989, is in the Minato-ku area of Tokyo, and was named to embody the three corporate aspirations of Technology, Ecology and Utopia, conforming to its avowed mission of creating the harmonious interaction of technology and nature (Figure 13.4). Maki accordingly kept the building footprint as small as possible. Inspired by the Centre le Corbusier, completed in Zurich in 1967, he conceived of Tepia as a pavilion, rather than a monumental corporate headquarters, and designed it to only occupy 40 percent of its site in deference to Jingo Gaien Park nearby. To accommodate the privacy required by the administrative staff as well as the need for an exhibition space and auditorium at street level, Maki followed the Corbusian model by creating two distinct wrappers, with upper-level offices under a triangular roof

Figure 13.4 Tepia
Source: Tomio Ohashi

and a more rectilinear base below, joined by columns so that a box-like language did not predominate. Mindful of the ecological emphasis of the brief, Maki was far ahead of the sustainability curve in also viewing this second roof as a cooling device, calculating that about 50 percent of the energy needed to heat and cool the building would be lost by using a conventional roof.

The intentional flatness of many of the exterior elevations of Tepia belies the extraordinary complexity of its detailing, and it required extensive documentation to convey the architect's intent to the contractor. His aim was to create "empty surfaces" that remove the personal reference provided by the hierarchy of scale, as well as to dematerialize the metallic wrapper, so that it becomes alluringly tactile, in much the same way as Tadao Ando treats concrete.[3]

A steel and glass Kofun

The Television Asahi Headquarters is located at the north corner of the Roppongi Hills complex in Tokyo, which was built by Minoru Mori. In addition to TV Asahi, this development includes a 54-story Condominium tower, as well as a museum, hotel, shops and restaurants. It provides yet another example of contextual response, because it faces a street on one side, and the Mohri Japanese Garden on the other, which has special meaning for the client because the family residence of the Mohri clan was once located there (Figure 13.5).

The veiled historical reference in this case, which only becomes obvious when looking at the site plan, is that of a keyhole-shaped Kofun tomb, and there is not inconsiderable irony in Maki's use of this potent symbol for a media headquarters, replacing one source of absolute historical authority with its contemporary

Figure 13.5 TV Asahi
Source: Fumihiko Maki

alternative. The Kofun morphology also provides the appropriate scale to stand up to this busy corner location, with elevations treated differently so that the flat base, with vertical mullions and an arcade, addresses the linear streetscape, and the rounded top faces into the quiet garden. This semi-circular, evenly gridded side encloses a 120-meter long, 30-meter high atrium, which acts as both an entrance for employees and reception area for visitors, as well as a public plaza, overlooking the garden beyond.

The city of memory

The Spiral, Kyoto National Museum of Modern Art, Tepia, and TV Asahi, as well as Hillside Terrace, Daikanyama, which was built in six phases, from 1969 until 2016, each interrogate a different issue that Maki has with Modernism. In his more ordered analog for the city on Omotesando, it is its relationship to

the sky, and by extension its distrust of nature. In the Kyoto Museum, he explores the possibility of refracting a traditional context. At Tepia tactility, and humanizing industrial materials and technology is key. Finally, Roppongi Hills is a statement about conforming to both a historical and contemporary condition. These all come together in his ongoing experiment at Hillside Terrace, which he has observed, like a king in his castle surveying his domain from his slender white redoubt at Hillside West (Figure 13.6).

Arata Isozaki: cultivating the other

Speaking through an interpreter to a relatively small, by invitation only, mostly British audience at the Royal Academy in London on June 10, 1995, Arata Isozaki began by saying: "You here this evening may regard me as being a repository of Japanese tradition, but I can assure you that it is as far from me as it is from you."[4]

Figure 13.6 Maki Office
Source: James Steele

national experience and down upon western Modernism. Isozaki, who was born in Oita in 1931, was named Arata, or new, by his father, who was a poet, and part of the Shinko, or new Haiku movement. He has certainly lived up to that name. Oita is far away from the hectic, cosmopolitan urbanity of the University of Tokyo, where he studied with Kenzo Tange, and he recalls always feeling like an outsider there. After graduating in 1954 he worked for Tange for nine years before establishing his own firm in 1963, most significantly being involved with the Tokyo Bay Plan, which had a seismic global impact among architects and planners at the time, as well as participating in founding the Metabolism Movement in 1959–1960.

This perception of estrangement has been compounded by the traumatic experience of both living through the war, and being a witness to its sudden end, which profoundly affected him to an extent that has not been verbalized by other architects, like Maki, who also endured it. His impressions, which help us better understand just how it affected him include this poignant memory of August 15, 1945, which was the day Japan surrendered, when:

> The sky over the archipelago was a cloudless blue . . . At that time as a boy in my mid-teens, I sensed that an era was ending. I had no idea what was beginning. All I knew was that the roaring had stopped and, for an instant, there was unmitigated calm.

And then: "that instance of total tranquility, when everything seemed to have stopped" was offset by the thought of

> the destruction of houses and buildings that we had considered mainstays of our way of life, the established belief of the national state with the Emperor at its head, and the social system that controlled even the smallest daily activities had collapsed and vanished, leaving behind only the void of the blue sky overhead.[5]

Since establishing his own firm, he characterizes his career trajectory in terms of decades, and has made no secret of the painful emotional metamorphosis that has accompanied each stage.

Although he then went on to detail many telling parallels between Japan and the United Kingdom because they share the experience of being island nations, that highly emotional opening statement kept silently reverberating, because his audience of course did indeed consider him to be an expert on the history of his nation.

In retrospect, his career trajectory, both before and after that lecture, clearly demonstrates his attempt to adopt the persona of an outsider, or more accurately an insurrectionist, simultaneously looking in on his own

His Oita Medical Hall, which was completed in 1960, while still in Tange's office, coincides with his Metabolism phase, and it is often included in anthologies of that movement. Yet, he views that project as the end of his exploration of Modernism, and the beginning of his determination to "dissolve" and "dismember" it.[6]

He was also actively involved in demonstrations against the Japanese-American Security Treaty at this same time, and while he was sympathetic to attempts to amalgamate traditional Japanese and Modernist spatial concepts, he sought political, not technological revolution, and viewed the utopian optimism of Metabolism as being both naïve, and inconsiderate of the natural processes they claimed to mimic, because he felt they also include decay as the inevitable corollary of growth.

In each 10-year cycle, Isozaki has used both writing and exhibitions, as well as the opportunity offered to his generation, to be able to propose almost any idea to a client and have it built, to work through his sequential impasses, and in the 1960s this took the form of a photomontage he produced for a magazine article entitled "Incubation Process," as did his article "The Invisible City" in 1966. In it, he places Japanese cities within a four-stage framework of urban planning from the beginning of rural urban migration at the beginning of the industrial age, up through the "functionalist" CIAM phase, and makes a convincing case that they resist discrete urban planning because they are in a constant state of flux. His "Electric Labyrinth" project at the 14th Milan Triennial, 1968, continued this theme as overt critique of modern urban planning, and all of these helped to liberate him from the conventional constraints that had impeded his personal growth.

The Osaka World Exposition in 1970 brought things to a head for him, since Kenzo Tange had put him in charge of both designing the technical facilities for the Festival Plaza and producing the opening day festivities. "I found myself," he said, "in the embarrassing position of being a critic of Modernism who was taking a professional part in Expo '70, a national event in which the Modernist vocabulary was the only one permitted."[7]

After recovering from the depressive cycle that this event precipitated, he became determined to actively pursue his "dismemberment" of Modernism by using the Constructivist tactic of inventing a new lexicon of architectural production, to reflect the altered reality he was confronting, and adopted the language of Platonic solids, which he has called maneire, or his Mannerist, way of doing so. He felt that a structure consisting of classical Euclidian geometry, including the cube, circle and equilateral triangle that preceded modern functionalism, and its prohibition of historical reference, was an effective critical device. Rather than using Platonic solids as a way of assimilating the Enlightenment project, which was not part of the Japanese experience, and trying to understand the alternative Western worldview that had brought his own identity into question, he has used them in a far more systemic way, to undermine it, and escape its consequences, by returning to this classical precedent. He was not the first to attempt this, considering that the Venetian architect Carlo Scarpa had done so as well.

Function follows form

Although there are multiple examples of his use of this structure, beginning with the robots he designed for the Expo '70 Festival Hall, the clearest are the Gumma Prefectural Museum of Modern Art and Kitakyushu Municipal Museum of Art, each completed in 1974. At Gunma, the building block is a cube with a 40-foot module, translated into a series that joined together to create a U-shaped sequence. One leg, which has two ranks of cubes split apart to provide an entrance corridor between them, contains galleries for temporary exhibitions, leading to permanent exhibition spaces for Western art in the right angle cross bar of the "U", and then the second leg, parallel to the entry with a gallery of Japanese art at its tip, canted at an angle over a reflecting pool to express difference.

At Kitakushyu, in Fukuoka Prefecture, the Museum is dramatically sited on a promontory and the parallel lines of cubes flanking the entry at Gunma become elevated box beams that cantilever out over the entrance. In each case, Isozaki's intention of using Euclidian geometry as an antidote to the strictures of Modernism is clear in the plan, in which structure is given preference over conventional ideas of museum space usage, and function is made to follow form, rather than the other way around.

Once this tactic of using classical Euclidian geometry to repress Modernist tendencies is understood, Isozaki's shift towards Postmodernism is less surprising, since it just amounts to the substitution of another, equally classical lexicon, which is used for the same purpose, as a rebellion against Modernism.

His 1983 Tsukuba Civic Center, examined earlier here, exemplifies the key difference between what many have seen as a crass act of appropriation of many different Western Post-modern images, and his more metaphysical attempt to carefully curate them to construct a message of difference. In that deeper reading, the sunken, eroding replica of the Campidoglio, without its statue of Marcus Aurelius, which is an idea that Jun Aoki claims he proposed to Isozaki while he was working for him, transcends being a mere copy of Michelangelo's plaza, and becomes a broader symbol of the loss of the res publica in the world in general and specifically in Japan, with the umbilicus mundi

replaced by a cultural vacuum. His choice of Ledoux's half circular and half square, which were used most famously at the Salt Works at Chaux, is also telling, since this was the first time that the Classical round column as tree was symbolically, rhythmically hacked apart by Euclidian squares, before being replaced altogether by rationally square columns.

As we have already seen, however, Fredric Jameson has made clear that Postmodernism was just another Americanized phase of the European ideology Isozaki sought to demolish, not a rejection of it, but it may have been too soon to see that.

Japan-ness

Throughout his long career, Isozaki has shown that his shocking statement on that spring evening in London in 1995, about his culture seeming to be as far away from him as it is from those who are not Japanese, was

Figure 13.7 Horyu-ji Museum
Source: Hartmut Poeling

disingenuous, at best. In addition to his remarkable book *Japan-ness*, in which he thoroughly dissects the Ise Shrine, Nandemon gate at Todai-ji and Katsura Palace as exemplars of Japanese spirit in architecture, he has proven this in so many other ways. One of these is his holistic understanding of the Buddhist belief that change is not linear and progressive but a cyclical process of creation and destruction, making it impossible to plan for the future in architecture or planning. Another is his advocacy of the substitution of Modernist, three-dimensional spatial organization with multivalent spaces consistent with the traditional Japanese concept of Ma. The artistic endeavor Isozaki used to help him most clearly enunciate this pre-rationalist condition was his "Ma: Japanese Time and Space" Exhibition held in 1978, which was further refined a decade later in a film entitled "Ma: Space/Time in the Garden of Ryoan-ji." He collaborated with director Takahiko Iimura, and musician Takehisa Kosugi on the film, and it clarifies how he views geometry as a mediator between these two important aspects of Japanese architecture.[8]

A Minimal pavilion in Ueno

Since he was born in 1937, Yoshio Taniguchi, who is the son of famous early Modernist Yoshiro Taniguchi, also joins the most well-known members of this generation who experienced both the run-up to World War II as well as its effects and aftermath and then went on to achieve global fame. Until he won a competition to redesign the Museum of Modern Art in New York City in 1997, which was his first project outside Japan at that time, he managed to keep a lower profile than the rest of this group, and like Maki, who was first drawn to the Modernist aesthetic by the houses of Yoshio's father, he was one of the few Japanese architects to pursue further education outside the country. He studied at Harvard's Graduate School of Design after he graduated from Keio University in 1960 until 1964 and in addition to Walter Gropius, he was also influenced by Josep Lluís Sert, who served as the dean of the GSD from 1953 to 1969. After returning to Japan, Taniguchi worked for Kenzo Tange from 1964 to 1972, completing his grounding in Modernist principles. His Horyu-ji Museum, or more technically Gallery of Ancient Treasures in Ueno Park, which houses 300 seventh- and eighth-century works from the venerable Buddhist temple in Nara, not only recalls Corbusian disciple Junzô Sakakura's similarly en-shrouded Kamakura Museum of Modern Art of 1951, but also confirms his Minimalist lineage (Figure 13.7).

Notes

1 Fumihiko Maki, "Maki on Architecture," in *On Maki Architecture/Maki on Architecture*, Exhibition catalogue for "The Architecture of Fumihiko Maki: Modernity and the Construction of Scenery" held at the Victoria and Albert Museum, 2001. Fumihiko Maki Traveling Exhibition Executive Committee, p. 56.
2 Fumihiko Maki, Lecture at the Bartlett, London, June 1993.
3 Ibid.
4 Arata Isozaki, "Island Nation Aesthetics," Fifth Annual Academy Lecture, Royal Academy of Arts, London, June 10, 1995, transcribed by the author.
5 Arata Isozaki, "Works in Architecture," Exhibition Catalogue, Academy Group Ltd., 1995, pp. 2–5.
6 Ibid., p. 10.
7 Ibid., p. 12.
8 Arata Isozaki, Takahiko Iimura and Takehisa Kosugi, "Ma: Space/Time in the Garden of Ryoan-ji," Program for Art on Film, Metropolitan Museum of Art and the Getty Foundation, 1989. As Isozaki says in the film: "Ma is emptiness or silence, the space between, rather than the thing or sound itself. This concept of time equals space is fundamental to the arts of Japan."

CHAPTER 14

Conflicting identities
Tadao Ando, Itsuko Hasagawa, Toyo Ito, Riken Yamamoto, Chiaki Arai and Shin Takamatsu

The architects in the second group to be discussed here were born just before World War II ended. They were very young when the bombing and surrender occurred, but most certainly experienced the American Occupation and its aftermath.

Tadao Ando, for example, was born in Osaka in 1941, just a few months before the start of World War II in Japan. He was sent to live with his maternal grandmother, took her family name and worked with a master carpenter while also attending school. He credits this early experience with teaching him to be precise to carefully examine each step in the building process, and fully appreciate the inherent quality of the materials used. After graduating from high school, he became a professional boxer and, during matches in Bangkok, Thailand, a visit to the Wat Phra Kaew piqued his interest in architecture. When he was 18, he started visiting Buddhist temples, Shinto shrines and teahouses throughout Kyoto and Nara, and was struck by the integration between architecture and nature in each one, finding the quiet peacefulness of the Zen garden at Ryoan-ji to be especially moving (Figure 14.1).

The first book on architecture that he bought, with great difficulty due to tight finances at the time, was *Oeuvre Complète* and he repeatedly traced the drawings in it to more thoroughly understand Le Corbusier's design approach. He also then visited local contemporary buildings, such as the Imperial Hotel by Frank Lloyd Wright, and found it to have "a strong mysterious power" derived from Wright's use of a variety of scales.[1]

Unlike some others of his age, he is not critical of Wright, but finds his approach to space to have a very Japanese quality, which he thinks stems from his respect for traditional architecture and close reading of *The Book of Tea*, by Okakura Kakuzō. Ando started out by designing furniture and interiors as well as small wooden houses, and in 1962 left on the first of a number of trips to Europe and the United States. His first was to France, and specifically to the Unite de Habitation, in Marseilles, which launched his career-long engagement with concrete. Subsequent travels led him to visit projects by Ludwig Mies van der Rohe and Louis Kahn, as well as Fallingwater by Wright, and this house reaffirmed his commitment to creating architecture that is in complete harmony with nature. He established Tadao Ando Architects & Associates in Osaka after returning to Japan in 1969.

Figure 14.1 Ryoan-ji
Source: James Steele

A Minimal model of things to come

His first project in the firm was his own office, where he has remained ever since, and soon afterward, in 1975, he designed a house for the Azuma family on an extremely tight, 3.3-meters-wide by 14.1-meters-deep, or 540-square-foot site in the Sumiyoshi-ku district in Osaka. It deserves special mention because it sets the tough, no-nonsense tone of all of his subsequent projects, and has been cited by Ando as containing many hints of principles that follow. Where many young architects make compromises to satisfy client demands, Ando divided this rectangular plot into three 4.7-meter-long segments, making the middle one a hikari-niwa or open courtyard, with a bridge connecting an entry/living space and bedroom above on the front, street end, and a ground-floor kitchen and bath with second upstairs bathroom at the back. In traditional Japanese houses, the inhabitants adapted to seasonal changes by adding or discarding clothing, or using more futon bedding, and this is Ando's attempt to reinterpret that attitude. This requires open air, all weather, day and night trips from one part of the house to the other, including bedroom to bath, which might not be acceptable to all clients. Of all of the other historical buildings he visited in his travels the Pantheon was one of the most impactful, because of its pure geometrical forms and connection to the sky through the open oculus in the middle, and that link is obvious here, in his determination to allow nature to penetrate the house. Another marker provided by this house is Ando's use of exposed concrete, which has become his trademark, and is further proof of the ability of Japanese architects to assimilate, transform and improve the ideas of others. Raymond, Le Corbusier and Kahn all used exposed concrete, with Kahn being especially keen to show the construction process by expressing the grain of the forms, and leaving the joints between the formwork and the holes visible, once the concrete had set and snap-ties were removed. The problem was that the form lines were often broken and the edges of the holes spalled or cracked, and so Ando set out to correct these flaws by not only concentrating on upgrading each of the ingredients in the mix, but also by taking the formwork to another level entirely. Realizing that leakage caused many of these faults, he used his experience as a carpenter to design stronger, more watertight corners, and now holds competitions between subcontractors for each project to see who can build the best forms. He also specifies the best wood for the forms and has it varnished for smoothness, striving for the tactile sensuousness of wood.

Whether or not Ando would still cite his Rokko housing complex in Kobe, which he started working on in 1978, as being most representative of his ideas as he did in a public forum in Osaka in the early 2000s is debatable, given the large number of stunning commissions he has completed since. Yet there is no question that it signals a turning point in both the scale of his work and his attitude about context. It is the culmination of a uniquely Japanese idea, shown here to be found throughout the traditional canon, that architecture, as he describes it, "is the act of introducing an autonomous object into the site, but at the same time it is the design of the site itself."[2]

In this instance, that melding was not quite as subtle as, say, that between Katsura Rikyū and its garden, because it required the removal of a large section of the Rokko mountain foothills. They are still at a daunting 60-degree angle by the time they reach this site, demanding an epic engineering feat that included stabilizing the entire hill with a below grade reinforced concrete post and beam grillage, on the same 4.8-by-5.8-meter grid as the first 20 units built above it.

His intention was to explore the possibility of returning the meaning he feels that Modernism, or more accurately, Le Corbusier, had stripped from the column and its use in a gridded frame by reducing it to an abstract grid. As such, it represents not only Ando's intentional departure from the Modernist application of what he refers to as a "universalized technology" by also coping with specific site conditions, but also embodies an obvious dichotomy, between a professed sensitivity to nature, and its extensive, rampant destruction.

As a result of this massive amount of cut and fill, however, the terraced units, which are individually designed within their identical framework, provide a different kind of jointly owned housing project with unmistakable Mediterranean overtones, in which everyone shares in the impressive views that unfold in an arc from Osaka Bay to Kobe port. Consistent with that regional reference, all of them are linked by small "streets" to a central "piazza" that Ando intended to be reminiscent of those in a Japanese village, as a true synthesis of East and West.

This first of what would eventually become three iterations of an innovative housing type recalls Fumihiko Maki's landmark *Investigations in Collective Form*, published while he was teaching at Washington University in St. Louis 14 years earlier, in 1964, as well as his own ongoing attempts to explore a union between Cycladian and traditional Japanese typologies at Hillside Terrace in Daikanyama.

A concrete Takasebune

In 1983, soon after this contextual breakthrough in Kobe, Ando designed the first of two Times buildings along the Takase river in Kyoto, in another deliberate attempt to more overtly integrate nature and architecture, interior and exterior and public and private space (Figure 14.2). He was once again inspired

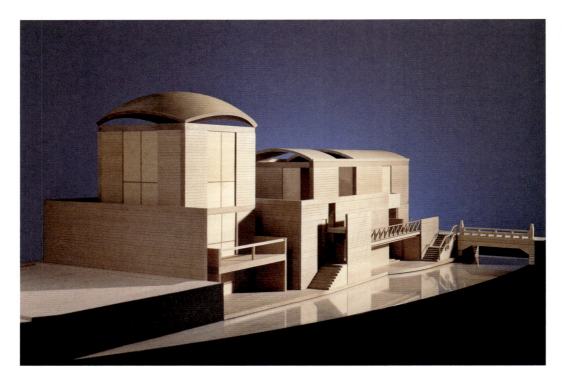

Figure 14.2
Times Model
Source:
Tomio Ohashi

Figure 14.3 Times
Source: Tomio Ohashi

by traditional references here, such as the boats, or Takasebune, that used to ply the canal, and the sliver thin Pontecho alley, running between Shijo and Sanjo-dori, parallel to the Kamogawa River, nearby; a street type unique to Kyoto because of tax laws that prevailed during the Tokugawa period (Figure 14.3). Placing the building so close to the water, and eliminating the boundary between it and his building is also reminiscent of the Isuzu River, which separates the sacred world of Ise Shrine from its secular opposite. Worshippers dip their hands into it before walking inside, and all of these memories and associations are consistent with Ando's wish to embed his architecture with multiple levels of meaning.

Church of the Light, 1989

Ando has always seemed more comfortable in working at a smaller scale and the enduring fame of the Church of the Light near Osaka, which is part of the United Church of Christ, and is formally called the Ibaraki Kasugaoka Church, completed in 1989, is proof of that (Figure 14.4). This small rectilinear worship space, created by aligning three 5.9-meter cubes, has a cross cut into the wall at the far end of the rectangle, which allows light to flood in through its open armature. It presents a powerful image after entering the space that draws worshippers toward it and is the most memorable mental image of those who visit the church only once.

Figure 14.4 Church of the Light
Source: Tomio Ohashi

Figure 14.5 Collezione Interior
Source: Tomio Ohashi

Figure 14.6 Collezione Exterior
Source: Tomio Ohashi

But the entrance is bisected by a 15-degree angle wall that slowly assumes added significance in subsequent visits, because it has been deliberately positioned to cast a sequence of cruciform shadows on the back wall. These slowly reveal themselves, as worshippers leave, as the reverberating penumbra of the cross of light in the front of the church, in an extremely subtle, and phenomenally sensitive manipulation of spectral contrast.

This was not Ando's first use of the cross as the centerpiece of a design, since it was the focal point of his Church on the Water in Hokkaido a year earlier, and also appears, upside down, in a secular context in his Collezione building in the Omotesando district of Tokyo in 1989 (Figure 14.5). This seven-story high-end commercial enterprise has a cylindrical drum at the entrance that guides visitors down into its four below grade floors, and Ando has used light wells and planting here to soften that marginally apprehensive experience (Figure 14.6).

Awaji Yumebutai

The earth needed to build an artificial surface in Osaka Bay for Kansai Airport was taken from Awaji Island and, at the urging of Tadao Ando, Hyogo Prefecture decided to establish an "Awaji Island International Park City" in 1999, to remedy the destruction of the natural landscape that this had caused. The timing of their decision also coincided with the need to create a memorial for the thousands of people who had died in the Kobe earthquake in 1995, and the idea of natural rebirth seemed an appropriate way to do that. The project includes the Awaji Yumebutai International Conference Center in the Westin Awaji Island hotel, the Hyakudanen or "hundred stepped gardens," and a terraced garden, with a hundred square planters containing flowers from all regions of Japan, which cascade down the slope that was decimated by excavation, with stairways in the middle and on both sides and corridors

Figure 14.7
Awaji Yumebutai
International Conference
Center
Source: James Steele

Figure 14.8 Awaji Yumebutai International Conference Center
Source: James Steele

between them (Figure 14.7). This method, of using raised planting beds, is part of the gardening history of this region, and is reconstituted, at a larger scale, by Ando here as a testament to local tradition. In addition to this centerpiece, Ando has also included an Observation terrace, as well as individual evocatively named pavilions such as the Shell Garden, the Seaside Corridor, the Mountain-side Corridor, the Oval Forum, the Circular Forum, and the Promenade Garden as well as an Open-Air Theater and the exciting "Awaji Yumebutai Plants Museum of Miracle Planet" which is also a machine-in-the-garden feat of high-tech bravado, in the midst of this verdant paradise (Figure 14.8).

This combination of gardens, folies and a conservatory, create an ecologically sensitive contribution to the public as well as the perfect architect's playground, just like Bernard Tschumi's Parc La Villette, where forms are often explored without concern for function.

A modern version of Philosopher's Walk

Two years after completing Awaji Yumebutai, Ando designed a small open-air museum called the Garden of Fine Arts in Kyoto within a rectangular site located near Shimogamo Hangicho, next to a Botanical

Figure 14.9 Garden of Fine Arts, Kyoto
Source: James Steele

Garden (Figure 14.9). To preserve the view of the Higashiyama mountains he created a ramp shaped like a compressed "X" with a central north-south spine bisected by another rotated at 22.5 degrees that guides visitors down to a series of station points, toward a waterfall that covers the entire retaining wall at the back of the site. These each overlook an individual artwork, reproduced on ceramic tiles to withstand the elements. These tiles were made by photographing the original painting to create a plate that was then incised onto a ceramic sheet. After it calcified they were cut and then put together, like a mosaic, to produce the final image.

Several of the works of art such as an Edo-period Scroll, on a wall on the way into the garden, "The Last Judgment" by Michelangelo Buonarroti, "The Last Supper" by Leonardo da Vinci, "La Grande Jatte" by Georges Seurat, and Claude Monet's "Water Lilies; Morning," which is shown flat, in the water, alongside the ramp rather than on a wall, have been reproduced at the same size of the original. Others, such as "Road with Cypresses and Star" by Van Gogh, and "On the Terrace" by Renoir, have quadrupled in size. Ando has

a habit of signing books about his projects with a quick sketch, and his autograph for the Garden of the Fine Arts consists of an overlay of a plan and perspective of the garden, which once again confirms his complete three-dimensional grasp of each concept.

Rational irrationality

Ando has been engaged in life-long polemical dialogue with Modern architecture that once again introduces the themes of Phenomenology and Critical Regionalism discussed elsewhere here. He has written eloquently and extensively about his attempt to balance what he has referred to as "abstraction and representation," which are at once vague but equally loaded terms that require a bit of unpacking. As far as abstraction is concerned, Ando not only assimilated the formal language of Le Corbusier and Louis Kahn but was affected by each of them in a profound way.

In addition to his formal language, he also credits Le Corbusier for teaching him the need for re-invention and persistence and the belief that the demanding training he endured as a young athlete could be transferred over into his architecture. This convinced him of the need for both psychological and physical strength as well as an adversarial worldview, which seems paradoxical given his heightened sensitivity and the deep spirituality evident in his work. It is also undoubtedly the source of its raw power.

Kahn, on the other hand, also taught him the joy of searching for beginnings, as well as the evanescent quality of light and shadow, and the possibility of achieving timelessness. Instead of being guided by Classical precedents, as Kahn was, however, his tutorials took place in the peace and quiet of Japanese gardens, in which dappled darkness offers spiritual comfort and the insight that they are changeable organisms that are never complete, but are "adrift in time."[3]

He has sought to apply all of these lessons to the formulation of architecture that conveys them, through abstract, rather than purely functional means, combining a clarity of logic with natural, historical and cultural factors, to show that not everything in life can be explained rationally.

The "representation" part of the equation is a bit trickier, since it holds a variety of meanings today. The first thing that comes to mind, however, is the use of that term by the late Dalibor Vesely, in reference to both the Humanist introduction of perspective during the Renaissance as the first indicator of Modernist elitism and individuality, as well as his concept of the subsequent divided representation of reality, between scientific positivism on one hand and human interaction with the natural world on the other.[4]

A remarkable achievement by Itsuko Hasagawa

One startling aspect of the youngest generation of architects presented here, among many others, is that a high percentage of them are women, either as partners in firms or sole practitioners, but such was not always the case in contemporary Japan.

So, the ability of Itsuko Hasagawa to both survive and thrive is nothing short of a miracle, given the difficulty that women had in making their way in such an androcentric profession since the beginning of the modern age, after the Meiji Restoration. The difficulty of doing so there was even greater than it was in the West, where the achievements of talented designers such as Margaret MacDonald, Charlotte Perriand, Lyubov Sergeyevna Popova, Ann Tyng and Denise Scott Brown have routinely been subsumed by their respective collaborators Charles Rennie Macintosh, Le Corbusier, Alexander Rodchenko, Louis Kahn and Robert Venturi.

Itsuko Hasegawa was born in Shizuoka in 1941, and worked with Kiyonori Kikutake after graduating from Kanto Gakuin University, before leaving to join the Kazuo Shinohara Lab at the Tokyo Institute of Technology in 1969, where she became a highly respected associate. She opened her own firm, Itsuko Hasegawa Atelier, 10 years later.

It should come as no surprise, then, that she shares many of the same beliefs that we have outlined as belonging to Shinohara, echoed throughout the scores of others discussed here who were influenced by him, such as a thorough knowledge of historical archetypes, a reductive exploration of the urban macrocosm within a minimalized microcosm, a cross-examination of functionalism, transparency and an attempt to anticipate the next cycle of technological determinism.

Of all of her many projects, her 1991 Shonandai Culture Center in Fujisawa, and the Museum of Fruit, in Yamanashi, West Tokyo, completed in 1996, are among the most representative of her view of architecture as a social art. Like Chiaki Arai, she relies heavily on extensive interviews with her clients to uncover aspects of a program that may not be readily apparent and then introduces Computer Aided Design methodology to test those findings. This results in an unusual balance between rationality and an almost childlike whimsy, acted out in layered materiality and unexpected juxtapositions of forms.

The Shonandai Cultural Center and Civic Theatre which is shaped by the idea of "Children, Community and Communication," was built in two phases, starting with a children's center, civic center and a spherical public auditorium which is 37 meters in diameter and has a map of the world etched upon it, in case anyone is unclear about the metaphor. Once these parts of the first phase were complete, client consultations resulted in alterations to the second stage, including the addition of proscenium stages, and an interactive museum for children including a planetarium to increase public accessibility. A forest of metallic trees surround the earth-like sphere and this, along with a metaphorical river running through the elongated central plaza, combine to convey the impression of a complete environment, rendered in aluminum.

The Museum of Fruit, which is Hasagawa's later version of a mechanized paradise, is in the Yamanashi district of West Tokyo, yet incongruously still within sight of Mt. Fuji. It was built six years after the Shonandai Center, and continues her translation of natural, ecological contexts into a technological matrix in a less urban setting. Three equally elegant, glass and steel envelopes, of different curvatures engineered by Arup Associates, seem to be haphazardly strewn across an orchard floor, like different, voluptuous varieties of metallic fruit, conveying the perfect image of machines in a garden.

Toyo Ito and his architecture of air

Toyo Ito is Japanese but was born in Seoul Korea, in 1941, because his father had a business there, and he moved the family back to his hometown of Shimosuwa-machi in Nagano Prefecture in 1943. He followed in 1945, and died in 1953, when Toyo was 12. When Ito was in the third grade of junior high school the family moved again, to Tokyo, and he transferred to Hibiya High School. Soon afterward, his mother commissioned Yoshinobu Ashihara, who had worked for Marcel Breuer's office in New York City, to design a house for the family, which left a lasting impression on him. He entered the Department of Architecture at Tokyo University and after graduating in 1965, worked for Kiyonori Kikutake & Associates. After six years there, he opened his own office, which he first called Urban Robot, or Urbot, before changing the name to Toyo Ito & Associates, Architects in 1979.

In 1971, his Aluminum House brought him considerable public attention. It is a deft compositional exercise, using square rooms of various sizes, within a square enclosure, and covering its wood frame structure entirely in aluminum, and also places him squarely

Figure 14.10 Steel Hut, Museum of Architecture on Omishima Island
Source: Miki Fujiwara

Figure 14.11 Silver Hut, Museum of Architecture on Omishima Island
Source: Iwan Baan

within the Shinohara orbit, which had such a powerful pull at that time.

His White U house of 1976, designed for his sister, heightened that interest and confirms that affiliation, since it is intended as an inner world for the family. It has since been demolished but the form provided a central courtyard that allowed everyone to have natural light, and to be in closer proximity to each other. Six years later he designed a house for himself next door, called the Silver Hut, using a vaulted aluminum structure to produce a much lighter, more diaphanous companion to offset the studier mass of the White "U." Each of these early projects underscores his stated intention of making an "architecture of air and wind" and his Silver Hut has since been replicated at his Toyo Ito Museum of Architecture on Omishima island on a breathtaking site overlooking the Seto Inland Sea (Figure 14.10).[5] The Museum also includes a Steel Hut in which Ito's work is exhibited with the Silver Hut reserved for social events (Figure 14.11).

His aluminum clad Yatsushiro Municipal Museum, which recalls the Silver Hut, was built in 1991, and certainly exemplifies his conviction to build lightly at a larger public scale, since it has a series of four vaulted, wing-like canopies that considerably lighten its mass, and make it seem to be airborne. These also visually progress upward toward a higher lozenge-shaped cylinder that owes a debt to Shinohara's Tokyo Institute of Technology Centennial Hall.

Structure mimics nature, with wiring

After many small local successes, each architect of note can usually point to one commission that brings them global fame, and for Toyo Ito that happened in Miyagi Prefecture in 2001, with the Sendai Mediatheque, in Sendai City. Arata Isozaki, who was consulted on writing the competition brief, takes credit for the unusual name encouraging the client to follow the French example of calling a library a bibliotheque,

Figure 14.12 Tower of the Winds, Day
Source: Tomio Ohashi

Figure 14.13 Tower of the Winds, Night
Source: Tomio Ohashi

to convey the fresh approach to disseminating information behind the project. This turned out to be a fateful decision, because it prompted Ito to adopt a digital metaphor, making this one of the first true expressions of the post-industrial, information age Modernism predicted by Kisho Kurokawa in the early 1990s.[6]

He had written much earlier about the difficulty of achieving an architectural language for the "microelectronic age" since it lacks the machine age avatars, of factories, automobiles, steam ships, and grain elevators so beloved of everyone from Le Corbusier to the Constructivists and Archigram and evocatively conjured up the image of "a city as a garden of microchips."[7]

The Tower of the Winds that he designed in 1988 over an existing reinforced concrete airway venting the Nishi-guchi Station in Yokohama was the first flower in this garden. The hollow octagonal Greek original in

the Agora in Athens is dedicated to Aeolis, the God of Wind, and has strategically placed openings that made air currents seem to be a divine voice (Figure 14.12). By placing openings in the existing concrete tube, attaching pressure-sensitive lights to it and encasing it in a perforated aluminum cylinder, Ito was able to create the perfect technological transformation of the Classical temple as a contemporary metaphor of our time with subway and train fumes as the holy zephyr (Figure 14.13).

The Sendai commission, however, was finally his chance to fulfill his goal of building one of those chips, by providing a free flow of information in a variety of media to everyone. To do so he eliminated the barriers usually encountered in a conventional library, by starting with six completely open reinforced concrete floors, within a 50-meter-by-50-meter glass enclosed cube, supported by 13 strategically located, vertical stent-like tubes of various thicknesses, which contain all of the services and also convey natural light into the interior. He located the four largest tubes at the corners, for stability, and made five of the smaller ones straight to accommodate elevators, the remaining four house ducts and electrical wiring.

Ito did not initiate the idea of inflating the columns in the grid that is such an essential component of Le Corbusier's Five Points, to allow them to contain functional uses. In his unrealized design for the Mikvah Israel Synagogue, in 1961, Louis Kahn did the same thing by placing columns at the corners of its clipped rectangular plan, and then inflating them and hollowing them out to accommodate worshippers inside. Kahn ran his office like a Studio, and when this project was in its generative stage, called everyone together to listen to him discuss it with resident critic Gabor, who rhetorically asked: "is it possible to inhabit the column?" Kahn was unable to realize what was for him a metaphysical way of becoming one with his structure, but Ito has made that wish a reality.

Expanding tree-like columns into spaces

Ito originally likened the hollow, stent-like columns in the Sendai Mediatheque to strands of seaweed billowing upward from the sea floor, but later reconsidered that metaphor, comparing them to a forest of trees, for the benefit of the people using the building. Trees obviously have deep significance in the Shinto tradition, and in Nagano, where Ito was born, he was deeply impressed by the Onbashira ceremony held at the Suwa Taisha Shrine which is among the oldest in Japan, and one of the few that does not have a Honden to house its deity, or kami, since it resides in the mountain itself. Four sacred logs are brought down the steep mountainside every six years to perpetuate the energy they emit, and kept in the Akimiya, which is one of the subsidiary shrines on site, which also include the Maemiya, Honmiya, and Harumiya.

With that life force in mind, as an antidote to the moribund grid of Modernism, he expanded the tree metaphor even more in his diminutive, TOD'S store, on Omotesando in Tokyo, in 2004, by using a branch-like pattern for the skin. Omotesando is the most exclusive High Street in Tokyo, and is known for its lush Zelcova trees. Ito used a digitized computer simulation of a sketch made over a photograph he took of one of them as the pattern for the wrapper for all six sides of the "L" shaped upscale fashion outlet and he kept the edges of the branches flush with the glass, which was an extremely difficult detail to realize (Figure 14.14).

Figure 14.14
TOD'S Omotesando
Source: Hartmut Poeling

Although it isn't as literally dendritic, he utilized the same approach in his Mikimoto Ginza 2 Store in 2005, anticipating, or more accurately initiating, a global trend toward the diagrid system subsequently used by Rem Koolhaas and Ole Sheeren on the CCTV Headquarters in Beijing in 2005 and the Olympic Stadium that Herzog and DeMeuron also designed there in 2008, in which a dendritic skin supports the entire structure (Figure 14.15).

In search of a new social realism

Riken Yamamoto, who was born in 1945 and received his master's degree in Architecture from Tokyo University within the Hara Laboratory in 1971, started out by concentrating on dwelling to an extent not evident in the careers of his contemporaries. After founding Riken Yamamoto & Field Shop in Kanagawa in 1973, he followed the Hara, and by extension the Shinohara pattern of using commissions for small houses, as the most "minimal social constellation" possible, to explore wider questions about the efficacy of spatial arrangements based purely on form-follows-function relationships. Like Shinohara and others in his orbit, Yamamoto was also very disillusioned by Expo '70 and the crass commercialization of earlier ideals that he felt it represented, and was equally disturbed by the riots that accompanied it, seeing them as exposing a glaring dichotomy between the fantasy of unlimited expansion and the reality of urban crisis, in which city dwellers were increasingly marginalized.[8]

After designing a series of houses from 1975 until 1985, he then expanded this singular investigation outward to include housing, partially moved by the dilemma of Danchi prototype that the Japan Housing Corporation (JHC) had launched soon after it was founded in 1955 to alleviate the severe housing shortage. They were inspired by Moscow's "Khrushchevki" apartment blocks, named after the Russian Premier who instituted these utilitarian units that were built in less than two months during the 1950s, and the JHC constructed 10,000 of the identical 45-square-meter units during the first year they were introduced. Although originally considered to be the height of modernity, because they also included new appliances, and unquestionably raised inhabitants' quality of life, Danchi were seen as slums by the early 1970s and were

in dire need of improvement. But, the new apartment type put forward as a substitute wasn't much better and actually lacked the small amount of cross ventilation provided in the original Danchi.

Making a habitable city

Yamamoto approached the question of improving social housing from the wider vantage point of how to restructure the city itself to make it more habitable, including inter-relationships between housing units, and the amenities needed to create a sense of community. He also expanded his original conviction about the causes of individual isolation as being the result of a Modernist concentration on configurations based on use, to a wider correlation with segregated CIAM style zoning.[9]

In 1986–1987 he was able to explore all of these new relationships between housing and the city in both of his relatively small mixed-use Gazebo and Rotunda projects in Yokohama. The Rotunda combines a store and storage-parking space at street level, a rental office on the first floor, rental apartments on the second, and a residence for owner Misao Shigemoto on the third and fourth, with an open deck at the top. Each of these is partially wrapped with stainless steel mesh to provide privacy and insulate against street noise, and each has tent-like polytetrafluoroethylene (PTFE) membrane roofs stretched over light frame steel trusses to cover courtyard spaces between units and the Gazebo owner's deck, giving them a light, open, airy feeling.

He realized a larger, more linear expression of similar usage, with an even more adventurous use of unit combinations, decks and membranes in his Hamlet mixed use project in Shibuya-ku, Tokyo in 1988 (Figure 14.16). This gave Yamamoto the confidence to finally challenge the Danchi mentality of focusing on the quality of the single unit itself and not on innovative ways of combining them in his Hotakubo Daiichi low income subsidized Public Housing, Kumamoto Prefecture, built between 1989 and 1991.

In it, he clustered 110 households around a sunken central grass courtyard, which is accessible by stairs leading down from a common plinth. As might have been anticipated, this common open front porch is now crammed full of the detritus of the daily life of its inhabitants, such as drying laundry, cooking grills,

Figure 14.15 Mikimoto Ginza 2
Source: Iwan Baan

Figure 14.16 Hamlet Yamamoto
Source: Tomio Ohashi

potted plants, outdoor furniture and children's toys. The central court idea itself is reminiscent of the debate that took place during the heady days of the Team 10 group in the 1960s resulting in housing estates such as Robin Hood Gardens in London by Peter and Alison Smithson and now demolished because of the intractable social problems it caused.

Each Hotakubo unit, however, also has an internal court or terrace, blessedly providing a private option to the community interaction that never seems to materialize within this idealized Commons, regardless of cultural context. As a cost saving measure, heavier concrete frame and block infill has also replaced the elegant stainless steel mesh, thin frame and PTFE membrane of the Rotunda, Gazebo and Hamlet precedents, yet an orderly series of five-story towers that punctuate the skyline of the internal court, spaced to strict building code requirements of allowing each inhabitant at least four hours of unobstructed sunlight,

do give a stately aspect to what might otherwise have been a depressingly clunky exterior.[10]

Seeking a nostalgic future

Chiaki Arai, who was born in Shimane in 1948, is part of that relatively small cluster of architects discussed in each of these three groups who sought to either formally or informally further their education outside Japan. After receiving his Bachelor of Architecture at Musashi Institute of Technology, now Tokyo City University in 1971, he left the student riots behind and joined the year long Louis I. Kahn Master's class at the University of Pennsylvania in Philadelphia 1973. Kahn selected a wide cross section of about a dozen international students a year for this class, which he taught, along with Norman Rice and Robert Le Ricolais from the time he was named the Paul Cret Professor of Architecture in 1966, until his death in 1974.

In spite of his growing fame, which increasingly required him to travel to job sites and deliver lectures all over the world, he rarely missed these sessions, which were held at the soaring top floor of the Frank Furness designed Fisher Fine Arts Library. He described this class as his "Chapel" and used it as both a seminar to share his enthusiasm for books he was reading at the time, such as Goethe's *Tragedy of Faust*, as well as an opportunity to explore ideas for potential projects, such as the master-plan for the Independence National Historical Park. Tadao Ando has said he assimilated Le Corbusier's thought process by tracing the drawings in the *Oeuvre Complète* and Kahn's students did the same by anticipating what he would say during long pauses before critiquing their work on the wall.

Arai spoke very little English at the time, but did absorb his intent, as well as Kahn's belief that a good question is better than the most brilliant answer. He won the coveted Schenk-Woodman Scholarship competition when he graduated, and then worked in Kahn's office for a short time before joining the Greater London Council in 1974. He established Chiaki Arai Urban and Architecture Design in 1980.

These two seemingly unrelated experiences nonetheless helped him to establish a coherent set of references, including the members of the so-called "Philadelphia School" that navigated alongside Kahn in these later years, such as Robert Venturi and Denise Scott Brown, Edmund Bacon, Ian McHarg, Romaldo Guirgola, John Bower, David Polk and Louis Sauer, as well as an equivalent number of luminaries that clustered around Archigram and the Architectural Association in London at the same time.

While there are notable exceptions, such as his impressive restoration of the Warehouse district in Yokohama into shops and restaurants in 2002, Arai has concentrated mainly on the highly technical task

Figure 14.17 Ofunato Civic Cultural Center
Source: Chiaki Arai

Figure 14.18 Ofunato Civic Cultural Center
Source: Chiaki Arai

of designing Cultural and Community Centers since 1995. These typically include concert halls, theaters and libraries of various sizes and his breakthrough came when he was commissioned to design the Kurobe International Culture Center in 1995.

After losing a major competition in 2003, and beset with mid-life doubts, he took a long break from practice to travel and think about future plans. He consequently decided to immerse his practice in the wide variety of digital programs now available, such as the Finite Element Method, or FEM system, to an extent not found elsewhere in many other Japanese offices today, combined with multiple physical models and then balanced this highly technical concentration with a sincere, concentrated attempt at public engagement through community workshops. Most architects view public forums as the nemesis of individual creative vision and only use them to justify personal wishes. But Arai has used them extensively as part of what he refers to as discovering the "topophilia" of any given situation and writing a "script" for the design that follows. He also uses analog 3-D simulation modeling combined with skilled Japanese carpenters to produce the formwork required to make the steeply stepped interior spaces he has become known for.

The Ofunato Civic Cultural Center and Library, also known as Rias Hall, which is located near the Rikuchu Coast National Park in Iwate Prefecture, is one of the first fruits of this combined, technological and popular approach involving more than 50 community workshops carried out over a six-year period before it was completed in 2008 (Figure 14.17). This sturdy, arcaded concrete monolith, inspired by Hans Scharoun's Berlin Philharmonic, fits seamlessly into the foothills around it. It was intended to mimic the natural rock formations of this part of the Sanriku Kaigan coastline, and has a high, striated tower in the center that covers its 1,100-seat Concert hall. The all-encompassing shell, with soaring interior spaces inside by deep sea canyons, also incorporates a theater, music studios, art galleries, a library, and a Japanese tearoom as well as other auxiliary spaces (Figure 14.18).

After the Tohoku earthquake and Tsunami devastated this coast on March 11, 2011 and more than 500 inhabitants of Ofunato took refuge inside its wide variety of spaces Rias Hall literally fulfilled Arai's aspiration that it serve as a Community Center, since it was occupied by most of Ofunato for many months afterward.

Of the many projects with similarly complex programs that followed, Arai's 2011 Kadare Cultural Centre, in Yurihonjo, Akita, as well as his Akiha Ward Cultural Center of 2104, and Odawara Performing Arts and Cultural Center, completed in 2015, continue to underscore his determination to use the latest technology possible to design structures that serve community needs. The stepped profile of the roof at Odawara, for example, which occupies the site of a long gone castle, combined with his formal reference to Hiroshige's woodcut "View of Lake Hakone" is especially instructive of his desire to "overcome Modernity" by creating architecture that evokes a "nostalgic future" by being both contemporary and richly laden with memory.[11]

Precisely machined testimonials to the past

Of all of the members of this second generation born during or just after the war, Shin Takamatsu undoubtedly presents the most opaque aesthetic face to Western sensibilities. He is proof of both the autonomy enjoyed by this early cohort of architects and the willingness of clients to both entertain and sponsor their novel ideas, as well as the relative lack of importance that functional conventions held for them.

Takamatsu established his practice in Kyoto after graduating from University there in 1971, followed by a PhD in 1980, but, like Arai, he was also born in Shimane in 1948, and it holds the key to his seemingly impenetrable creative vision, because the Shinto shrine of Izuzu is located there.

It may now been seen to be axiomatic that many Japanese architects make reference to a shared historical tradition in a wide spectrum of ways that range from subconscious allusion to deliberate omission, but Takamatsu reminds us that this heritage has many facets and does not always conform to widely held clichés.

While others revere the refined Austronesian pedigree of the Ise Shrine, or Katsura Rikkyū, his taste trends toward the Shrine dedicated to Ōkuninushi-no-mikoto and associated with Susano-o, rather than that of Amaterasu. His contrarian taste also extends to

Figure 14.19 Origin I, Kyoto
Source: Tomio Ohashi

Figure 14.20 Kirin Plaza, Osaka
Source: Tomio Ohashi

the fat, drum-like body of the pagoda of the Koyasan Temple in Kyoto rather than the staged elegance of the original prototype at Horyu-ji, the eclecticism of Hideyoshi's Hiunkaku Flying Cloud Pavilion at Nishi Hongan-ji instead of Katsura as well as the ornate excess of Nijo-jo and Toshugo Shrine, and as such he provides a warning that the collective tradition is profound and not everyone shares an affinity for the same parts of it.

The aspects of these alternative traditional precedents that are relevant to his work are presence, similar to the awe-inspiring quality of the sublime, distinct from beauty, identified by Edmund Burke and Immanuel Kant, the immediacy of the sensuality of form, the feeling of tension and fear of the unfathomable implicit in the interaction between the natural and the artificial construct inserted into it, and his appreciation of decorative handicraft.[12]

Although he has now built large projects all over the world, his earlier work best exemplifies this transference. His first "Origin" series, for example, was designed for the Hinaya textile company in Kyoto that specializes in making obi for Kimono, and conceals offices and showrooms behind an imposing, sharply sculpted and polished dark red granite street elevation punctuated with shiny, stainless steel bossing (Figure 14.19).

His 1987 Kirin Plaza commercial center in Osaka continues this disconnect at an even more intense urban scale, by using four square glass towers inserted into a black stone and heavy metal base to create a subliminal presence that would project a corporate image, rather than the function of the entire assemblage. Takamatsu took advantage of its corner location to make it a landmark that completely changed character after sunset to become an illuminated totem of pleasure in the midst of the crowded Shinsaibashi entertainment district (Figure 14.20).

Kirin Plaza was unfortunately demolished in 2009, and, like several other of Takamatsu's early buildings, it was yet another victim of an unsympathetic economic equation that stands in stark contrast to a clearly demonstrated reverence for traditional icons that have inspired Takamatsu and gives preference to land cost and potential profit over architectural importance.

Notes

1 Lecture by Tadao Ando, translated by Noriko Miyagawa, "Tadao Ando Exhibition 2009: The City of Water/Osaka vs. Venice", given at the Suntory Museum, Osaka, June 2009.
2 Ibid.
3 Ibid.
4 Stylianos Giamarelos, "Interdisciplinary Reflections and Deflections of Histories of the Scientific Revolution in Alberto Pérez-Gómez's Architecture and the Crisis of Modern Science," *Journal of Architectural Education*, Vol. 69, No. 1, 2015, pp. 17–27.
5 Toyo Ito, "The New Real," Lecture at UCLA, Los Angeles, December 10, 2007.
6 Kisho Kurokawa, *New Wave Japanese Architecture*, Academy Editions/Ernst & Sohn, London 1993.
7 Toyo Ito, "The Architectural Image of the Micro-electronic Age", in *Toyo Ito*, JA Library, Summer No. 2, 1993, pp. 4–7.
8 Riken Yamamoto, *Cell City*, INAX Publishing, Tokyo, 1993.
9 Riken Yamamoto, *How to Make a City*, Architektur-galerie Lucerne, Sulgen, Niggli, 2014.
10 JA Housing Special Issue, No. 3 Autumn 1991, p. 13.
11 Although introduced by John Betjeman, Arai uses the term as refined by Yi-Fu Tuan and described by his disciples in Paul C. Adams, Steven Hoelscher, and Karen E. Till, (Eds.), *Textures of Place: Exploring Humanist Geographies*, Minneapolis: University of Minnesota Press, 2001.
12 Shin Takamatsu Lecture at SCI-Arc, Los Angeles, September 27, 1989. See also Mark Linder: *Less than Literal: Architecture after Minimalism*, Cambridge, MA: MIT Press, 2004. This helps clarify the distinction between presence and the concept of appearance.

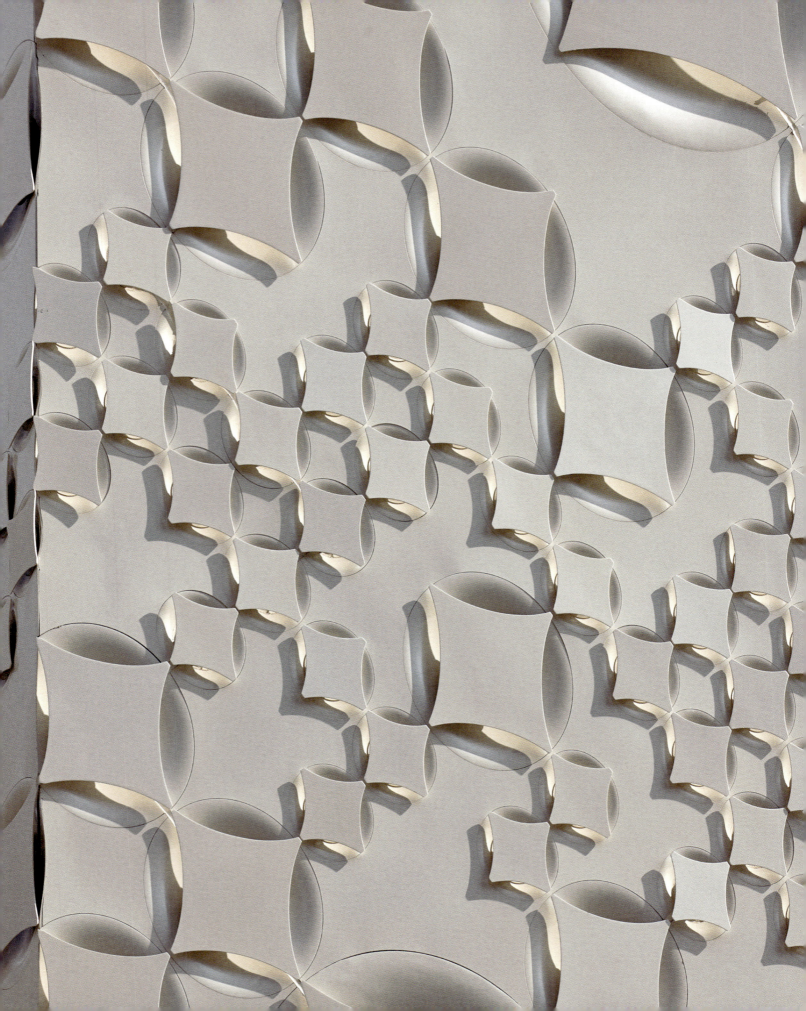

CHAPTER 15

Relief and rebuilding
Kazuo Sejima, Kengo Kuma and Jun Aoki

There is a third cluster of Japanese architects who were born in the mid-1950s, that are also part of this post-war firmament and therefore have also exerted a powerful influence on the youngest generation today. Because they didn't experience either the run-up to the conflagration or the devastation it caused, their worldview seems to be more liberated and less tied to issues of history and conflicting identity.

Kengo Kuma, for example, is one of the few architects in each of the three groups reviewed here to study extensively outside Japan. He was born in Yokohama in 1954 and after graduating from Tokyo University in 1979, and working for several corporate firms in Tokyo, became involved in research at Columbia University in New York City. He characterizes his professional career as being divided into three stages, beginning with his return to Japan after leaving Columbia in 1986, in the midst of the boom. Postmodernism was at its height in the United States while he was there, as well as Europe, and in 1989, as further proof of the aesthetic latitude that architects still enjoyed just before the bubble burst, he designed a large Mazda showroom in Tokyo centered around an inflated, stylized Ionic column called M2. It was intended as a deliberate, exaggerated caricature of the style, which he saw as a form of Western capitalist expansionism, but nobody seemed to share his sense of humor, and he was widely criticized for it. M2 has now found a new, more appropriate role as a funeral parlor.

A small, collage-like bathhouse in Izu, Kamo-gun, in Shizuoka Prefecture, however, completed two years earlier, begins to hint at his deeper intention, to seek out a non-Western, Japanese alternative to both Modernism and Postmodernism, by translating the chaos of Tokyo into architecture. If this sounds familiar, it is because, as outlined here previously, Kazuo Shinohara, as well as Hiroshi Hara and others, had reached the same conclusion more than a decade earlier, after the evanescent Metabolist vision of a newly urbanized archipelago, born of the economic miracle of the 1960s, confronted the cold war reality of choosing sides between equally distasteful, diametrically opposed political and economic systems in the 1970s. Instead of creating new utopias, Shinohara, and Hara, whom Kuma considers a mentor, as well as numerous other followers, chose to map the macrocosm of the city within the microcosm of the house.

Kuma, however, was frustrated to find that Tokyo was maddeningly resistant to formal translation, and then, in the late summer of 1990, the Nikkei Stock Index went into free-fall. By late 1991, property values followed, and economic growth came to a standstill. The bubble had burst, and Kuma no longer had the luxury of searching for meaning in disparate urban order.

During this second phase, his main concern was survival, and he then unexpectedly received two projects far away from the city that helped him do so. The

Kirosan Observatory, and Yusuhara Visitor's Center, which are both in Shikoku, and were each completed in 1994, forced him to "erase architecture and to confront materials" without having to answer to the project manager of a large construction company as he would be forced to do in Tokyo.[1]

His way of "erasing" these two projects was to bury the Kirosan Observatory inside its mountaintop site, and to use a very light tensile structure, supporting an airfoil shaped roof to make the Visitor's Center seem weightless. He added an equally exquisite wooden bridge and museum to this Center in 2012, which is inspired by Tokugawa-era Hanebashi bridges using the dou-kung method of bracketing by interlocking timber beams without metal fasteners, also hints at a new-found admiration for traditional wisdom that can be traced back to that trying time (Figure 15.1). Finding inspiration in both the Shinto and Zen Buddhist traditions, Kuma figuratively revisited the Ise Shrine, as the ultimate example of erasure and recon-

sidered the Buddhist warning about desire and the attachment to physical objects, which is created by the mind and illusory. Ise reveals that it is the knowledge about how to build a building and not the artifact itself that endures, and the idea, and not the object that is important. Because the Shrine is only a periodically reconstructed illusion, the confines of the site are irrelevant.

Throughout the 1990s Kuma continued his efforts to "erase" architecture, which conforms to the zeitgeist of anti-materialism in the post-bubble era. This is most evident in his Water-Glass House in 1995, which is suspended by a lightweight steel frame structure over an infinity pool, and seems to levitate weightlessly above it. This was also the first time that he used louvers, which have since become one of his design signatures, since they visually break down surfaces and fragment them into strips.

By 2000, Kuma started to achieve wider recognition and was asked to be part of the Commune at the Great

Figure 15.1 Yusuhara Visitor's Center
Source: Kengo Kuma

Figure 15.2 Bamboo House, Great Wall Commune, Badaling, China
Source: James Steele

Wall project in Beijing that same year. Because of the political climate at the time he was surprised that he was selected by developer Zhang Xin of SOHO China Limited to participate in the design of one of 12 houses on this extensive site near the Badaling section of the wall intended to showcase a cross section of Asian talent, and to be rented out on a short or long term basis.

Architects selected their sites by lot and they are stung out along the steep winding road ascending upward from a clubhouse and administrative office building near the entrance. Because it is bisected by a ravine, Kuma's site is less than ideal, but he made a virtue of adversity by using his "Bamboo house" as a deferential metaphor for the Great Wall itself, which seems to snake effortlessly across hills and valleys in the near distance, becoming thicker or thinner as the topography requires. By using bamboo, he also alludes to a brisk trade in different species of this commodity between China and Japan in the past, suggesting a long tradition of collaboration between the two nations.

Figure 15.3 Chokkura Plaza
Source: Kengo Kuma

His Stone Museum in Nasu, built in 1998, was much more challenging in terms of erasure, given the inherent heaviness of the material, but he made it seem lighter by using long, thin slabs and leaving gaps between the horizontal layers, to allow light into the interior. He was also prompted to use stone at Chokkura Plaza in 2006, because of three pre-existing masonry storage barns on the site, and integrated his building with these old Oya stone warehouses, once used to store rice. This stone, which Frank Lloyd Wright also used for his Imperial Hotel in Tokyo, is soft and easy to carve when first excavated, and hardens after exposure to air. Kuma used a diagonal metal frame to support it.

His attempt to break down building mass continued in 2012 with his design the Asakusa Culture Tourist Information Center, located on a 326-square-meter corner site directly across from the outer Kaminari-mon Gate of the Sensō-ji Temple.

It is primarily a tourist information center, to promote interesting sites in Tokyo and throughout Japan but also has an exhibition space, offices, a conference room and auditorium. In this instance his anti-materialistic strategy includes a series of roofs that visually slice the tower into eight horizontal sections according to function, as well as first attempt at using vertical louvers to fragment the surface into strips.

As recognition increased, Kuma had to push back against the growing international tendency toward singular computer generated and constructed objects, with no apparent ties to their site, climate or cultural context. His counterinsurgency against objectification and its economic association with commodification, which he believes to be a central characteristic of Western architecture, has revolved around "recovering place" and its temporal and natural relationships, as well as a Japanese sense of lightness and transparency.[2]

Figure 15.4 Asakusa Tourist Center
Source: James Steele

The feminine factor

Kazuo Sejima, who is the first major female architect since Itsuko Hasegawa to achieve superstar status in Japan, was born in 1956, two years after Kengo Kuma. Unlike Hasagawa she has spoken more openly about the challenges of making her way in a male-dominated profession and her selection of Japan Women's University, rather than another more mainstream provider of professional training hints at her early awareness of emphasizing gender identity. It is a private institution founded in 1901 as *Nihon Joshi Dai-Gakko* by Jinzo Naruse, who studied at Andover Theological Seminary

and Clark University in the United States and was dedicated to promoting higher education for women.

After receiving her master's degree in 1981, Sejima joined Toyo Ito and Associates and remained with him until establishing Kazuyo Sejima & Associates, in 1987. She later formed SANAA with former employee Ryue Nishizawa in 1995. The trail that both Hasagawa and Sejima blazed in Japan has subsequently widened considerably, consistent with a general trend of more women entering architectural schools and the profession in both Japan and throughout the developed world. In addition to Sejima, Ito also has named former employee Maki Ohnishi, as part of the younger generation in his "constellation" of influence. Her firm Onishimaki and Hyakudayuki architects, which she founded with Yuki Hyakuda in 2008, will be seen here to be a new normal in Japan today. She joins other female members of the latest generation in partnerships featured later here, such as Yui Tezuka of Takaharu and Yuki Tezuka Architects, Chie Nabeshima with Makoto Takei of TNA Architects, and Momoyo Kaijima, who established Atelier Bow Wow with Yoshiharu Tsukamoto, in addition to sole practitioners Kumiko Inui and Hiroshi Nakamura, among many others.[3]

Along with Ito, and by extension the Shinohara circle that their ethereal architectural lexicon recalls, Sejima also somewhat surprisingly cites Modernists from the heroic phase of the movement, such as Mies van der Rohe and Le Corbusier as inspirations. Once revealed, however, that seemingly contradictory nexus helps us to make sense of her distinctively different, prescriptive approach to programming, as a mild form of social engineering, rather than the descriptive method favored by Modernist functionalism.[4]

The 1991 Saishunkan Seiyaku Women's Dormitory in Kumamoto, which is her first major design, begins to explain the difference. It houses 80 new employees of a pharmaceutical conglomerate in two parallel two story 4.5{—}meter-wide by 45-meter-long apartment blocks flanking a 9-meter-wide atrium that is as high as the apartment blocks on either side of it. Residents are housed four to a room and must collectively use bathroom facilities on the second floor as well as the central social space, in an attempt to nurture camaraderie and build team spirit during their first year with the company. The bathroom block levitates within an

Figure 15.5 Gifu Kitagata Apartment
Source: Hartmut Poeling

enclosed pod that seems to hover above the central social space, and it, along with rectilinear mechanical towers that punctuate the atrium, especially recall Shinohara's preference for purely abstract geometric forms.

The Gifu Kitagata Apartment Building underscores Sejima's success in establishing both a high professional profile and a well-defined gender identity, since master-planner Arata Isozaki chose her in 1998 to be one of the four members of an all-female cast of architects that he selected to help promote public awareness of women's role in creating the built environment today.

Sejima contributed the south-eastern component of this extensive residential complex, which, moving clockwise around the rectangular site, also includes American architect Elizabeth Diller of Diller-Scofidio to the north-east, fellow Japanese colleague Akiko Takahashi of Akiko and Hiroshi Takahashi/Work-

station at the north-west corner and Christine Hawley of the British firm Cook+Hawley on the south-west corner of the internal park designed by Martha Schwartz.

Re-testing a preference for privacy

Gifu also re-affirms Sejima's re-invention of Modernist, and specifically Corbusian tropes and her deliberate use of prescriptive programming, in that it is clearly inspired by the Unité de Habitation, in Marseilles, yet varies from it in significant ways. Like this post-war precedent, her fish-hook shaped section, which is splayed out along an east-west axis to receive as much north light and cross ventilation as possible, is raised up on piloti to allow for parking underneath, and is one unit deep, with internal space modulated by different section heights. Rather than using a central double loaded corridor, however, she has located public circulation along an exposed corridor connected to a sequence of fire stairs that animate the internal façade facing into the park, and has distributed living spaces among a series of parallel partitions perpendicular to it, connected by an adjoining internal corridor of their own, along the external wall on the other side.

In addition to the wider mission here, of continuing Riken Yamamoto's search for a new, more liberated social housing prototype for Japan, to replace the timeworn Daichi model, the prescriptive program in this case relates to her assignment of one of these front-to-back spaces as a double height "terrace" with full knowledge of the distinct possibility that occupants would use it to hang out laundry to dry there, or stack boxes in it, in full public view, given the lack of laundry and storage space in the complex as a whole. As such, this repetitious and constantly changing exhibition of clothing preferences and packed belongings adds an especially personal and colorful note to the elevation, as questionable artwork of the same genre as Tracey Emin's unmade "My Bed" that was shortlisted for the Turner prize in 1999, and sold at Christie's for just over four million dollars in 2014.

Another of Le Corbusier's principles, of creating a processional, is in evidence at the Ogasawara Museum, or O-Museum, Nagano, which Sejima and Nishizawa completed in 1999. It is a long slender rectilinear building that is little more than an enclosed viewing pavilion raised above the ground as a gesture of respect for a fourteenth-century castle that used to occupy the site. It deliberately demarcates the space between a lush bamboo forest on one side and a restored and listed Samurai house that it is intended to showcase on the other and gradually rises from the parking lot, where visitors arrive, to direct them toward the ticket booth at the other end. In direct contradiction of Modernist practice once again, however, visitors are then led underneath the museum onto a ramp moving in the opposite direction on the other side, which takes them up and into the gallery itself. Once inside it becomes clear that the repetitive vertical fret pattern on the glazed, entry elevation actually mimics the striated stalks of the bamboo that line the ramp and this visual

Figure 15.6 21st Century Museum in Kanazawa
Source: Iwan Baan

Figure 15.7 Museum in Kanazawa, Corridor
Source: Iwan Baan

reverberation is further enhanced by the view of the house in the near distance.

The historical and contextual allusions at Ogasawara also contradict Modernist resistance to historical reference, and extend beyond the deference shown to both the memory of the castle and the residential artifact honored here, as well as the crystalline echoing of the bamboo forest, to a more subliminal but nonetheless obvious parallel with the Karesansui Zen garden of Ryoan-ji, mentioned often here as having inspired many other Japanese architects, where an earthen wall is used as a datum that separates a gravel foreground from the forest beyond.

The much larger 21st Century Museum of Contemporary Art in Kanazawa, which followed soon after Ogasawara in 1999, took four years to complete.

It set SANAA on the path of similar commissions of this type to follow, such as the Glass Pavilion at the Toledo Museum of Art received in 2001, the remarkable extension to the Instituto Valenciano de Arte Moderno in Valencia, Spain, ongoing since 2002, and the New Museum of Contemporary Art in New York City in 2003. But Kanazawa best illustrates Sejima's continued exploration of the same kind of prescriptive programming and informed contradiction of Modernist conventions discussed earlier.

The museum typology is foreign to Asia in general, since it is a product of the Enlightenment attempt to categorize and classify the natural world and artifacts and art within it. Even the idea of a "Cabinet of Curiosities" that predated the type in Europe was unknown in Japan, where the very thought of attempting to capture culture seemed incomprehensible due to the Japanese tradition of viewing culture as a living entity not something to be displayed publicly for analysis. That changed during the rush to develop, accompanied by a desire to emulate Western institutions, but even then a preference for what are essentially shrines to natural elements and forces remained, as illustrated by Tadao Ando's 1994 Museum of Wood, in the Mikata-gun Forest in Hyogo Prefecture, Kengo Kuma's aforementioned Stone Museum in

Nasu, and the Nakaya Ukichiro Museum of Snow and Ice among others. And yet, museology has never been a perfect fit in Japan, as evidenced at Gunma, where Arata Isozaki fits function into form and deliberately turns the terminal Japanese wing at an angle to underscore its otherness.

At Kanazawa, Sejima turns that hesitation about collection into a legible narrative about the artificiality and pathology of this compulsion, by turning the galleries into boxes of different sizes and heights that project up through a circular roof as a symbol of acquisitiveness. Eight years later, she also used the same metaphor in her design of the New Museum in New York City, but simply stacked them there, due to site constraints. To offset the effect of effete abstraction often induced by viewing art, she has approached the Kanazawa museum as a village in miniature, with an encompassing circular corridor, and side streets branching out from an internal main spine, passing by four central courtyards. This provides more freedom and a feeling of community than the single entrance that security usually dictates, as do the library and restaurant for public use.

The glazed, circular perimeter at Kanazawa is the most lyrical part of Sejima's reinterpretation of the type since it seems to be intended for both seeing and being seen. This shows her awareness that people watching, and the possibility of a chance meeting, are both the strongest motivations for going to a museum today, especially in privacy-prone Japan, and this wide perimeter street contributes to the feeling of community she wants to establish.

Constructing a new system of architecture

Jun Aoki, who was born in 1958, is the relative youngster of this distinguished tripartite family of postwar architects, connected to them primarily through his extended apprenticeship with Arata Isozaki from 1983 to 1990, before establishing his own firm. He continues the dialogue initiated by Kazuo Sejima at both Ogasawara and Kamakura in surprisingly similar and dissimilar ways at his Aomori Museum of Fine Art completed in 2006, inspired by excavations at the Sannai-Maruyama site near the museum, which have uncovered the ruins of a 5,500-year old Jomon village.

The similarity is that Aoki, like Sejima, was also guided by Le Corbusier and in this instance layered over the concept of the concrete present interlocking the earthen past with the precedent of the Sainte Marie de La Tourette priory near Lyon. He has described his interpretation of Le Corbusier's intention as "to not adopt an existing coordinate system" but "to transform, displace and modify that coordinate system, or better yet, to construct an altogether new coordinate system" in which "two worlds define each other, as if bound in a reversible figure ground relationship."[5]

He diverges from Sejima's path by commemorating this history in a more visceral way, as a series of crisscrossing trenches covered by a lid that is flat on top but variegated underneath, creating a series of jagged interstitial spaces between the ground and the roof that are used as galleries. Rather than the transparency that defines the social concept of the Kanazawa museum, he reinterprets the curtain wall differently by concealing the joints of the brick wrapper to make it appear to levitate, recalling the enduring historical context around it.

The Aomori Museum begs the question about Aoki's own position on the Modernist sensibility. Japanese critic Kenjiro Hosaka has described it, in turn, by invoking Ernst Cassier, discussed earlier here as one of the favorite philosophers of the Metabolists because he attempted to integrate scientific Positivism and hermeneutics. According to Hosaka, Aoki's architecture conforms to Cassier's notion of mythic thinking which "configures into the world" as opposed to scientific and by extension modernist attempts to "configure the world" and as such it avoids Platonically complete forms and rejects functionalism in favor of the interstitial and what Aoki refers to as "mutation," or the manipulation of space, which incidentally results in architecture.

Using ornament to unlock the subconscious

Aoki has also designed a series of stores for Louis Vuitton in Japan and those on Omotesando in Tokyo in 2002, in the Tenjin district of Fukuoka in 2011 and the Louis Vuitton Matsuya store in Ginza in 2014, each of which continue this dialogue with context and the past. At Omotesando he has used a composition of interlocking horizontal windows to conjure up the ghost of the early modernist Dojunkai Apartments that once stood nearby, before being demolished to make way for Tadao Ando's Omotesando Hills in 2005. In Fukuoka, the light arcing across the exterior louvers intentionally recalls the ripples on Hakata Bay.

The three level Louis Vuitton boutique in Ginza, which attaches to the corner of the Matsuya Department store, not only pays homage to the history of this storied district but also engages Japan's interaction with the West, since Ginza is adjacent to the first railway station at Shimbashi, which was the gateway to Tokyo for foreign visitors from Yokohama port and has always been associated with contemporary trends. To assimilate this history Aoki has used elegant interlocking aluminum lenses on the façade that are coated with opal beige pearlized fluoropolymer paint and are raised from a translucent inner wall to create delicate shadows during the day and allow interior and LED lights behind them to emerge through their scalloped

edges and illuminate the façade at night. In addition to evoking the Vuitton logo, it also recalls the komon, or fine print pattern, produced in this district favored for the Kamishimo, or formal attire worn by the Daimyo and Samurai during the Muromachi period in Edo.

Imbedded lessons moving forward

Each of the distinguished individuals in the three post-war periods just described are distinctively different, and yet each of them has quite surprisingly also addressed the same liturgical pairing of tradition, as the social analogy of cultural habit and affinity to nature over time, and the incursion of the Western Modernist technological imperative that has threatened to reconfigure it. Without summarizing each of their positions, it has been astonishing to discover the multitude of ways in which they have each responded to this nexus and this serves as a warning against making superficial assumptions.

Figure 15.8 Aomori Museum of Art, Jun Aoki & Associates
Source: Daici Ano

Figure 15.9 Louis Vuitton Matsuya Ginza
Source: Daici Ano

The generation that follows them has had to confront the harsh reality of severely diminished expectations, due to the after effects of the bursting of the bubble economy of the 1980s. And yet, they have proven to be exceptionally resilient and have found innovative ways to survive and thrive. In doing so, they have not only resuscitated certain aspects of Japanese tradition, such as a preoccupation with materiality and surface, the search for the sublime and a preference for interstitial space, but have also revitalized the seemingly anti-thetical pairing of objective positivism and intuitive heuristics by reinventing Modernism and finding ways to synthesize the technology that accompanies it with the natural environment.

Notes

1   Kengo Kuma, *Studies in Organic*, Tokyo: Toto, 2009, p. 30.
2   Kengo Kuma, *Anti-Object: The Dissolution and Disintegration of Architecture*, trans. Hiroshi Watanabe. London: AA Publications, 2008.
3   Alexandra Lange, "MoMA Offers Japanese Navigators in an Architectural Firmament," *New York Times*, March 31, 2016, p. 2.
4   Yuko Hasegawa, Interview with Kazuo Sejima and Ryue Nishizawa, "The Roles of Architecture and Art in Creating a New Tomorrow," in Takuya Miyake, ed. *Architectural Environments for Tomorrow*, Tokyo: Access, p. 200.
5   Kenjiro Hosaka, "Ethics for Architecture, Architecture for Ethics," in *Jun Aoki: Complete Works 1: 1991–2004*, tr. Hiroshi Watanabe, INAX, Tokyo, p. 27.

PART V

The next generation

CHAPTER 16
Doing more with less

The explosion of the Bubble Economy in 1989 resulted in the precipitous decline of the Nikkei Stock Market and collapse of real estate values over the next three years, causing a protracted financial crisis and bringing the "Economic Miracle" to an end. During the "Lost Decade" of the 1990s that followed, only government intervention kept banks and corporations from failing.

The power and status that had accrued to architects that had come of age in Japan during the period of extraordinary growth that followed the utter devastation of World War II was over. They had headed offices with multiple projects of monumental scale that were being designed and built at the same time all over the world, and were once able to dictate decisions to clients, and use each building design to explore lines of formal inquiry that interested them throughout many projects over time, and refuse commissions at will. But young architects born just before this crash face a future predicated upon hugely diminished expectations.

Severely diminished expectations

Signs of this change in worldview abound and are hinted at in the book *Pet Architecture* by Atelier Bow-Wow, in which its principles Yoshiharu Tsukamoto and Momoyo Kajima have thoroughly catalogued the inventive, vernacular solutions that entrepreneurs must now resort to by fitting their shops into urban spaces that would be considered un-buildable elsewhere. This isn't a new phenomenon in cities like Tokyo, where property values still remain relatively high, and while

the more established architects just discussed have been able to secure commissions abroad, younger practitioners are now under pressure to identify such sites and propose them to prospective clients to survive.[1]

Atelier Bow-Wow was founded in 1992 by Tsukamoto, who graduated from the Tokyo Institute of Technology in 1987, and Momoyo Kaijima, who, like Sejima, also received her undergraduate degree from the Faculty of Domestic Science at Japan Women's University. After graduating in 1991, she received her graduate and post-graduate degrees from Tokyo Institute of Technology in 1994 and 1999. Their office, on a typically small back street in Tokyo, conforms to the Pet Architecture profile, since it is skillfully inserted into the houses around it, making it virtually unrecognizable as an office from outside. The A-frame enclosure serves as a tight-knit communal live-work environment for the partners and their employees who use every inch of space efficiently (Figure 16.1).

Kajima and Tsukamoto have resuscitated and re-directed the study of Behaviorology that was in vogue among programmers configuring functional relationships during the late Modernist period in the West. As with all of other adaptations of Modernist principles by Japanese architects already described here, however, this permutation transcends the form follows function mantra and emphasizes nature, and the inter-relationships between those they are designing for and engagement with the natural and local environment.[2]

Figure 16.1
Atelier Bow-Wow Office
Source: Atelier Bow-Wow

Conforming to tight parameters

The Mosaic House, by TNA, the "House and Garden" project by Ryue Nishizawa, which are both in Tokyo and the 2004 House by Hideyuki Nakayama in Matsumoto, Japan, also clearly illustrate these tight site constraints in the different urban contexts. The Mosaic House was built in 2006 two years after Makota Takei and Chie Nabeshima founded TNA Architects and typifies this telescoping down of project size with residential or mixed use neighborhoods. Unlike the Atelier Bow-Wow office, it stands alone on its small trapezoidal lot, and four-story high buildings on the south side of the site and commercial activities nearby dictated solid sides for privacy and an entirely glass roof that directs light into the middle of the small residence by arching it toward the sun. The curve also describes the complex zoning codes in force here and

all of these parameters combined to shape the interior layout, which is completely oriented toward the sky (Figure 16.2).

Ryue Nishizawa, who graduated from Yokohama National University, and joined Kazuyo Sejima as a partner in SANAA in 1995, before establishing his own firm in 1997, has taken an entirely different approach in his five story "House and Garden" complex on a busy Tokyo commercial street. It is wedged into a 4-meter wide space between two other buildings and to increase the sense of space and yet retain privacy in this live-work environment for two writers he has used only glass walls and has placed planters on balconies at the front of each of the floors. The bedrooms are located on the first and third floors, and the office spaces are in between (Figure 16.3).

Hideyuki Nakayama, on the other hand, initially had a bit more breathing room when he started to design

Figure 16.2
Mosaic House
Source: TNA,
Daichi Ano

Figure 16.3 Nishizawa Garden House
Source: Iwan Baan

his 2004 House, located on what was initially a relatively open residential area of Matsumoto. It was not only named for the date it was built, but also to commemorate the point at which he became determined to re-think the entire process of what an architect goes though in intervening in the natural environment, establishing what are essentially artificial boundaries, and establishing a home (Figure 16.4).

When he first visited the site he was struck by the thick carpet of clover that covered it but during the design process, the entire area started to be developed. Two-story houses were built close to his site and grass

was replaced with gravel. He responded by reconfiguring the house, turning it into a solid boxcar shaped enclosure, making the exterior siding an ironic generic commentary on residential materiality, raising the box up on a glass plinth base and re-planting clover around it. He then used half, or split levels inside so that the floor of the living area is only one meter above grade. This brings the inhabitants face to face with the green frame so that when gazing down from the living room floor, the remains of the ground seem like a specimen stored in a glass box, so that each leaf of clover can be seen as a cat would see it, or like when one is laying on the ground.[3]

Figure 16.4
Hideyuki Nakayama, 2004 House
Source: Toshiyuki Yano

Figure 16.5 Shuhei Endo, Springtecture, Matsumura Yoshiharu
Source: Shuhei Endo

Finding new materials

Confronting limitations has also led young architects like Shuhei Endo to adopt less expensive materials and to use them in new ways. His single-family "Spring-tecture" houses on the outskirts of Nagahama in Shiga Prefecture, on the north-eastern shore of Lake Biwa are a graphic example of this heightened level of innovation. He has used standard sized sheets of corrugated galvanized sheet steel, bolted together and curved to become both the exterior enclosure and inner surface of each house, consistent with the idea of partially shared elements, or bunyutai. Additional materials, such as glass, brick walls and earth berms combine to complete the forms (Figure 16.5).

Notes

1   Atelier Bow-Wow, *Pet Architecture*, Tokyo: World Photo Press, 2002.
2   Yoshiharu Tsukamoto, Momoyo Kajima, Atorie Wan, with Terunobu Fujimori, Washida Menruro, Yoshikazu Nango, *Behaviorology*, New York: Rizzoli, 2010.
3   From a description provided by Hideyuki Nakayama.

CHAPTER 17

On the surface

The elusive qualities of surface tension and tactility have been a consistent feature of Japanese architecture, as seen in the subtle sheen of the Hinoki planks on the Ise shrine, the golden and shou-sugi-ban-sided retreats of the Ashikaga shoguns outside Kyoto and the shoji screens of Katsura Rikyū, in pre-Meiji eras, as well as the metallic glitter of Shinohara's Centennial Hall, the seductive planarity of Fumihiko Maki's Tepia Science Center, the silken concrete of Tadao Ando and the kaleidoscopic enclosure of Toyo Ito's Tower of the Winds, in recent times.

The elusive allure of flatness

Planar two-dimensionality is the inextricable component of this appeal, mentioned earlier in reference to the tightly compressed façade of the Morigo Office building in Tokyo, which Togo Murano designed in 1931 and can now be seen to be the progenitor of many contemporary buildings in cities throughout the archipelago (Figure 17.1). This cultural preference for flatness also recalls cautionary advice about the difference between Japanese and Western concepts of space offered by Kazuo Shinohara, Kisho Kurokawa and Arata Isozaki, among others, who all allude to floor-level views though multi-layered interiors framed by a succession of shoji screens toward exterior gardens as the antithesis of form follows function articulation.[1]

The historical reason for this divergence has been exhaustively explored by Alberto Pérez-Gómez and Louise Pelletier, who have traced it back to the advent of Humanism during the Italian Renaissance, and the objectification of the architectural artifact that followed, due to the use of perspective representation which preferences the individual, looking toward a personal horizon line, rather than the more holistic worldview of an amorphous collective.[2]

The wabi-sabi of controlled rust

Weathering steel, which is made of special alloys that eliminate the need for painting and is allowed to rust naturally, seems to have been adopted by many young Japanese architects as the ideal contemporary material to convey the spirit of tactility and aging so central to the illusive Zen concept of wabi-sabi. It has been adapted in a number of different ways by young architects including a Natural Science Center in the Matsunoyama region of Niigata Prefecture by Tezuka Architects, an Environmental Education Center in Hyogo and Tsunami Disaster Prevention Center in Minamiawaji City by Shuhei Endo, and a private museum in Shiogama, Miyagi Prefecture, by Hitoshi Abe.

Niigata, where the Kyororo Natural Science Center by Tezuka is located, is also known as yukiguni, or snow country, and its angular profile was inspired by wooden structures in the Matsunoyama region that shield local roads from snow, as well as a submarine-like 160-meter-long serpentine plan that follows a well-worn

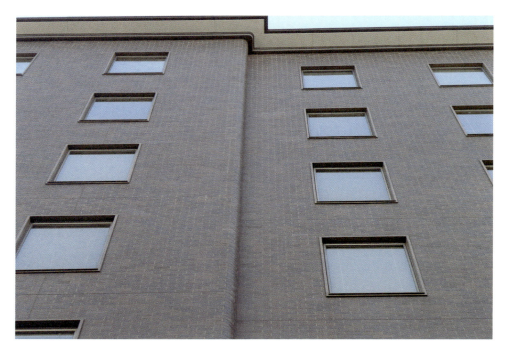

Figure 17.1 The Morigo Office building
Source: James Steele

Figure 17.2 Abe, F-town
Source: Daichi Ano

Figure 17.3 Environmental Education Center in Hyogo
Source: Matsumura Yoshiharu

Figure 17.4 Tsunami Disaster Control Center
Source: Matsumura Yoshiharu

Figure 17.5 Abe, Kanno Museum
Source: Daichi Ano

Figure 17.6 Tezuka, Matsumoyama, Kyororo Natural Science Center
Source: Katshuhisa Kida, Fototeca

path around the site that is sometimes buried under snowdrifts of up to seven meters deep. The skin is 6-millimeter-thick welded Cor-Ten plate steel, which can withstand a 2,000-ton snow load (Figure 17.2).

At strategic points, large floor-to-ceiling windows provide breathtaking views of the exterior snow-scape and a 34-meter tower also offers a view over the tree-tops. The weathering steel skin, which was welded on site, was conceived to change over time, so that it will eventually look like a ruin emerging from the forest, or snow.

Shuhei Endo's Environmental Education Center in Hyogo shares similar animistic characteristics and educational goals with the Kyororo Natural Science Center, but because the Kansai region is far warmer than Niigata, its distinctively caltrop shape has been carefully fitted into the hilly site to lessen its environmental impact. Endo designs in series and this is part of his "Bubbletecture" group, with a 1.2-millimieter thick weathering steel skin and green roof of local moss, over a Hinoki frame (Figure 17.3).

Endo's Tsunami Disaster Preventive Control Center in Minamiawaji City is elevated at the end of a dock in Fukura port to provide clear sightlines toward the water and the floodgates beyond, and remain above Tsunami waves. It is part of another "Looptecture" series, using 7.3-meter-wide continuously curved walls to dissipate structural stress. It is also sheathed in weathering steel, in homage to industrial landscape around it and circular windows around the perimeter complete the metaphor (Figure 17.4).

Hitoshi Abe has also chosen to use a rusted steel carapace for his Kanno museum, overlooking the Pacific Ocean on a hillside in the small town of Shiogama in Miyagi Prefecture, but has returned to the requisite precedent of flatness and quilted it to give it additional tactility. This private gallery is a repository for the permanent display of just eight sculptures within a 10-meter square by 12-meter high container. Abe arrived at the internal spatial configuration by doing soap-bubble studies inside a similarly proportioned box and has cut a triangular window into the south-east corner of the steel container, to offer views toward the ocean below (Figure 17.5).

He has also used angular flatness and quilted steel, but painted white in this case, in a series of seven stacked rectilinear restaurants and bars of various heights, cryptically called F-town in the middle of the entertainment zone in his hometown of Sendai. They hover above a glazed street-level entry, seeming to defy gravity by spiraling upward around a central core (Figure 17.6).

Mercantile salvation

Commercial applications, or more specifically store-fronts, are another of the latest, even more prosaic, equivalents of the transformation of the traditional Japanese preference for flatness realized by Togo Murano on the Morigo façade, offering young architects a fitting canvas for creativity that is also suitable to the new reality of budget contractions.

While the extensive use of computer programs is surprisingly rare among young Japanese designers except for highly complex projects such as the theaters and concert halls designed by Chiaki Arai, discussed earlier, those creating these façades use them effectively, as Jun Aoki's Louis Vuitton store in the Ginza district of Tokyo illustrates. It sets an elegantly high standard for this typology, with the well-known monogram impressed on sheets of aluminum coated with pearlescent fluoropolymer paint. The sides of the panels are perforated, letting the light from inside spill around the edges (Figure 17.7).

Kumiko Inui has also contributed to this genre with her multi-layered design for Dior, which is also in the Ginza district of Tokyo. The outer aluminum skin is drilled with innumerable holes of various sizes that allow light from the inner layer to shine through (Figure 17.8). Consistent with the modest commissions offered to young architects today, and their ability to leverage them into larger projects, Inui got her start with a commission for a monument, which she approached as an opportunity to reinterpret what monumentality means. Her version is a play on domesticity, since it is an abstract recollection of shelter, with openings deliberately sized to recall residential windows, and serves as a somewhat protected sitting area on the plaza in front of the Shin-Yatsushiro Shinkansen Station. The entire house-shaped structure is made of ultra-thin fiberglass reinforced concrete with many square openings of various sizes that are strategically sized and located to accommodate structural stresses, and to frame interior views of surrounding houses (Figure 17.9).

Ginza is also blessed with yet another stunning façade by Hiroshi Nakamura for a Lanvin Boutique that is far more articulated than either of the flatter Vuitton or Dior examples and appears to be carved into an older brick enclosure at the first floor of the high-rise tower it graces. It is also made of metal, with holes of various sizes drilled through it, but in contrast to the other two, it is only one layer thick and as a study in black and white, the dark matte exterior comes alive after dark, when internal light shines through, just as the white

Figure 17.7
Louis Vuitton Matsuya Ginza
Source: Daici Ano

Figure 17.8 Dior
Source: Daichi Ano

Figure 17.9
Shin-Yatsushiro
Monument
Source: Daichi Ano

Figure 17.10 Lanvin Boutique
Source: Daichi Ano

interior does during the day, when sunlight streams through into the shop itself (Figure 17.10).

A rubberized cage

Keiichiro Sako and Takeshi Ishizaka of SAKO Architects have departed from this patterned, perforated metal trend in their Beijing Shop for the Romanticism chain, which has other locations throughout China. They asked Sako then to create a design that could not be copied, which is of obvious concern for a prominent brand there, and he certainly rose to the challenge.

Sako worked for Riken Yamamoto for eight years, starting with his housing project near Ryokuen Toshi Station in Izumi Ward, near Yokohama and ending up as the project manager on the Nishi Fire Station in Hiroshima, the Shinonome Canal Court in Tokyo and the huge Jianwai Soho project at 39 East Third Ring Road, in the Chaoyang District in Beijing, which Yamamoto won in a competition in 2000. He met a client for his own Cube-Tube Transport building there, and established his own office in Beijing on the strength of that commission.

He also has a second office in Tokyo now and travels back and forth between China and Japan. The Jianwai Soho project led to this commission, which is relatively modest for him, and Sako responded by creating an all-enveloping net made of steel rods wrapped in Styrofoam and glass fiber and then coated in epoxy resin and covered with a water paint finish. He intended to

Figure 17.11 Romanticism
Source: NACSA

Figure 17.12 Mt. Fuji Sakura House
Source: Ryota Atarashi

establish an organic relationship between human and spatial form and the clothing on display, implying that each is, or has a skin (Figure 17.11).[3]

Metallic Ise-Katagami

Back in Japan, Masahiro and Mao Harada of Mount Fuji Architects Studio have contributed substantially to the residential equivalent of the perforated metal retail genre in their Sakura home-office in the upscale, yet cluttered Meguro neighborhood in Tokyo.

Inspired by the autonomy provided by the forests surrounding both the Farnsworth House by Ludwig Mies van der Rohe, and the Glass House of his disciple, Philip Johnson, and certainly unable to replicate the real

thing in such tight quarters, they decided to create a delicately punctured microcosmic steel equivalent of a cherry orchard here, to provide maximum privacy for their clients (Figure 17.12).

To achieve this sensation they have used a free-standing 5-meter high wall layered in front of another 7.5-meter high backdrop and each of these screens is made of 3-millimeter-thick steel with holes punched out in cherry blossom pattern. This mimics a traditional paper stencil technique called Katagami, or Ise-katagami, used for dyeing textiles and kimonos. This art, which has now been designated to be an Intangible Cultural Property in Japan, originated in Suzuka in Mie Prefecture and examples dating back to the Nara period have been discovered in the Shōsōin at

Todai-ji. It involves combining several layers of washi paper together with persimmon-based glue and then cutting them into stencils with dōgu-bori. The combination of these two heavily laden metaphors, of cherry blossoms and Katagami stencil-work, underscores the enduring mnemonic power of such cultural forms within the younger generation of Japanese architects as well.

Tumescent beacons in Shibuya and Minato-ku

Masaki Endoh and Masahiro Ikeda, of Endoh Design House & MIA, have created their own remarkable testimonial to the national tradition of tactility with their tubular Natural Ellipse House, which is appropriately located in the midst of the entertainment district of Shibuya and was completed in 2002. They have used 24 elliptical flat steel bars that were laser cut to form an elongated metal cage to envelope the house, and then wrapped this substructure in a seamless fiber-reinforced polymer sheet to enhance the feeling of plasticity. Fiber-reinforced polymer sheets are typically used as roofing insulation, so its use as an external skin here is unusual, and in addition to its raw power, another obvious benefit is that it enhances translucency and eliminates the need for internal insulation (Figure 17.13).

Hiroshi Nakamura & NAP Co. Ltd., who designed the Lanvin Boutique described earlier, which conforms to the planar sensibility in question here, have contributed their own, overtly marsupial version of this more

Figure 17.13 Masaki Endoh and Masahiro Ikeda, Natural Ellipse House
Source: Hiro Sakaguchi

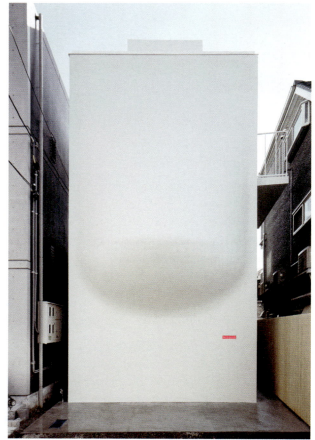

Figure 17.14 House SH, Exterior
Source: Daichi Ano

Figure 17.15 House SH, Interior
Source: Daichi Ano

atavistic approach in their 2006 House SH in Minato-ku which also seems to breathe from within, in spite of being made of inert materials. While they are certainly not flat, each of these houses attests to an enduring need to express the inner essence of materials, in a sensual way (Figures 17.14 and 17.15).

Notes

1   See, for example, Kisho Kurokawa, *Re-discovering Japanese Space*, Weatherhill, 1989.
2   Alberto Pérez-Gómez and Louise Pelletier, *Architectural Representation and the Perspective Hinge*, Cambridge, MA: MIT Press, 2000.
3   Keiichiro Sako, "Mr. Blunt: An Interview with Keiichiro Sako," Mark Magazine, No. 20, June–July 2009.

CHAPTER 18

Interstitial space
The new engawa

There are several vernacular solutions to the problem of integrating open space into a building enclosure. The courtyard, which is the most ubiquitous, has ancient roots in many different cultural settings throughout the world, due to climatic advantages, such as its ability to collect cool night air and distribute it by convection during the increasing heat of the day, mitigating extreme temperatures in harsh climates. The breezeway, called the taktaboosh in the Middle East and the lanai in Hawaii, operates in much the same way, transferring air collected in a landscaped area overnight to a paved area that heats up during the diurnal cycle, allowing people sitting under an overhang in the middle to enjoy the air flowing between them.

The engawa, however, has a profoundly social as well as environmental purpose and is only found in Japan. This interstitial space, which has been mistakenly referred to as a either a deck, a terrace, or a nure-en, for taking off shoes before entering, serves an altogether different purpose, of erasing the strict boundary between the enclosure and open space. As such, it is the physical manifestation of an inclusive attitude toward nature, of integration with it as opposed to the distancing and distrust that are characteristic of Eastern architecture.

The Hall of Immortal Poets

There are many traditional examples, but the engawa at Shisendo will serve to illustrate its purpose of seamlessly blending inside and outside together. A Samurai named Jozan Ishikawa built this sukiya-style retreat. He was a proficient swordsman and was selected to be a bodyguard for Tokugawa Ieyasu at the Battle of Sekigahara. He left his post to help friends surrounded by the enemy, and was only spared from execution because of the courage and loyalty he displayed. After his discharge, he went to care for his dying mother, and then bought a small parcel of land on a hillside on the outskirts of Kyoto.

In the interim, he departed from the Samurai preference for Zen Buddhism because of its minimal immediacy and joined the Cheng-Zhu school of Neo-Confucianism. He commissioned Kano Tan'yu to paint portraits of 36 Confucian poets that he selected, and wrote an inscription below each of them, giving this house the name Shisen no ma, or Hall of the Immortal Poets (Figure 18.1).[1]

He built it in 1641, at age 59, and lived there until his death 31 years later, conforming to the Confucian ideal of the hermit scholar. The engawa, between the Hall and the dry sand and satsuki azalea garden in the foreground of the garden and shakkei or borrowed landscape of incrementally higher trees further on, must have been the perfect place for him to meditate. A bamboo shishi-odoshi that fills with stream water and clacks down on a rock when it is full, used by farmers to scare deer away, is the only thing that breaks the silence, perhaps meant to intentionally interrupt his concentration, as a metronome to help pace his days and serve as a reminder, in the midst of his meditations, that life remains to be lived.

Mediating between alternative spatial realities

Azaleas also play an important role in another famous garden across the Pacific, at the Getty Museum in Los Angeles, completed by Richard Meier in 1997, and it serves as a particularly apt reminder of the essential difference between this paradigmatic example of the traditional Japanese attitude about the importance of the integration of architecture and nature, and the Western, Modernist aversion to it. The controversial design of the azalea garden by installation artist Robert Irwin is located between the museum and the Getty Research Institute (GRI) on the vast hilltop that also includes the Getty Conservation Institute, the Getty Foundation and the J. Paul Getty Trust. The Museum commissioned the garden after the complex was

Figure 18.1 Shisendo
Source: James Steele

complete to offset an impression of aloofness, and soften the edges of the complex. It is fittingly shaped like a lightning bolt, penetrating through the sterile perimeter of the Modernist citadel, offering a textured contrast to the idea that nature should be kept at a distance and only seen in distant views through framed openings.

In 1991, Tomohiro Yokomizu designed an entirely different kind of museum near a village north of Tokyo, in Azuma, which stands in sharp contrast to this deliberate distancing from environmental context. It is named for artist and poet Tomihiro Hoshino, who has overcome a tragic disability and is dedicated to the belief that nature can be irrational but not arbitrary and operates on principles that simply can't be explained.

It is sited along a lakeshore with mountains in the distance, and houses a permanent collection of 100 pieces of his work (Figure 18.2).

Inspired by soap bubbles, Yokomizu has flipped Kazuyo Sejima's use of boxes, as containers of art within a circle, in her 21st Century Museum in Kanazawa, by using circles of various sizes as the galleries, within a rectangular frame, to convey Hoshino's idea of interdependence. Consequently, the interior, with its interstitial spaces between circles, does meet the architect's wish to have it seem to be like a walk in the woods, creating a childlike sense of wonder and expectation. This marks an important evolution in the original notion of the engawa, since it is the areas of space between the circular spaces, not at the periphery

Figure 18.2 Tomihiro Museum
Source: Christoffer Rudquist

of the museum, that are the critical interstitial zones in the building (Figure 18.3).

Yokomizu has used a similar strategy of utilizing the gaps between curvatures to define differences in his NYH house, designed for a couple in Nagoya. In this case, the fissures symbolize the blurred boundaries between the living and working zones in the small residence. Thin, curved walls made of 9-millimeter-thick steel plates also allowed the entire building to be manufactured at a factory eight blocks away from the construction site and assembled very quickly (Figure 18.4).

Sou Fujimoto has invoked the engawa in a different way by skillfully weaving internal and external spaces together in his two-story Musashino Library, connected to a newly renovated Art Museum for the University (Figure 18.5). He has used a spiraling bookshelf to hold 100,000 volumes, with another 100,000 in closed archives, erasing conventional notions of differentiation between reading, reference and circulation areas and creating a seemingly endless layered landscape of shelving, light, glass and trees in all directions (Figure 18.6). He has also used bookshelves as the structure, also turning them outward and covering them with glass as a metaphor of the changing role of physical books in this venerable institution (Figure 18.7).

He has also explored spatial layering and the elimination of boundaries at a smaller scale in his remarkable House N in Oita, completed in 2008 (Figure 18.8). By using three nested envelopes he tests the concept of "in-between" since the outer skin, which covers the entire house, creates an indoor/outdoor garden, while the second is more restricted and the third defines interior space (Figure 18.9).

Two other residences that offer completely different interpretations of the engawa form are the Yomiuri Miyagi Guest house of 1997, an early work by Hitoshi

Figure 18.3 Tomihiro Museum
Source: Christoffer Rudquist

Figure 18.4 NYH House Yokomizu, NYH model
Source: Makoto Yokomizu

Abe in Zaou Miyagi Prefecture, and a house in Buzen, by Makoto Tanijiri of Suppose Design Office.

In his Yomiuri project, which is sheathed in dark cedar that gives it an ancient appearance, Abe has used the internal rotation of internal volumes to create fissures for circulation between them, ending in a clearly legible external engawa, screened from public view. By rotating the plan, however, he has been able to transform the established, linear quality of this type of space into a series of progressive, angular equivalents that remain true to the spirit of an intermediary zone, but amplify its intention (Figure 18.10). This is a markedly different approach than that taken in 2002 in his Town Centre Hall in the Shiki district in Reihoku in which vertical surfaces are angled to make origami-like forms that mitigate between internal and external space (Figure 18.11).

In his Buzen house, on the other hand, Makoto Tanijiri has interrogated the relationship between inside and outside differently by using an all-encompassing flat glass roof to cover a series of volumes, or rooms with pathways between them that seem to be randomly distributed beneath it, but have an internal logic of their own. These paths become wider courtyards or narrower slits to accommodate the daily life of the young family using them, making it possible to experience an outdoor ambience in the most inclement weather (Figure 18.12).

Each of these completely different, highly inventive re-interpretations of the engawa clearly demonstrate the seemingly endless ways that creative young Japanese architects today have been able to re-discover historical formulations, and to present them in new configurations.

Figure 18.5 Musashino Library plan
Source: Sou Fujimoto

Figure 18.6 Musashino Library
Source: Iwan Baan

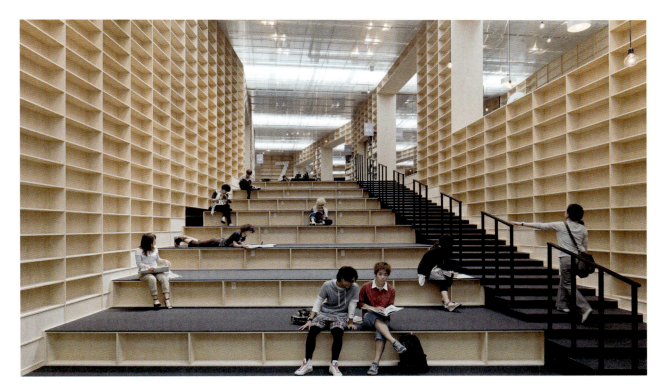

Figure 18.7 Musashino Library
Source: Iwan Baan

Figure 18.8 House N in Oita
Source: Iwan Baan

Figure 18.9 House N in Oita
Source: Iwan Baan

Figure 18.10 Yomiuri Miyagi Guest House, Daichi Ano
Source: Hitoshi Abe

Figure 18.11 Reihoku Town Hall, Daichi Ano
Source: Hitoshi Abe

Figure 18.12 Buzen House, Suppose Design Office photo
Source: Makoto Tanijiri

Note

1 J. Thomas Rimer, Hiroyuki Suzuki and Jonathan Chaves, *Shisendo: Hall of the Poetry Immortals*, Weatherhill, 1991.

CHAPTER 19

Reinventing Modernism

Modernism, in its full multitude of permutations, has been shown here to be one of the most pervasively recurring themes in the contemporary history of Japanese architecture. It is an enduring and endemic preoccupation among several younger practitioners and because of its past importance and enduring appeal, specific background information seems to be needed before reviewing their current work.

The movement is tied to the first "Machine Age" industrial economic cycle, and a compressed sequential chronological history is difficult because it evolved in different ways within the nations leading the Industrial Revolution that launched it.[1] A rough approximation, however, has it beginning in the United Kingdom and France, with the Crystal Palace, as the centerpiece of the Great Exhibition in London, 1851 and its French equivalent, the Galerie des Machines at the Universal Exposition built along with the Eiffel Tower, in Paris in 1889, marking the apogee of the declaration of manufacturing prowess by both countries.

Rather paradoxically, the beginning of the Modern movement itself, however, can be traced to Augustus W.N. Pugin, John Ruskin and William Morris and their conscientious awareness of the social problems caused by industrialization. Their outrage is perhaps best enunciated by Ruskin in his "Nature of the Gothic" chapter in his *Stones of Venice* trilogy, and the Arts and Crafts movement that finally emerged was formalized by Charles Robert Ashbee, at the Guild and School of Handicraft in 1888 and Peter Davey has made a

convincing case that this is the source of the Modern movement as it later emerged in Germany.[2]

The torch is passed to Germany

Having just united in 1871, Germany was eager to match the industrial production of the United Kingdom and France, and architect and diplomat Hermann Muthesius was sent to London in 1896 as a Cultural Attaché at the German Embassy to determine the reasons for British manufacturing might. He summarized his findings in *Das Englishe Haus*, (*The English House*), published upon his return in 1904. In it, he attributes British success to the simplicity of the Arts and Crafts aesthetic.

After his return to Germany, Muthesius joined the Prussian Board of Trade as a Privy Councilor and using this position as a platform, he advocated that Arts and Crafts principles be institutionalized as part of a national educational policy, called the Kunstgewerbeshule, or Schools of Arts and Crafts. These had been anticipated by earlier efforts, such as the Dresdener Werkstatten fur Handwerkskunst or Workshops for Artistic Craftsmanship, in Dresden, founded by Karl Schmidt in 1898, the Darmstadt Artist's Colony on the Mathildenhohe, supported by Grand Duke Ernst Ludwig of Hesse, in 1899, the new Workshops established in 1901 by the Wurttemberg Minister of Culture at the Stuttgart School of Applied Arts, run by Otto Kruger and Bernhard Pankok, and Peter Behrens's

United Workshops for Art in Handicraft (Kunst im Handwerk) in Dusseldorf of 1903. These workshops, such as the Kunstgewerbeshule at Dusseldorf, the United Workshops for Art in Handicraft in Munich and the Grand Ducal Saxon School of Arts in Weimar, directed by Henry van der Velde, were introduced into schools with pre-existing handcraft curricula and prominent artists and architects were appointed to direct them.

The founding of the Deutsche Werkbund

After openly criticizing the quality of German manufactured goods in a lecture in Berlin in 1907, Muthesius was accused of being unpatriotic by the National Association for the Economic Interests of the Arts and Crafts. This prompted him to establish the Deutsche Werkbund, or German Work Federation in Munich that same year, as a collaborative effort between design and industry to achieve what Muthesius described as "the ennoblement of commercial activity." Many of the 12 founding members of the Federation, and an equal complement of corporate affiliates, were later instrumental in the establishment of the Modern Movement in Germany, which shared its mission to create a new Kunstgewerbe, or "aesthetic culture" for the fledgling nation state.[3]

A legendary debate on Arts and Crafts principles

While all Werkbund members agreed that Germany needed to improve the quality of its product design in order to make it more competitive on the world market, there was a deep internal rift on how to achieve that goal, striking at the very core of the Arts and Crafts ethic of handicraft.

This conflict erupted at the first Deutsche Werkbund Exhibition held at the Rheinpark in Cologne early in 1914, just before the outbreak of the First World War. This fundamental difference of opinion over the issue of the extent of mass production was finally aired in a now legendary debate at the Exhibition over the issue of mass production, between Hermann Muthesius, as the proponent of creating types, or the standardization of the industrial process and Henry van de Velde, who advocated individual artistic freedom. Although it has now been reduced to the shorthand of "Norm versus Form" or type versus individuality, this argument involved the degree to which the individual worker should be allowed to participate in the manufacturing process. The basic agenda of the Werkbund was to improve efficiency, cut costs and to make products more saleable, without compromising high aesthetic standards. The economic potential inherent in finally balancing the equation, which William Morris and the British Arts and Crafts movement had failed to solve, of how to provide the highest quality products at a price that the common person could afford, was uppermost in the minds of the Werkbund members. New research has uncovered a more nuanced reading of this debate, which places Muthesius' advocacy of types or Typisierung, as opposed to Alois Reigl's theory of Kunstwollen or "will to form" as espoused by van der Velde, not just within the context of Wilhelmine hopes for commercial growth, but also its strategy for colonial expansion. In this recent reading, advocates of Muthesius' theory of Typisierung also supported increased government control of the Werkbund, to allow more efficiently organized production.

The rise of the Modern movement

Archduke Ferdinand of Austria was assassinated in Sarajevo on June 20, 1914. Emperor Franz Josef I of Austria then signed a declaration of war with Serbia, causing Russia to come to Serbia's defense. Because of treaty obligations with Austria and fear of a combined British, French and Russian attack, fueled by Russian mobilization, Germany declared war on Russia on August 1, and France on August 3, 1914. The devastating conflict that followed, which toppled the Austro-Hungarian Empire and led to the Russian Revolution, and lasted until the Armistice of November 11, 1918, was labeled "the Kaiser's War" by the tragically decimated remnant of the generation that experienced it, but the full extent of his blame is still being debated. What is incontrovertible is that after it ended, riots now referred to as "the November Revolution" broke out in Berlin in 1918 and Prince Maximilian of Baden, or Max von Baden, who was then the Chancellor of Germany, demanded the abdication of the Kaiser because of a lack of popular support for his rule. In a series of deft political maneuvers, Max von Baden arranged for power to be passed to the Social Democrats, led by Friedrich Ebert. As a result, Wilhelm II, the last Emperor of Germany and King of Prussia, was deposed and the reign of the House of Hohenzollern ended with him.

To avoid the ongoing factional struggle in Berlin, a national assembly was convened in Weimar on August 11, 1919, where a new constitution was drafted and ratified as the basis for a liberal parliamentary democracy. This new Deutsches Reich, which was called the Weimar Republic after the city where it was founded, lasted for 14 years before being displaced by Adolf Hitler and the National Socialist German Workers Party. It has three distinct phases, beginning with a period of crisis plagued by hyperinflation and political challenges from the right and left, from 1918 to 1922, followed by the "Golden Twenties" under the leadership of Gustav Stresemann from 1923 until 1929 and a final phase of decline from 1930 until the advent of National Socialism.

The first phase of the Weimar Republic

Little more than five years after the assassination of Archduke Ferdinand, Germany was forced to accept full responsibility for the First World War as stipulated in Articles 231 through 248 in the Treaty of Versailles, signed on June 28, 1919. In these "war guilt" clauses, Germany was required to pay 269 billion gold Marks in reparations, the equivalent of 100,000 tons of pure gold, which led to crippling economic hardships. In addition, its national borders were redrawn, and German territory was ceded to Denmark, Czechoslovakia, Belgium, France and Poland. Its overseas colonies were also divided up by several of the Allied powers and the loss of raw materials that they supplied as well as the destruction of its urban infrastructure by the war made economic recovery extremely difficult. After Germany defaulted on its reparation payments in January, 1923, French and Belgian troops occupied the Ruhr valley and remained there for two years to insure deliveries of coal that were part of the payment arrangement. To give a sense of the amount of the reparations required, it took Germany 92 years, until October 2010, to finally pay them in full.

Crippling reparations demanded in the Treaty of Versailles, which amounted to a version of economic warfare that replaced military conflict, drastically reduced the German capacity to buy goods. It also caused the value of the currency to fall, and the price of those goods that were available to rise. As people started to access their savings to augment their devalued income, billions of Marks entered the economy during the period right after the war causing a cycle of devaluation and inflation that caused hyperinflation.

The second phase of the Weimar Republic: the Golden Twenties

The second phase of the Weimar experiment was fueled by the financial stability that Gustav Stresemann, who was appointed Chancellor in 1923, was able to provide by resetting the value of German currency. He replaced the highly inflated Papiermark with the Rentenmark, bringing the exchange rate back to its prewar level. Stresemann also balanced the national budget by making deep cuts in government spending. The Dawes Plan of 1924, which allowed the United States to loan Germany the money it needed to bring its reparation payments up to date, also eased the path to financial recovery. In addition, Stresemann also negotiated the end of French presence in the Ruhr during this phase, made diplomatic progress with Russia and perhaps most importantly for internal stability, managed to keep both the Communist and National Socialist parties at bay.

This 10-year period, in the midst of the Weimar Republic, framed by the appointments of Gustav Stresemann as Chancellor in 1923 and Adolf Hitler in 1933, is now referred to as "the Golden Twenties" because it was also a time of cultural revival and greater creative freedom in the arts, mirroring the general relaxation of social mores that characterized the 1920s as a whole.

This halcyon age also provided a fertile, liberal atmosphere in which modern art and architecture could grow, in ways that had profound repercussions for the future. In architecture, this translated into the rejection of the familiar forms and techniques of the past.

The Modern movement found its full identity in Germany during this remarkably brief, decade-long period, building on the framework that the Deutsche Werkbund had provided. It wasn't an entirely new theoretical construct, but the final reconfiguration of that collaborative, resulting from the progress that the Federation had made, leavened by the shift of public sentiment away from the exclusive use of standardization. It was the culmination of the deliberate process of the institutionalizing of culture inaugurated by two Emperors, before the Weimar Republic started. Many of the leaders of the Movement, such as Walter Gropius and Ludwig Mies van der Rohe, fought in World War I and passionately believed that the production ethic of the Deutsche Werkbund, in combination with craft, contained within it the seeds of both the social redemption and physical reconstruction of the German state.

The Bauhaus

The remarkably brief timeline of the Staatliches Bauhaus, which has become synonymous with the beginning of the Modern movement in Germany, parallels that of the Weimar Republic, revealing how instrumental the liberal policies of that government were in fostering new artistic endeavors. Walter Gropius established the Bauhaus in 1919 at the Grand Ducal School of Arts and Crafts in Weimar, designed by Henry van der Velde in 1905.

In retrospect, the curriculum that Gropius instituted was a re-calibration of the Van der Velde-Muthesius, Typisierung vs. Kunstwollen debate, in his attempt to balance handicraft and standardization and finally integrate art and industry. Gropius was the consum-mate public relations expert and he ensured that the new school was heavily and very successfully marketed, which partially explains its legendary status today. It wasn't a coincidence that the cover of the first brochure produced in this concerted advertising campaign was a woodcut of a Gothic Cathedral, by Lyonel Feininger. The image of a cathedral, along with the subtle implication of the name Bauhaus, is clearly an allusion to German Gothic heritage.

Der Geist der Gotik, written by Karl Scheffler in 1917, provided the theoretical framework for the practical marriage that Gropius had in mind. It was published just before the end of World War I and in it, Scheffler goes much further than John Ruskin did in his chapter "The Nature of the Gothic" in *The Stones of Venice*, in not only equating the style with a communal spirit, but also with the ethnic essence of an entire nation. In *Der Geist der Gotik*, Scheffler equates the evolution of Gothic form with the German geist, or spirit, using an argument that is remarkably similar to that put forward by Wilhelm Worringer in *Formprobleme der Gotik*, or *Form Problems of the Gothic*, six years earlier. The word *geist* is difficult to translate but can mean either time, spirit or ghost depending on its context. It was popularized by Georg Wilhelm Friedrich Hegel in *Phänomenologie des Geistes*, or *The Phenomenology of Spirit* or *The Phenomenology of Mind*, in 1807.

Contrary to popular belief, the Bauhaus was not initially intended to be a school of architecture, but rather the realization of the Werkbund ideal of the pursuit of industrial excellence to improve German society, through the design and the fabrication of better products. The concentration on architecture increased after the school moved to Dessau in 1925, but at the outset the curriculum had a simple, two-part structure. The first section lasted for six months and involved painting and experiments with form; presented in the legendary "Vorkurs" or foundation course by Johannes Itten, who taught at Weimar from 1919 to 1922. It concentrated on the characteristics of different materials, as well as composition and color theory. The second phase of the curriculum involved three years of workshop training, divided between art and craft, under the supervision of experts in each field, as well as courses in the theory of architecture and field experience in construction.

During its short 14-year history, the Bauhaus revolutionized architecture and the educational system related to the profession. The Weimar Bauhaus, which started in 1919, was dissolved due to political and budgetary issues, moving to a new Gropius designed building in Dessau in 1924. This second school was supported by Mayor Fritz Hesse and the City Council and incorporated into the Municipal Schools of Arts and Crafts and Trade.

A sudden end but an enduring legacy

Gropius resigned as Director in 1928, two years after the completion of the Dessau Bauhaus, and chose Hannes Meyer to replace him. Meyer, however, proved to be very controversial and divisive because of his radical political views and was fired by Mayor Hesse in 1930. Gropius then appointed Ludwig Mies van der Rohe to replace Meyer in the hope that he could calm things down, but by then the balance of power in Dessau had shifted to the National Socialists and in 1932 the City legislature voted to dissolve the school and cancel all of its contracts. Mies van der Rohe attempted to re-open the Bauhaus in Berlin but was once again forced to close it in 1933.

With the 1929 Stock Market Crash in the United States and the Great Depression that followed, American assistance ended, which led to renewed unemployment and political instability in Germany. In the September 1930 elections the National Socialist German Workers Party received slightly more than 18 percent of the popular vote, making it the second largest party in the *Reichstag*. President Paul von Hindenburg then appointed three Chancellors in rapid succession until further instability forced him to dissolve the parliament twice in 1932 and appoint Adolf Hitler as Chancellor in January 1933.

Disseminating an ideology

The Weimar experiment and the artistic freedom it had fostered ended with that fateful appointment, and while Europe was embroiled in war, the next act of the Modernist movement then opened in the United States, with two of its leading proponents ensconced in important academic positions at both Harvard and the Illinois Institute of Technology. This led to sweeping changes, from Ecole des Beaux Arts to Modernist curricula at schools of architecture as well as the adoption of the position by many architects throughout the United States immediately after the war. The Case Study House Program in Los Angeles is but one of many possible examples of the proselytism that occurred during that time.

In the meantime, Le Corbusier, who had remained in France during the war and remained viable through an as yet unexamined relationship with the Vichy government, evolved his own Ecole-based strain of Rationalism, and opened up another front for the Modern movement that we have seen to be especially attractive to Japanese architects.

Many Modernisms

This abbreviated outline is intended to show that the term "modernism" as it relates to architecture is heavily freighted with complex layers of ideological inference, dating back to the industrial revolution, involving specific national agendas that are not relevant to external conditions and yet have produced formal constructs and attitudes that have proven to be irresistible to others for a variety of reasons.

Charles Taylor helps to unlock the puzzle of earlier Japanese overlays, as well as helping us to evaluate the recent work shown here, and separate it from this heavy ideological baggage, by offering up the possibility of "multiple modernities." In his view, in addition to other obvious exceptions in the developing world, such as Russian Constructivism, Dutch De Stijl, or other famous variants in Cuba, Czechoslovakia and Brazil, there are many non-Western entities, such as Japan, that have modernisms of their own that cannot be understood in the context of previous constructs. They do not conform to the process of "subtraction" from religious systems and metaphysical beliefs and the rise of individuality that Western Modernism engendered, in which economics and the idea of social equality displaced traditional social values. They do not share the same "social imaginary" or way that they envision their collective existence, and do not see themselves as part of an economy in the Western sense, of being part of "an interlocking set of activities of production and consumption which form a system with its own laws and dynamic."[4]

The high-tech factor

In addition to Taylor's useful admonition, and in addition to other mainstream variants in Germany, France and the United States, it is also necessary to factor in the influence of the British High-Tech refinement of the Modernist position that distills its essence, since this is also legible in recent work in Japan. There are several clearly identifiable features of this particular approach, filtered through the historical course of progressive constructs in the United Kingdom since the Industrial Revolution and the rapid completion of the Crystal Palace of 1851. These are a tendency to celebrate and flaunt technology by treating a building as a large piece of equipment as well as a self-contained Arcadia, or all-encompassing Utopia that can be dismissive or free of its context and all other cultural iconography, and the habit of perpetuating the mythology of the efficacy of prefabrication, rapid construction and ultimate flexibilty as a panacea against future irrelevance.[5]

The mantra of prefabrication

This last position, of valorizing prefabrication, is most visible in a small, five story apartment building in the Shibuya district of Tokyo, completed by Kumiko Inui

in 2005, in which she has derived one unit type which switches position on each floor plate, as does the stair core, to increase the sense of variety and space (Figure 19.1). It is also apparent in the NYH house by Makoto Yokomizo, which is a private four story studio and residence on a very narrow site in the densely urban Naku district in the middle of Nagoya, mentioned earlier as a contemporary example of the use of the traditional Japanese concept of the engawa (Figure 19.2). Yokomizu had the interlocking metal panels, used to divide the spaces on each of its four floors, manufactured and factory assembled and then transported and craned into place on site.

Déjà vu in Beijing

Keiichiro Sako has used prefabrication to great effect at a much larger scale in Beijing in a mixed use, housing and commercial project that is in the best tradition of

Figure 19.1 Kumiko Inui Apartments
Source: Daici Ano

Figure 19.2 NYH House
Source: Makoto Yokomizo

Figure 19.3 BUMPS, Model
Source: Keiichiro Sako

the Japanese Metabolists (Figure 19.3). In designing his BUMPS building, which combines commercial use on the lower level, with four residential towers above, he contradicted a local feng-shui convention of orienting houses in a north-south direction because of density issues to allow maximum sunlight into each residence and shorten circulation routes by rotating them 45 degrees off this axis. The towers are 80 meters high, with many of top floors of the two-story units cantilevered forward by two meters, to create shade for those below (Figure 19.4). Black and white color-coding, which recalls that used in Sako's free-standing BEANS Bookstore in Kanazawa, Japan, built two years earlier in 2006, also creates a strong visual image. All windows are one meter square, adding to the stacked shipping container image so beloved of advocates of prefabrication (Figure 19.5).

Figure 19.4 BUMPS, Beijing NDC Studio, Inc
Source: Misae Hiromatsu

Figure 19.5 BEANS
Source: Tomio Ohashi

A fluid internal landscape, and three houses

The high-tech emphasis on flexibility also appears, with an important qualification, in an unexpectedly modest way in the Lotus beauty salon in Kuwana City, in Mie Prefecture, by Hiroshi Nakamura and NAP architects. In this relatively modest project, he has achieved a sense of openness by carefully balancing a unifying structure with enclosures that would provide each customer with a sense of privacy and his solution was to use a long, lid-like roof supported by thin columns, covering a serpentine wall that curves into protective niches that enfold the reception area and each work station (Figure 19.6).

The private residence, however, has always been gold standard of Modernist sensibilities, and this remains true with the latest generation of Japanese architects as well. Three houses by Makoto Tanijiri, and

Suppose Design, in Otake, Bishamon and Kitakamakura, are clear indicators of consistency as well as reinterpretation.

His Otake house is sited on a high ridge overlooking the Seto Inland Sea and Miyajima adjacent to the ruins of Kamei Castle near Hiroshima (Figure 19.7). To take advantage of spectacular views from the hilltop, he flipped conventional public/private stacking and located the bedrooms on the ground floor of the square footprint, below the living, dining and kitchen functions, with a sizable patio, under a six-meter wide eave, facing north toward the Sea. To provide a sense of surprise, most of the entire exterior is coated in a black waterproof wrapping except for the fragile glazing of the northern side of the house, which contrasts dramatically with the closed, southern entry elevation (Figure 19.8).

Tanijiri has used a similar strategy of closing down the entrance elevation at the back, and opening up toward views in the front in his mixed use Bishamon project also located on a similarly breathtaking overlook near Hiroshima. In this case, however, a steep slope required that it be elevated on pilings, and the lower level is given over to a café and domestic uses above (Figure 19.9).

The sloping site of the Kitakamakura residence, in Kanagawa, was even more difficult to negotiate, forcing him to create a series of retaining walls to hold back the hill and use steel beams bridging between two concrete pillars to sequentially elevate the floors of the rectangular plan, with the long sides perpendicular to the slope, while still minimizing excavation as much as possible. Unlike his two Hiroshima houses, he has placed the entry at the bottom of the slope here, and has located the private zone at the top, encased in a concrete shell that literally anchors the house to the site, and the way it angles outward is very reminiscent of the 1965 Inter-University Seminar House, in Hachioji Tokyo by Le Corbusier's disciple Takamasa Yoshizaka (Figure

19.10). The glass sides of the long rectangle are the most eloquent and elegant part of the concrete and wood frame house; the interior in an ever-changing rainbow of light (Figure 19.11).

A critical difference

The topic of Critical Regionalism concludes this highly selective and necessarily compressed review of the contemporary renewal of the final episode of the first cycle of the Modernist saga.

Tzonis and Lefaivre founded a multidisciplinary research institute at Delft University of Technology in 1985, which led to their realization of a reaction to the growing phenomenon of globalization in architecture and urban planning. Through a series of books, articles and conferences over the next 20 years, they honed the idea of "region" as well as the interaction between social and cultural resources they considered necessary to define one.

Figure 19.6 Lotus Beauty Salon
Source: Hiroshi Nakamura

Figure 19.7 Otake House
Source: Toshiyuki Yano

Figure 19.8 Otake House
Source: Toshiyuki Yano

Figure 19.9 Bishamon
Source: Toshiyuki Yano

Figure 19.10 Kitakamakura
Source: Toshiyuki Yano

After initial articles about Critical Regionalism appeared in "The Grid and the Pathway" and *Fur Eine Andere Architektur* by Fisher-Taschenbuch Verlage they published a series of books on this topic, which are now classics.[6] Their encyclopedic knowledge of Western history lends credence to their theory and, in addition to these essential texts Tzonis has provided important extemporaneous references to help explain it, in his public lectures, and these deserve parenthetical mention because they offer a deeper insight into the core idea of Critical Regionalism.

He suggests, for example, that the regionalist imperative against global similarity isn't new, but started as far back as the Roman Empire, since it was the first truly global power and imposed a uniform economic structure, language, legal system, cultural norms and set of architectural typologies over the entirety of its vast territorial enterprise. The devastation and the economic collapse that it left in its wake is proof of its unifying might, since over the next century, people simply forgot that it took the Romans centuries to learn about building. As a result, the Western world was cast back into autonomous regions, intensifying the need to bring back a universal political system.

Different regions and proto-national entities began to compete culturally to become the New Rome, and this desire for an organized system later became manifest in French garden design. In its attempt to recover classical rules and translate them into landscaped space, it provides an important insight about the connection between societal organization and attitudes toward nature. The dissemination of this kind of highly formalized garden started to eliminate diversity, and like the imposition of Roman order, once again separated

Figure 19.11
Kitakamakura
Source: Toshiyuki Yano

society from the reality of nature. The formal French garden of the Ancien Régime was unable to conform to the new historical trend toward market economics that first began to emerge in England during the Industrial Revolution, while British gardens, which were designed to look organic, even if they were highly structured, were also the landscaped equivalent of the political and economic systems at the time.

Tzonis feels that Johann Wolfgang von Goethe is one of the best examples of Regionalist imperative in the national sphere since he was a key figure in the National Romantic movement and emphasized local customs, values and traditions because he was stung by French and Italian characterizations of Germans as being barbarians. He turned to German Gothic architecture, and specifically toward the Cathedral of Strasbourg, as a clear indication of how a building can reflect traditional values and yet reflect the advances of its own time and still allow the architect to have creative freedom. Goethe used it, and his intellectual interaction with the building, as a way of gaining confidence, seeing it as a symbol of the genius of the people, not through rules, but through irrational emotion. He said architecture creates dreams and visions, and out of those establishes identity.

Tzonis also lists John Ruskin as another good example of the Regionalist ethos because of his idea that architecture is not just a visual but also an economic art revealed by the process of production. Ruskin introduced the principle that the role of architecture is to both create and sustain communal relationships and lifestyle, and took his inspiration from the regional domestic buildings of the past, which he saw as an antidote to the social problems related to a modern, capitalistic society, addicted to consumption.)

These seemingly disparate insights by Tzonis and Lefaivre tell us that beyond the specific examples of architects who are attempting to synthesize Modernist principles with local traditions that they describe in their books, there is a deeper, historical meaning to Critical Regionalism related to resistance against the growth of global capitalism, which is directly associated with national pride.[7]

Evoking the Lord of Sendai in concrete

Hitoshi Abe personifies that mixture, because he has approached the question of how best to re-interpret the classic Modernist language in a uniquely Japanese way, by using formal juxtapositions that bridge the gap between the two. He first gained international recognition by winning the competition in 1992 to design and build Miyagi Stadium in Sendai, Japan, while still a student at Sci-Arc in Los Angeles and working in an office there. He based his concept on the curved shape of the helmet of the Daimyo Date Masamune, who is a local hero in Sendai, and controlled the region from the late sixteenth to the mid-seventeenth century, by pushing back against encroachment by both Hideyoshi Toyotomi and Ieyasu Tokugawa (Figure 19.12).

On the other hand, his Sasaki-Gishi Medical Services Offices, which was completed in 2004 and includes a factory for the production of prostheses, explores the traditional courtyard typology, re-interpreted here as a six meter square glass enclosure in the center of the complex that allows both physical and visual interaction between office and factory workers.

Figure 19.12 Miyagi Stadium, Shunichi Atsumi
Source: Hitoshi Abe

Figure 19.13 Sasaki-Gishi, Daichi Ano
Source: Hitoshi Abe

The exterior precast concrete walls, which are made of post-stressed concrete and then stacked, however, clearly follow the Modernist conceit of revealing how they were made, creating the contrasting dialogue between regional and global methodologies that Tzonis and Lefaivre explicate (Figure 19.13).

A concrete, steel and glass machiya

These qualifications are also well represented by the work of Waro Kishi, who was born in Yokohama in 1950 and received his degree from the Department of Electronics from University of Kyoto. In 1973 he established Waro Kishi, Architect & Associates, in Kyoto, followed by Waro Kishi + K. Associates/ Architects, also in Kyoto, from 1992 until the present.

Although Kishi technically fits within our earlier discussion about other architects of his generation,

such as Kazuo Sejima, Kengo Kuma and Jun Aoki, he has been included here because he embodies both the economic and national dimensions that Tzonis and Lefaivre refer to, since he has been particularly adept not only at recognizing the value of Western technology, but also pushing back against it to express a uniquely Japanese aesthetic.

He politely rails against the Modernist label that started to be applied to him soon after he completed his first notable commission, for a house in Nipponbashi in 1992, simply because this superficial reading fails to recognize this inherent duality. One reason for all the attention, however, was that he managed to fit this "eel's nest" into an impossibly small 2.5-meter wide and 13-meter deep site in downtown Osaka. It recalls the typical shop-houses that graced the city during the Edo period, with the retail space facing the street, and the living area behind an open courtyard

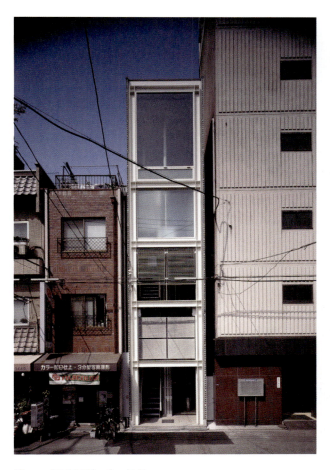

Figure 19.14 Nihonbashi House
Source: Hiroyuki Hirai

Figure 19.15 Nakagyo, Waro Kishi
Source: Hiroyuki Hirai

Figure 19.16 Nakagyo, Waro Kishi
Source: Hiroyuki Hirai

in the middle. This house is a refined translation of the machiya, in Modernist materials (Figure 19.14). In spite of site restrictions, Kishi has also managed to provide his elderly clients with a dignified, generously proportioned upper level by suppressing the lower three floors, and in doing so has also courageously defied stereotypes about confining the elderly to the ground floor, in this clear statement that age is as much a mental as a physical state. The top floor, which has a 6 meter high ceiling, includes an open-air terrace, occupies a large portion of the entire envelope, and seems detached from the urban chaos below.

Like the select few who have also travelled extensively outside Japan, Kishi also sought out Le Corbusier and Louis Kahn, and the roof garden, which is the last of the five points, which Kishi has described as being revolutionary, was an obvious inspiration here as well as elsewhere.

The roof garden refined in Nagakyo

He has distilled this concept of the detached and lofty aerie in a 4.2-meter wide and 13.4-meter long three-story house on a corner of the mixed-use commercial and residential district of Nakagyo in the southern part of Kyoto (Figure 19.15). It was designed for an antique dealer, with public space on the ground floor and a residence above, and in spite of its constricted space, Kishi was able to carve out an open central courtyard in the middle of the lot, which includes the stairs leading up to the bedrooms and living-dining area above (Figure 19.16). The upper floor was inspired by Le Corbusier's little-known Beistegui House, which is essentially a deck with a flat roof, facing the Arc de Triomphe and the Champs Elysees. Kishi adapts it here in a space that seems to float above the city below, presenting the skyline as a distant panorama, and proves his willingness to assimilate Modernist spatial concepts.

Notes

1   See Reynar Banham, *Theory and Design in the First Machine Age*, Cambridge, MA: MIT Press, 1980.

2   Peter Davey, *Arts and Crafts Architecture*, London: Phaidon, 1997.

3   Hermann Muthesius, *Style-Architecture and Building-Art: Transformations of Architecture in the Nineteenth Century and Its Present Condition*, Chicago: University of Chicago Press, 1996, p. 62.

4   Charles Taylor, *Modern Social Imaginaries*, Durham: Duke University Press, 2004, p. 162.

5   Peter Buchanan, "High-Tech," *Architectural Review*, July 1983, pp. 34–37.

6   See Alexander Tzonis and Liane Lefaivre, *Critical Regionalism, Architecture and Identity in a Globalized World*, Prestel, 2003 and *Architecture of Regionalism in the Age of Globalization, Peaks and Valleys in the Flat World*, Routledge, 2011.

7   Alexander Tzonis, "Critical Regionalism," Architectural Forum of Southwest China, the China South West Architectural Design Institute (CSWADI), the Museum of Contemporary Art, Chengdu, January 10–11, 2015.

CHAPTER 20

Technology as nature

A subconscious reminiscence of the forest that once covered Japan seems to still be a defining part of the collective memory of the nation. This narrative began with instances of its origins, starting with the Shinto foundation myth itself, when creators Inazagi and Izanami descended to Onogoro-shima, which was the first island to emerge after droplets from the spear they dipped into the primordial ocean started to form an archipelago below. They built a dwelling around a central pillar there, and circled around it in opposite directions, while exchanging their vows.

Later in the myth, trees are also central to the memorable story of how deities gathered on Takama-ga-hara, or the "high plain of heaven" to find a way to lure the daughter of Izanagi and Izanami, the Sun Goddess Amaterasu out of a cave she had hidden in to escape the brutality of her brother Susano-o, and bring light back to the cosmos. They sent a delegation to Mount Kaga to dig up, rather than cut down, a large sasaki tree to avoid disrupting its life force and after placing it in front of the cave, festooned its upper branches with jewels, placed a long mirror in the middle, and strung blue and white ornaments around the bottom. Then Ama-no-Uzume, the Shinto goddess of revelry, performed an erotic dance for the entire group, wearing only a moss sash and sasaki leaf headdress. When Amaterasu heard the music and the raucous laughter and saw the jewels and her reflection in the mirror on the sasaki tree through a crack in the rock sealing the cave, she came out, and a shimenawa, or rice straw rope, was placed across the mouth of the cave to prevent her from returning.

Shinto myth also holds that the "three treasures" of the mirror, or Yata-no-Kagami, the jewels, or Magatama, and a sword called Kusanagi-no-tsurugi, given to Amaterasu by Susano-o to atone for his bad behavior, were passed on by Amaterasu to her son Ame no Oshihomimi no Mikoto, and then to her grandson named Ninigi-no-Mikoto, and then to Jimmu, the legendary first Emperor of Japan. It also maintains that the sword is kept at the Atsuta Shrine in Nagoya, a single jewel at the Imperial Palace in Tokyo and the mirror is at the Grand Shrine of Ise. The cyclical renewal of the Ise Shrine, which includes the relocation of this mirror, from one representation of Amaterasu's earthly shelter to another, also centers around the reconstruction of a "heart pillar" or shim-bashira, considered to be the conduit of her spirit between heaven and earth.

The Izumo Shrine in Shimane Prefecture, which is associated with Susano-o, has also been described here as being organized around a central pillar, while four equally ancient structures that comprise the Shinto Shrine at Suwa in Nagano, recall the Sasaki tree and shimenawa in another way, through reference to a himorogi, or "divine fence," or square area, with a sasaki tree at each corner and shiminawa between, and a single sasaki tree, or yorishiro in the middle, representing the kami, or deity in the center. Himorogi are still common on building sites in Japan, and a Shinto priest asks the Kami to forgive disruption of the earth in a jichinsai ceremony before construction begins.

The Onbashira Festival at Suwa, which is held every six years rather than following the 20-year cycle at Ise, dates back to the seventh century, and first involves the Yamadashi, or cutting down of 16 enormous trees for the corner posts of each of the shrines, and then the Kiotoshi, in which they are pushed down a steep slope from the forest to the site below. During this second ceremony, the people ride on the backs of the logs, or "Onbashira", to wild applause from more than a million onlookers.

As these ancient cultural associations suggest, trees have always had sacred meaning for Japanese carpenters who are renowned for being able to elicit the essential character of the wood they work with. A personal recollection of a story told to me by architect Kazuhiro Ishii gives an insight into this unusually high degree of sensitivity, related to his experience as a student volunteer during the restoration of the roof beams of the Daibutsu at Todai-ji, between 1976 and 1980. He remembers hearing the huge roof beams groan as they straightened after the heavy clay tiles were removed from them, convincing him that they were still alive, and inspiring him to work primarily with wood from that time on.

The Daibutsu certainly marks the apogee of Buddhist influence in Japan during the Nara period, as well as the use of wood for a single project, since thousands of acres around it were stripped of the giant hinoki trees that were used in the great hall, as well as the two pagodas and numerous entry gates of its first iteration. More were felled for its smaller main hall, rebuilt in 1181, by the Buddhist monk Shunjôbô Chôgen. It was re-built once again in the early eighteenth century at an even more reduced scale, but still ranks as the largest wooden building in the world.

Wood continued to be the primary construction material throughout the nation until the systematic adoption of Western values took place during the Meiji Restoration. In yet another remarkable internal transformation, Japanese carpenters then re-directed their ancestral skills toward industrial alternatives. Their guilds were similarly re-organized into groups that eventually morphed into the "big six" construction companies, which are Kajima Corporation, Takenaka, Obayashi Corporation, Kumagai Gumi, Tasiai Corporation and Shimizu, today.

After World War II ended, the urban transformation of Japan, from cities of wood to concrete, steel, aluminum, brick and glass, was complete, and the architecture described previously here confirms that radical shift, with architects attempting to excel in the use of these inert materials. The only difference has been in the degree of resistance to or adaptations of external paradigms. In these singular lexicons, tile was applied to concrete to make it more resistant to humidity, or the ingredients of the mix, the crafting of forms and sharpness of the edges of the snap-tie holes were emphasized to re-invent it, or the level of concentration once lavished on wooden joints was transferred to the way steel beams and joists meet.

What has changed, however, is there has now been a subtle shift toward an attempt to re-imagine how architecture can be re-united with nature that seems prevalent throughout the contemporary period in Japan, in commemoration and recognition of the immutable cultural relationship between the two, and this has now been distilled in more literal and reflective ways that reveal a new aesthetic.

Visually slicing the forest into strips

Takei-Nabeshima Architects (TNA) have contributed to this perceptible shift, for example, with their design of a tower-like residence they have called the Ring House, on the exclusive enceinte of Owner's Hill 185 miles north-west of Tokyo (Figure 20.1). It takes its name from the alternating belts of wood and glass that enclose it that paradoxically allow it to blend into the Karuizawa forest around it. These bands, which were sized according to the amount of openness or privacy that was necessary inside, act like the stripes on a zebra to de-materialize the house. They are faced with wood and stained black, and because the vertical supports holding up each floor are white, the solid rings seem to hover.

An alternative reading, however, is that rather than stitching architecture and nature together, the rings visually manage to systematically eliminate the surrounding forest when seen from inside, because they slice it into disjointed horizontal panoramas. Like the different times of the day, and in each season of the year,

Figure 20.1 Takei-Nabeshima Architects (TNA) Ring House
Source: Daichi Ano

adapting perfectly to fog, or rain or snow, just like the woodland it shares (Figure 20.2).

Hugging the trees

Young architects Hiroshi Nakamura and Takaharu and Yui Tezuka have each taken a different approach, seeking to integrate with, rather than blend into the terrain by building around it.

In his lyrically named "Dancing Trees, Singing Birds" project for example, Nakamura sought to erase what he has termed the "dichotomy" he believes exists between architecture, people and the natural environ-

ment in this housing complex in Tokyo, by saving as many of the trees in a large wooded grove on the sloping site as possible. He started by consulting an arborist to determine how close to the roots of the existing trees he could place the foundation of the relatively large building without damaging them (Figure 20.3). He also constructed a three-dimensional digital map of the root system, as well as recording all trees with branches over 15 centimeters and then used computer simulation to predict how his intervention would perform within this ecosystem, as well as in extreme weather events. This resulted in irregularly shaped rooms based on both current conditions and simulated growth

Figure 20.2 Takei-Nabeshima Architects (TNA) Ring House, Interior
Source: Daichi Ano

patterns, so that large trees are now interspersed with the houses and are visually present throughout the complex (Figure 20.4).

Takaharu and Yui Tezuka have similarly sought to save as much of the existing landscape on the site of their Fuji Kindergarten project in the Tachikawa district of Tokyo as possible, finally managing to allow three large Zelkova trees to remain, which project through the roof of the oval school. They have conceived of it as a small, enclosed village for 500 students with an open courtyard in the center that allows them to play safely, and the trees provide them with a constant physical connection with the environment (Figure 20.5).

Accessible abstraction

Instead of saving trees in his design for the Kanagawa Institute of Technology or KAIT, Junya Ishigami has designed a forest of 305 steel surrogates of his own. He first imagined this facility as a place where students could work within a colonnade, laid out on a regular 4-meter grid, within a single, 2,000-square-meter rectilinear space. As time went on and the client reacted by requesting spaces of various sizes, he began to feel constricted by it, and changed direction, seeking freedom from geometric rules following patterns of omission, rather than repetition (Figure 20.6).

Figure 20.3 Hiroshi Nakamura, Dancing Trees, Singing Birds
Source: Hiroshi Nakamura and NAP

Figure 20.4 Hiroshi Nakamura, Dancing Trees, Singing Birds, Interior
Source: Hiroshi Nakamura and NAP

Figure 20.5 Takaharu and Yui Tezuka, Fuji Kindergarten
Source: Katsuhisa Kida, Fototeca

Figure 20.6 Kanagawa Institute of Technology or KAIT, Junya Ishigami
Source: Iwan Baan

Figure 20.7 Kanagawa Institute of Technology or KAIT, Junya Ishigami, Column plan
Source: Junya Ishigami Office

Figure 20.8 Sou Fujimoto, NA House, Tokyo
Source: Iwan Baan

He found instead that trying to replicate a forest was more difficult than he imagined, and realized that

> just to contemplate one of the columns is to deal with 304 others with which it actually has a specific and equal relationship ... I had the feeling the space would not work unless I tried to find a way to connect such things as imagery and perception, directly to some undetectable system of shaping spaces and environments.[1]

While he started with very free hand drawings, his final, extremely precise computer renderings of each column location belie his desire for randomness, but he did succeed in creating the feeling of a forest. The glazed

wrapper also reflects the cherry trees surrounding the Institute, when they are in bloom, completing the culturally specific metaphor (Figure 20.7).

A tree-house or a house like a tree?

Sou Fujimoto has also tried to recreate the feeling of living within a forest in his NA House in Tokyo, which also is a continuation of his singular, experimental search for previously untested architectural experiences. This fanciful version of a tree has 21 individual floor plates representing the branches intended to provide spaces for different kinds of activities. These vary in size from 2 to 10 square meters, and are each connected by stairs or ladders of different types. As in

Figure 20.9 Tree House, Mount Fuji Architects Studio
Source: Kinchi Suzuki

a tree, noise also carries and individuality is intentionally relative, to juxtapose the feeling of privacy with connectivity, and amplify the experience of unity within it (Figure 20.8).

In addition to the inter-relationship between architecture with the city, Fujimoto also started investigating its connection with furniture very early in his career. During a visit to a large market hall in Vietnam he was inspired by a shopkeeper who was sleeping on the counter of her stall and realized that furnishings can be reinvented, depending on circumstances. He has implemented this overlap in the scale of the platforms used throughout this house, in which each acts like a room, and the steps between the floors serve many functions.

A spiraling replica

Also motivated by the need to reintroduce nature, or at least an artificial facsimile of it, into the midst of the visual disarray of Tokyo, Mount Fuji Architects Studio has also attempted to create an arboreal replica in their own Tree House on an extremely small 80-square-meter lot hemmed in on all sides by other buildings.

Rather than using platforms, however, the branches in this case increase in scale as they swirl outward from a massive central core, to conjure up bucolic scenography within a very small frame. More specifically this "column-beam" frame structure is made of 32 laminated veneer members, each 51 millimeters thick, rotated 11.25 degrees into a complete circle. As they do, each "branch" is 55 millimeters higher than the previous one, creating an elegant spiral (Figure 20.9).

In spite of the different approaches used by each of these architects, their projects offer ample evidence of a discernable reverence for and recollection of the part that nature and the Shinto tradition has played in Japanese history and the enduring relationship between the two.

Note

1   Junya Ishigami, *Small Images*, LIXIL Publishing, 2008, pp. 33–34.

CHAPTER 21

Searching for the sublime

Enclaves of idealism continue to survive in various parts of the world today that are typically still in the midst of the industrializing cycle and some architects in them still adhere to the belief that they serve a common good, and that what they do has the capacity to change people's lives.

In Brazil, for example, which is mid-way through a particularly bumpy development curve, it is still possible for those of a certain age to experience a strong sense of déjà vu, as if entering a parallel universe that hasn't changed in 50 years. Its capital, Brasilia, is the most obvious instance of this anomaly, but Sao Paulo, which is the financial hub of the nation, is also caught in an architectural time warp, as well.

It is the birthplace of the eponymous Paulista School, founded by João Batista Vilanova Artigas, Oswaldo Bratke, Joaquim Guedes and Paulo Mendes da Rocha in response to the curvilinear Carioca School of Oscar Neimeyer, Affonso Eduardo Reidy, Sergio Bernardes and the three Roberto brothers, based in Rio de Janerio. Paulista architecture is characterized by a brooding, rectilinear, overtly Brutalist monumentality, as seen in 2006 Pritzker Prize Laureate de Rocha's Museum of Brazilian Sculpture, in Sao Paulo (Figure 21.1). He has placed a majority of the museum underground, beneath an impressive, 97-foot long, 39-foot wide horizontal beam that cuts diagonally across an open plaza above that recalls the outstretched arms of the equally gravity defying Cristo Redentor or Christ the Redeemer statue at the top of Mount Corcovado in Rio de Janerio. Like that recent addition to the Seven Wonders of the World, Mendes da Rocha's massive concrete span also seems to welcome everyone, in spite of socio-economic background, to come forward, but in his case beckons them into a museum, which is often seen as an enclave of privilege.

This is consistent with his egalitarian principles, and those of the movement he represents, in which deliberately non-representational, rectilinear forms proclaim a socially responsible architectural ideology similar to that first established in Germany in 1918. High seriousness is called for in it because it contends that the well-being of the collective souls of humankind are at stake, leaving no time for whimsy, which seems to be another preoccupation of young architects in Japan today. That new tendency also seems to include a palpable yearning to discover the essence of the sublime, as Edmund Burke defined it, as the ineffable aura inherent in natural forces, capable of moving us more profoundly than beauty because it instills apprehension, as the perfect antidote to ennui.

Disillusionment transitioning to frivolity

Having now survived the throes of rapid development, this generation is no longer burdened by idealism, having exchanged it for post-industrial disillusionment several decades ago. But quite paradoxically, the cynicism that is an endemic part of the contemporary

Figure 21.1 Paulo Mendes de Rocha, Museum of Brazilian Sculpture, in Sao Paulo
Source: James Steele

condition now seems to have morphed into an attempt to find an alternative, in a search for subliminal intangibility. While other architects of their generation elsewhere in the world are increasingly relying on a rapidly expanding menu of computer aided design software and often start exploring formal solutions on screen almost immediately, their counterparts in Japan largely resist the lure of this technological imperative. Instead, they adopt an almost child-like approach to design, typically prefaced by illusory sketches, and this has resulted in a total rejection of conventional rules and assumptions to an extent not seen in earlier generations.

Their rejection of the computer during the conceptual stage seems counter-intuitive, since Japan has the reputation of being the most electronically wired nation in the world, and all the more noteworthy for that reason, begging the question of why this is so. It is a difficult premise to prove but may stem from an intuitive understanding of the essential dialectic that has been a leitmotif throughout this narrative, of an innate historical awareness of the dangers inherent in allowing algorithms to paralyze instinct.

Random order to calm the mind

Several projects by Sou Fujimoto help us to understand this subliminal search. He was born in Hokkaido, and was immediately struck by the difference between its relatively unspoiled natural beauty and the visual chaos of urban life when he started studying architecture at Tokyo University. After graduating in 1994, he resisted the typical trajectory of either apprenticing in an office or pursuing further education and simply decided to take time out to think about the current state of his profession, and how he wanted to engage with it. As he got to know Tokyo better, he began to see similarities rather than diametrically opposed differences between small details, such as the canopies, branches and leaves of the trees in the forests he liked to explore back home and the minutiae of streetscapes, such as the visual cacophony of telephone poles, layered signage and overhanging wires he encountered during this peripatetic interlude, having to do with scale and intensity. Inspired by the British artist Richard Long, who has also explored the idea of creating landscapes by walking, connecting a disparate number of places together over time, Fujimoto came to realize, as Louis Kahn put it, that the street itself is a room. He decided to rent several spaces along his daily route to serve his several different needs of studying, sketching, sleeping, eating, washing and sleeping, connected by alleyways as corridors, thereby challenging the conventional idea that a house need be a single object or structure.

The house as the city, the city as a house

The relationship between this realization and the experience of the sublime, caused by natural forces, begins with an apartment complex that he has designed for Shunzo Ueda, who needed to generate rental income on a small property he owned in Tokyo after a family medical emergency forced him to give up his regular job.

To contend with the extremely tight 83-square-meter site boundary, Fujimoto conceived of the collective cluster as four individual two-room houses, including one for the owner, stacked up into an artificial mountain. These are connected by both interior and exterior stairways that are intentionally precarious to convey the feeling of scaling a peak, reinforcing Burke's concept of transcendence. Achieving this sleight of hand, of making each apartment seem to hover almost weightlessly above the other, required considerable effort and skill, with a structural system that is mostly hidden from view (Figure 21.2). Each unit also conforms to a universally understood, gable-roofed shape, recalling Robert Venturi's description of his iconic design for his mother's residence in Chestnut Hill as a "child's drawing of a house," as well as Kazuo Shinohara and his insight that a singular dwelling contains within it all of the essential elements of a city. Fujimoto also views this collective as Tokyo in microcosm and as the background landscape for residents looking out at it from their mountaintop aerie.

In attempting to make this connection, Fujimoto also joins other young architects and firms who are pushing back against urban constriction, such as Mt. Fuji, discussed earlier in Chapter 17, who have used perforated steel plate stenciled with images of a cherry tree orchard enveloping their Sakura house in Meguro, to conjure up a forest, or Hitoshi Abe, whose as yet unrealized 2,165-square-meter Bouno House in the Ohji section of Tokyo, designed in collaboration with Masahige Motoe, also conveys the impression of a mountain (Figure 21.3).

Between nature and architecture

The idea of the house as a city, and architecture as landscape, also helped to formulate Fujimoto's Children's Center for Psychiatric Rehabilitation in his birthplace in Hokkaido Prefecture, which was conceived of as having both the intimacy of a house, and the collective liveliness of a small city. To realize this paradox he has used blocks of the same size scattered about in what seems to be what he calls an "accidental landscape," which actually has a precise internal logic of its own. This allows for high density, yet also provides a sense of open-ended unpredictability and infinity variety, in which children can play in groups, and find privacy, if they want to (Figure 21.4).

Louis Kahn rhetorically asked: "how far is too far and how near is too near," in placing many different elements within an artificially constrained boundary in referring to his unrealized design for the Motherhouse for the Dominican Congregation of St. Catherine de Ricci in Media, Pa, which also has a deceptively hectic plan.[1] While he uses elements with the same square shape, without a discernable perimeter, Fujimoto's site plan has a similar sense of rightness and appropriate distances between spaces. There are multiple centers within this similarity, for both the staff and the patients, all under a single roof, which is not legible from the jagged perimeter (Figure 21.5).

The primordial hut

Fujimoto has only used one cube for his Wooden House in Kumamoto, made by stacking up 350-millimeter or roughly 14-inch square beams to create an enclosure, with irregularly spaced gaps between them for louvered glazing. In addition to the walls, these beams also serve as the internal structure, the walls, floor, ceiling and furniture, erasing all previous distinctions between these categories. This creates what he describes as "an amorphous landscape" in which inhabitants experience "a new and different sense of distances" and rather than being proscribed, "these various functionalities create an existence akin to

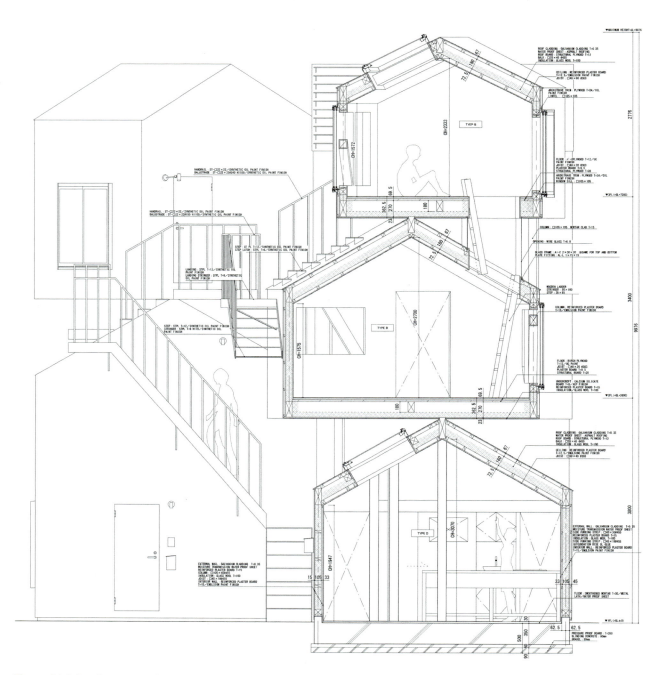

Figure 21.2 Sou Fujimoto, Tokyo Apartment House Section
Source: Sou Fujimoto

Figure 21.3
Hitoshi Abe, Bouno House

Source: Atelier Hitoshi Abe

Figure 21.4 Sou Fujimoto, Children's Center for Psychiatric Rehabilitation
Source: Daici Ano

Figure 21.5 Sou Fujimoto, Children's Center for Psychiatric Rehabilitation, Plan
Source: Sou Fujimoto

primitive conditions before architecture. Rather than just a new architecture, this is a new origin, a new existence" (Figure 21.6).[2]

As with several other iconoclastic projects by Fujimoto discussed here, the Wooden House is intended to raise important questions about functionality. They challenge our conventional perception about what is necessary or appropriate in architecture and remind us that while it is an art, which alters our world-view, it must also serve the people that inhabit it. This diminutive cellulose cube once again raises intriguing questions about cultural differences and what may be an innate, psychosexual predilection for tight spaces (Figure 21.7).[3]

A dreamscape in Daikanyama

Akihisa Hirata also has also sought to achieve this dreamlike state in his 2007 Saragaku commercial complex across from Fumihiko Maki's extended Hillside Terrace project in the upscale Daikanyama district of Tokyo. Because of local codes that prohibit big-box retail stores, as well as a very tight trapezoidal site, Hirata adopted the metaphor of a forested mountain range of layered small stores around the perimeter and pedestrian pathway as valley through the middle, which allows for excellent people-watching from walkways above, and vibrant advertising displays, as the "trees." Vertical windows, which extend up through several floors, are carved into each of the various retail clusters,

Figure 21.6
Wooden House in
Kumamoto
Source: Iwan Baan

Figure 21.7 Wooden House in Kumamoto,
Model
Source: Sou Fujimoto

Figure 21.8 Akihisa Hirata, Saragaku
Source: NACSA

contributing to the impression of walking through a secret wooded landscape (Figure 21.8).

The last act: Para-modernism?

Finally, these attempts to commune with the subjective side of our consciousness also bring to mind a distinction made by Shuhei Endo that while Modernism is dead, and all that often remains is the style, without the ideology that nurtured it, the methodology behind it still remains as a foil against which many young architects continue to treat new, experimental ideas. Endo refers to his work as "Para-modern" because even though he respects those first principles, he is also sensitive to the place we occupy on the cyclical timeline laid out for us by the theorists analyzed earlier. Global society and all of the various permutations of built environment it has created; as well as the natural equivalent it has

destroyed, has radically changed the equation. If the agricultural revolution was the first wave of human evolution, the industrial age, when Modernism was born, the second, and the Information Age the third, we are well into the fourth, rushing headlong toward Singularity. Japanese architects have proven to be very adept at amending foreign influences such as Modernism, and making them conform to cultural conventions, and have made it abundantly clear that the familiar allegories surrounding generalities such as tradition and capitalism must now change.

Notes

1   Personal notes taken during the Louis Kahn Master's Class, University of Pennsylvania, 1968.
2   Sou Fujimoto, provided by the architect.
3   Molly Young, "Tiny Spaces," *New York Times*, May 8, 2016, pp. 22–23.

Glossary

Ama-no-Uzume: "Heavenly, Alarming (or Whirling) Woman," the Shinto goddess of elation, who is famous for performing an erotic dance that lured Amaterasu from a cave and restored light to the universe. In early Japan, female Shamen dedicated to Uzume were called *miko*, personified by the legendary quasi-mythical Queen Himiko.

Amaterasu, or Amaterasu-ōmikami: "She who shines – spirit above all others"; the Shinto sun goddess, enshrined at Ise, Mie.

Bakufu: "tent government"; first used in reference to the government of Minamoto no Yoritomo, who established the first Shogunate in Kamakura in 1192.

Buke-zukuri: The much simpler, more austere military alternative to the aristocratic shinden-zukuri, with more space allowed for retainers, and a watchtower.

Byōbu: Japanese folding screen, originally intended to deflect the wind.

Chang'an: Now Xi'an, was the capital of China for many Dynasties, which reached its height during the Tang Dynasty (618–907). It was laid out on a grid plan, reflecting the hierarchy of Chinese society of the time, with the palace of the Emperor at the top. The Tang Dynasty had an enormous influence on Japan, and Chang'an was used as the model for Heian-Kyo, established by Emperor Kanmu in 794.

Chidorihafu: A roof gable with slightly curved sides inspired by the wings of a plover.

Chigaidana: Literally means "staggered shelves" built into the wall of a shoin.

Chigi: Crossed finials, like horns, placed at the gable ends of Shinto shrines for apotropaic purposes, to ward off evil.

Cho: A traditional unit of measurement equal to 109.9 meters.

COR-TEN: Registered trademark name for a steel alloy which is chemically treated to allow it to weather naturally to form a protective rust-like coating, so it doesn't require painting.

Daiku: Carpenter.

Daimyo: As Shogun, from 1368 to 1394, Ashikaga Yoshimitsu established shugo, or provincial constables, who gained considerable power during the Muromachi period, second only to the Shogun himself. These regional lords later became known as Daimyo. After the battle of Sekigahara in 1600, the victorious Tokugawa Shogunate divided into the fudai daimyo, the hereditary vassals who supported them before and during the battle, and the tozama daimyo or "outer lords" because they were then relegated to fiefs, the distant parts of Japan, who joined them either at the end or afterward. As a classic example of long historical memory, it was the tozama who, 267 years later, instigated the fall of the Tokugawa regime by supporting the young Emperor Meiji.

Dōgu-bori: Tools, similar to the hollow, cone-shaped metal tips used by pastry chefs for piping icing onto a cake, used for cutting the paper stencils for the dyeing of textiles, such as kimono, in the hand craft known as katagami or Ise-katagami. The paper is made of many layers of washi, or mulberry bark, glued together with persimmon juice, and is then smoke cured.

Doken Kokka: The term used for the construction state in Japan, in which profit from development supports social welfare programs. (See: Gavan McCormack, "The Construction State: The Pathology of the Doken Kokka" in *The Emptiness of Japanese Affluence*, East Gate Books, London: Routledge, 2001, pp. 25–78.)

Doma: "Dirt place" or earthen floor between exterior and the raised wooden floor of the interior of a traditional Japanese farmhouse, where the kamado, or fireplace was located, to prevent combustion.

Dou-kung: Interlocking wooden "cap and block" bracketing, assembled without any metal fasteners, borrowed from Chinese architecture, that allows the extension of roof gables in a column and beam structural system.

Engawa: The closest Western analogy to this fabled and distinctively Japanese space would be a deck, or patio, but the engawa is covered by a roof, is typically much narrower, and runs the entire length of the garden side of a building. It mitigates between the interior and nature, so is intentionally interstitial in character.

Ent-fernung: Absence, or distance.

Feng shui: "Wind-water" geomancy of aligning architecture with ch'i, or natural forces.

Fushin bugyo: Officials in charge of construction projects during the Tokugawa Shogunate.

Fusuma: A sliding door, more solid than a shoji screen.

Hachitama: The spheroid Observation Deck of the Fuji TV Studios Building, in Tokyo.

Himorogi: Literally means "divine fence," a Shinto enclosure consisting of columns erected at each of its four corners, with an enclosing rope, or shimenawa then strung between them.

Hinoki: Japanese cypress.

Hiwada-buki: Cypress bark thatched roofing.

Hongawara-buki: Tiled roof.

Honmaru Goten: Like the Donjon of a European castle, the last bastion of defense.

Irori: Sunken, earthen hearth in a traditional Japanese house.

Ishigaki: Dry stone wall.

Izanagi and Izanami: (He and she who beckon, or invite.) Not the first deities in the Japanese pantheon, but a brother and sister who stood on the bridge of heaven and, as the Kojiki says, were asked to create islands out of the primordial soup. "Now the spirits of heaven all commanded the mighty one He Who Beckoned and the mighty one She Who Beckoned with mighty words proclaiming: 'Make firm this drifting land and fashion it in its final form!'" *The Kojiki*, Compiled by Yasumaro Ō no, translated by Gustav Heldt, Columbia University Press, 2014, p. 16.

Jichinsai: A land purification ceremony, which has three parts.

Jitō: Estate managers during the Kamakura and Muromachi Shogunates.

Jokamachi: Means "the town below the castle," these were sizable cities in their own right.

Jomon: Indigenous people of Japan, who take their name from the rope-like patterns on their pottery, predominant from about 14,500 BC to the Yayoi intervention around 300 BC.

Jūkyo shūgōron: Villages all over the world, studied by Hiroshi Hara, Tōkyō Daigaku, Seisan Gijutsu Kenkyūjo and Hara Kenkyūshitsu, published in a series of volumes entitled *Jūkyo shūgōroni* by Kajima Kenkyūjo Shuppankai, Tokyo, 1974. Those in Japan have exquisite photographs by Tomio Ohashi.

Kami: Deity or spirit.

Kara-hafu: Roof with a curving gable.

Karesansui: A Zen rock garden.

Katachi: Form, shape or pattern.

Katagami or Ise-katagami: See Dōgu-bori.

Katsuogi: Heavy, cylindrical weights placed across the ridge of a Shinto shrine, to protect it from wind.

Kaya: Misicanthus reed used for thatching roofs at Ise shrine.

Kayaoi: The curved eave of a roof, especially a pagoda.

Kegare: Shinto term meaning defilement.

Ken: Traditional unit of measure equivalent to 6 shaku, or approximately 1.82 meters.

Kenchikushi: Architect.

Kiotoshi: Riding the Onbashira or pillar during the Yamadashi Festival during the renewal of the Shimosha Shrine.

Kojiki: A collection of ancient Japanese myths commissioned by the Empress Gemmei and compiled by Ō no Yasumaro in 711 AD.

Kokera-buki: Thin wooden shingles made of cypress.

Koku: Measurement of rice weighing 150 kilograms, used as a means of barter and payment, of salary or tax in the past.

Kondo: The "golden hall" or main hall, which is part of a Buddhist temple.

Kusanagi-no-tsuru: The name of the sword that is one of the "Three Treasures" of Japan.

Lanai: A verandah. Common in Hawaii.

Ma: An extremely important concept in Japanese architecture, which requires elaboration. It is technically defined as the space between, an interval, pause or a void, but involves a Japanese perception of space-time that is substantially different from the Western idea of continuity, in being one of equivalence. Initial interest in the concept in the Western architectural media can be traced to a 1966 issue of *Architectural Design* guest edited by Guenter Nitschke, entitled "MA: The Japanese Sense of Place" (March 1966, Vol. 36, pp. 116–156), but many Japanese architects were already trying, and continue to attempt to clarify the meaning of this elusive concept.

Arata Isozaki has been foremost among them, since he designed an entire exhibition entitled "MA: Space-Time in Japan" for the Cooper-Hewitt Museum, in New York in 1976, which took on a life of its own, following a circuitous route around the world and then finally opened in Japan in 2000 as the "MA Exhibition, 20 Years After." Isozaki also later collaborated as author with director Takahiko Iimura, and musician Takehisa Kosugi on a film entitled "MA: Space/Time in the Garden of Ryoan-Ji," commissioned by the Program for Art on Film (PAF), a New York organization co-sponsored by the Metropolitan Museum of Art, and the Getty Foundation.

In his original "MA: Space-Time in Japan" Exhibition, Isozaki offered nine different variations, interpretations, or refinements of this in-between state, which help to understand it, which he has identified as: Himorogi, Hashi, Yami, Suki, Utsuroi, Utsushimi, Sabi, Susabi and Michiyuki. A Himorogi, as previously defined here, literally means "divine fence" and is a Shinto enclosure consisting of columns erected at each of its four corners, with an enclosing rope, or shimenawa then strung between them, with folded paper markers hung from it to designate a sacred space. So the variation of Ma here is a space set apart. Beyond its usual meaning of bridge or chopsticks, Hashi, which is the second variation, also connotes a threshold, or boundary. The third variation, of Yami, means dark, referring to the Shinto belief in the kami, or spirits emerging in darkness. During the final eight-year period of renewal which occurs at the end of the twenty year cycle of the reconstruction of the Ise Shrine, for example, the final act is Sengyo no Gi ritual, or the moving of the deity Amaterasu Omikami, from the old dwelling to the new one. This takes place just after sunset, when all lights are turned off as the priests perform the mitama-shiro or transference of the object in which her divine essence is thought to reside, which in this case is a shintai, or mirror, carried behind a silk enclosure and hidden from view. Since Yami refers to the second half of the diurnal division, Ma may more accurately be that point at which the sun, as Akira, or brightness, has just set.

Suki, as the next nuance of Ma, is also part of the term sukiya, also defined here, but in this case means a room, or enclosure. Utsuroi is described by Isozaki himself as "the moment when nature is transformed, the passage from one state to another." In the interior of houses in the past, when people moving at night cast reflections on rice shoji screen dividers, Isozaki feels that "the flickering of shadows and the transience of shifting planes allude to the changing world of nature" in which

"Ma is the expectant stillness of the moment" that accompanies it.

Isozaki completed his refinements of the concept of Ma, with Utsushimi, the spaces in which people live, Sabi, which is often paired with Wabi, as the passage or movement of time, Susabi, as the place or space where things appear and disappear, and finally, Michiyuki, as the co-ordination of movement through a space, by things that regulate it, such as the stepping stones in a Japanese garden. (Arata Isozaki and Ken Tadashi Oshima, *Arata Isozaki,* Phaidon, London, 2009, pp. 158–161.)

Macha: Finely ground Japanese green tea.

Magatama: A claw-shaped jewel that is one of the "Three Treasures" of Japan.

Mie gakure: A term used in Japanese gardening: seen and unseen, or hide and reveal.

Mon: Similar to medieval heraldry, family insignia.

Mono no aware: Sadness caused by an awareness of transience.

Mujokan: From mujo, or impermanence.

Nagayamon: A nagaya, or long house, was where poorer Samurai lived and the nagayamon was its gate.

Nihon: The etymology is "the origin of the sun," the name for Japan, and the Japanese call themselves Nihonjin.

Nijiriguchi: The small doorway of a Japanese teahouse, as a reminder of humility.

Ninomaru: The five-part section of Nijo-jo, in Kyoto; see Tozamurai.

Nure-en: A veranda.

Ohiroma: The public audience hall in a shoin-zukuri.

Pagoda: A tower that evolved in Temples in China and then elsewhere in Asia as a variation of the Indian Stupa, which was originally intended to contain a relic of the Buddha. While originally having only small ridges, such as the Wild Goose Pagoda in Xi'an, pagodas in Japan eventually had many gracefully curved eaves.

Raku: Hand formed, lead glazed Japanese pottery fired at low temperatures, to create a rough surface, usually used for tea ceremonies.

Rikyū: Refers to cultural icon Sen-no Rikyū, a Buddhist priest who perfected the tea ceremony, and became an advisor and confidant of Shogun Hideyoshi Toyotomi, before offending him, and being required to commit suicide.

Ritsuryō: A legal system based on Confucian philosophy, comprising a more centralized government that combined the ritsu, or criminal code, and ryō, or administrative and civil codes. It was imposed during the late Asuka period and prevailed during the Nara period from 710 to 794, before being relaxed by the Imperial Court in Heian-kyo.

Sabi: The second part of the Wabi-Sabi duality, that appreciates things that are imperfect, as part of the cycle of life.

Sakaki tree: The evergreen Cleyera Japonica, celebrated in Shinto myth as the tree that was brought down from the mountains above "the high plain of heaven" and festooned with jewels, mirrors and ornaments to lure the sun goddess Amaterasu from her hiding place in a cave and restore light to the universe. *See also*: **Ama-no-Uzume**.

Samurai: As the ritsuryo state weakened during the Heian period, farmers began to arm themselves and a code of ethics, or Bushidō, followed. After the Genpei war, Minamoto clan leader Yoritomo appointed *shugo* and *jito* as administrators and tax collectors, and this group eventually emerged as the Samurai class in Japan. The Kamakura Shogunate of Minamoto no Yoritomo started in 1192. After the Tokugawa Shogunate unified Japan and warfare essentially ceased, the Samurai became administrators, until they were dissolved at the beginning of the Meiji Restoration in 1868, bringing the history of these fabled warriors to an end.

Sankin kotai: The law of "alternate attendance" in which Daimyo were required to travel from their own domain to Edo at regular intervals depending on their status, and retain a second residence there, to essentially ensure that they were financially unable to mount any resistance to the Tokugawa regime. A network of roadways developed throughout Japan as a result.

Sekigahara: Decisive battle on October 21, 1600, in which Shogun Tokugawa Ieyasu defeated the Western army of Ishida Mitsunari, to finally unify Japan.

Sencha: Japanese green tea made by infusing the whole leaves in hot water, rather than the powder, which is used in matcha.

Shakkai: "Borrowed landscape" using higher trees and shrubs in the background of a garden, which may be located over the property line to create a feeling of larger space.

Shaku: A traditional unit of measure based on the length of a forearm, but now standardized as 11.9 inches.

Shikinen sengu: The term referring to rebuilding of Ise Shrine, which occurs on a 20-year cycle.

Shimenawa: "Enclosing rope" are lengths of rice straw rope used for ritual purification.

Shinbashira, or Shim-no-mi-hashira: Central pillar, or column, which refers to the central column of the Ise shrine, Izumo-grand-shrine and Kamosu-shrine. The column has sacred significance because the *Kojiki* relates that after forming the first island of Onogoro, Izanagi and Izanami descended to it from the bridge of heaven, constructed a hall with a pillar in the middle of it, circled it in opposite directions, and were married.

Shinchintaisha: The Japanese term for Metabolism.

Shinden, or **shinden-zukuri:** A residential typology that was developed by the aristocratic class during the Heian period in Kyoto, which had a south-facing rectangular hall or shinden in the middle, flanked on either side by perpendicular wings, connected by a covered corridor.

Shishinden: A long, wide throne or ceremonial hall best seen at the Kyoto Imperial Palace, which is the first hall encountered after entering the Shomeimon gate. The building type was supposedly first introduced into Japan at Ninna-ji in 886.

Shōen: A manor house during the feudal period in Japan, typically exempt from taxes.

Shoji: Sliding rice paper screens in a wooden frame.

Shoin zukuri: A style of Japanese architecture that developed during the Muromachi Period – roughly between the fourteenth and the sixteenth century –

characterized by the use of *tatami* mats, square columns, sliding doors, coffered ceilings, and the integration of spaces in which to display art. Literally, "book room" or a "study."

Shoshin: The Zen concept of "beginner's mind," or letting go of previous mental constraints.

Shou-sugi-ban, or Yakisugi: charred cedar used for siding to make it fire-resistant.

Shugo: Provincial governors appointed by the Shogun.

Sugi: Japanese cedar, cryptomeria japonica.

Sukiya: A style of architecture inspired by the rough, impermanent materials used in the Japanese teahouse.

Susanoo no Mikoto, or simply Susano-o: The Shinto god of storms, and brother of Amaterasu the goddess of the Sun, and Tsukuyomi, the god of the Moon.

Taika: "Great Reform"; refers to reforms instituted by Emperor Kotoku in 645, based on Chinese, Confucian principles, to consolidate Imperial power after the fall of the powerful Soga clan.

Takama-ga-hara: The Shinto "high plain of heaven."

Taktaboosh: A breezeway between a garden and paved courtyard.

Tatami: A thick, woven rice straw mat, with fabric edges, that is twice as long as it is wide, and varies in size according to region. Rooms of traditional houses were laid out according to this module.

Tenshu, or tenshukaku: The central tower of a Japanese castle.

Tokonoma: An alcove in a shoin-zukuri for the display of art, and calligraphy.

Torii: The gate to a Shinto shrine, with two uprights and a curved lintel, denoting the transition from a profane to a sacred space.

Tozamurai: The waiting room for retainers in a shoin. At Nijo-jo, the Tokugawa Castle in Kyoto, for example, it is the first section encountered after entering the gate, followed, in the diagonal "flying geese" plan, by the Shikidai-no-ma, or formal reception room, the Ohiroma or Grand Rooms, the Kuro-Shoin, or Inner

Audience Chambers, and finally, the Shiro-Shoin, or living quarters of the Shogun.

Tsuke-shoin: A bay window, located next to the Tokonoma in a Shoin-zukuri.

Tsumi: A legal or moral offense. Violation of a law, or socio-religious rule.

Wabi: Simplicity.

Washi: Paper made from mulberry bark.

Yamoto: Around 300 AD, the Yayoi were subverted by a new polity, called the Yamoto, centered around Ise-shi.

Yata-no-Kagami: The mirror that is one of the Three Sacred Treasures of Japan, which also include the sword Kusanagi no Tsurugi and the jewel, Yasakani no Magatama.

Yayoi: People of disputed origin who displaced the indigenous Jomon population around 100 BC, introducing intensive rice farming and iron production.

Yorishiro: In Shinto, objects felt to attract spirits, or kami.

Zaibatsu: Large corporate conglomerates, in Japan; typically refers to the "big four" companies of Mitsui, Mitsubishi, Sumitomo, and Yasuda.

Zelkova: Deciduous tree of the elm family. The Zelkova serrate is found throughout the country.

Zukuri: A suffix, added to indicate something that is made, which comes from the verb (tsukuru) which means "to make, to manufacture, to grow." This suffix is used in several expressions to mean something which is created or made, such as Shiden-zukuri, a mansion made in the shinden style.

Bibliography

Kimimasa Abe. Early Western Architecture in Japan, *Journal of the Society of Architectural Historians* 13:2, 1954, pp. 13–18.

Kimimasa Abe. Meiji Architecture in Naoteru Uyeno. Japanese Arts and Crafts in the Meiji Era, Centenary Culture Council Series: Japanese Culture in the Meiji Era, 8. Tokyo: Pan-Pacific Press, 1958, pp. 177–198.

Mitsuaki Adachi, Ed. *Kunio Maekawa: Sources of Modern Japanese Architecture*, Tokyo: Process Architecture, 1984.

Cassandra Adams. Japan's Ise Shrine and Its Thirteen-Hundred-Year-Old Reconstruction Tradition, *Journal of Architectural Education*, 1998, pp. 46–60.

Paul C. Adams, Steven Hoelscher, and Karen E. Till, Eds. *Textures of Place: Exploring Humanist Geographies*, Minneapolis: University of Minnesota Press, 2001.

Theodor W. Adorno and Max Horkheimer, *Dialectic of Enlightenment*, New York: Verso, 1979.

Shinobu Akahori and Waro Kishi. Modern Houses II, *Japan Architect*, 29, Spring 1998, Special Issue.

Yoshiaki Akasaka. New Aspects in Modernism, *Japan Architect*, 14, Summer 1994.

Alfred Altherr. *Three Japanese Architects: Maekawa, Tange, Sakakura*, Berlin: Academy Editions, 1968.

Tadao Ando. From Self-Enclosed Architecture to Universality, *The Japan Architect*, 3011, May 1982.

Tadao Ando. *Buildings and Projects*. New York: Rizzoli, 1984.

Ioanna Angelidou. Intertwinements, *MAS Context*, 9, Networks.

Ezrin Arbi, Austronesian Vernacular Architecture and the Ise Shrine of Japan: Is There Any Connection?, Department of Architecture, Faculty of the Built Environment, University of Malaya, Kuala Lumpur, 2013.

Takashi Asada and Mitsuo Taketani. Genbakujidai to Kenchiku ("Architecture in the Atomic Era"), *Shinkenchiku*, 10, August 1955, pp. 77–86.

Yoshinobu Ashihara. *The Hidden Order: Tokyo Through the Twentieth Century*. Tokyo and New York: Kodansha International, 1989.

William George Aston. Nihongi; Chronicles of Japan from the Earliest Times to A.D. 697. Collected Works of William George Aston, Bucarest: Ganesha, 1997.

Jonathan Morris Augustine. *Buddhist Hagiography in Early Japan*. London: Routledge Curzon, 2005.

Cemil Aydin. Japan's Pan-Asianism and the Legitimacy of Imperial World Order, *Asia-Pacific Journal: Japan Focus*, 11, March 2008.

Shigeru Ban. *Shigeru Ban*, New York: Princeton Architectural Press, 2001.

Shigeru Ban and David N. Buck. *Shigeru Ban*, Barcelona: Gustavo Gili, 1997.

Reynar Banham. *Theory and Design in the First Machine Age*, Cambridge, MA: MIT Press, 1980.

Reyner Banham. *Megastructure: Urban Futures of the Recent Past*, New York: Harper & Row, 1976.

Reyner Banham and Hiroyuki Suzuki. *Contemporary Architecture of Japan 1958–1984*, New York: Rizzoli, 1984.

Graeme Barker and Candice Goucher, Eds. *The Cambridge World History: Volume 2, A World With Agriculture, 12,000 BCE-500 CE* p. 376.

Gina Barnes. *State Formation in Japan: Emergence of a Fourth Century Ruling Elite*, Abingdon, Oxon: Routledge, 2007.

Roland Barthes. *Empire of Signs*, trans. R. Howard, New York: Hill and Wang, 1982.

Bruce Batten. Foreign Threat and Domestic Reform: The Emergence of the Ritsuryo State. *Monumenta Nipponica*, 41, 2 (Summer 1986) pp. 199–219.

R. Bellah. *Beyond Belief: Essays on Religion in a Post-Traditional World*. New York: Harper and Row, 1970.

Peter Bellwood, James J. Fox, and Darrell Tryon, Eds. *The Austronesians, Historical and Comparative Perspectives*, Canberra: Australian National University Press, 1995.

Ruth Benedict. *The Chrysanthemum and the Sword*. Boston and New York: Houghton Mifflin, 1974.

Leonardo Benevolo. *History of Modern Architecture, Volume 2: Modern Movement*, Cambridge, MA: MIT Press, 1977.

Massimo Bettinotti, Ed. *Kenzo Tange 1946–1996: Architecture and Urban Design*, Milano: Electa, 1996. London: Routledge and Kegan Paul, 1971.

C. Blacker. *The Japanese Enlightenment: A Study of the Writings of Fukuzawa Yukichi*, Cambridge: Cambridge University Press, 1964.

Werner Blaser. *Structure and Form in Japan*. Zurich: Artemis-Verlag-Aktiengesellschaft, 1963.

Peter Blundell-Jones. Where do we stand? A lecture about Modernism. Post-Modernism and the Neglected Possibility of a Responsive Architecture, *Architecture and Urbanism* 3, 198. March 1987 (text in English and Japanese).

Brian Bocking. *The Oracles of the Three Shrines: Windows on Japanese Religion*. Richmond, Surrey: Curzon, 2001.

Botand Bognár. *The Bubble and Beyond: The New Japanese Architecture*. London: Phaidon, 2008.

Botand Bognár. *Hirosi Hara: The Floating World of His Architecture*. London: Academy Editions, 2001.

Botand Bognár. *Nikken Sekkei: Building Future Japan 1900–2000*. New York: Rizzoli International, 2000.

Botand Bognár. Nikken Sekkei and the Evolution of Modern Japanese Architecture, in *Nikken Sekkei: Building Future Japan 1900–2000*. New York: Rizzoli, 2000.

Botand Bognár. Design in the Land of 'Creative Chaos': The Emergence of New Modernism in Japanese Architecture, in Helen Castle (Ed.), *Modernism and Modernization in Architecture*, London: Academy Editions. 1999.

Botand Bognár. Surface Above All? American Influence on Japanese Urban Space, in Heide Fehrenbach and Uta Poiger (Eds.), *Transactions, Transgressions, Transformations: American Culture in Western Europe and Japan*. New York: Berghahn Books, 1999.

Botand Bognár, Ed. Japan At The Cutting Edge, *New Architecture* 3, October 1999.

Botand Bognár. *An Architecture of the Unknown and Unknowable in Takasaki Masaharu: An Architecture of Cosmology*. New York: Princeton Architectural Press, 1998.

Botand Bognár. The Japanese Example – The Other 'End' of Architecture, *New Architecture*, 2, August 1998, pp. 49–63.

Botand Bognár. From Group Form to Lightness: Maki's Architecture "Up" to the Next Millennium, in Fumihiko Maki, *Buildings and Projects*. New York: Princeton Architectural Press, 1997.

Botand Bognár. What Goes Up, Must Come Down: Recent Urban Architecture in Japan, in *Durability and Ephemerality: Harvard Design Magazine*. Cambridge, MA.: Harvard University Graduate School of Design, Fall 1997, pp. 33–43.

Botand Bognár. *World Cities: Tokyo*. London: Academy Editions of John Wiley and Sons, 1997.

Botand Bognár. *Togo Murano Master Architect of Japan*. Introduction by Fumihiko Maki. New York: Rizzoli International, 1996.

Botand Bognár, Ed. and principal author. *Minoru Takeyama. Architectural Monograph No. 42*. London: Academy Editions, and New York: St. Martin's Press, 1995.

Botand Bognár. *The Japan Guide*. New York: Princeton Architectural Press, 1995.

Botand Bognár. Revisiting the 'City in the Air' – Thoughts on Hara's New Umeda Sky Building. *SD, Space Design*, January 1994, Special issue on Hiroshi Hara, pp. 87–96.

Botand Bognár. The New Phenomenalism in Japanese Architecture, *A+U, Architecture and Urbanism*, 280, January 1994, pp. 2–9.

Botand Bognár. From Ritualistic Objects to Science Fiction Constructs: The Enigma of Shin Takamatsu's Architecture, in Paolo Polledri (Ed.), *Shin Takamatsu*. New York: Rizzoli International, 1993.

Botand Bognár. Critical Intentions in Pluralistic Japanese Architecture, *Free Space Architecture, AD Profile 96*, 62, 3–4, 1992, pp. 72–96.

Botand Bognár. Fumihiko Maki: Making of an Urban Architecture, Fumihiko Maki, *World Architecture*, 16, Profile: Japanese Issue, 1992.

Botand Bognár, Ed. and principal author. *Japanese Architecture II. AD Profile 99*, London: Academy Editions, and New York: St. Martin's Press, 1992.

Botand Bognár. Architecture, Nature & A New Technological Landscape: Itsuko Hasegawa's Work in the 80s: Aspects of Modern Architecture, *AD Profile 90*, London, 1991.

Botand Bognár. *The New Japanese Architecture*. Introduction by John Morris Dixon. New York: Rizzoli International, 1990.

Botand Bognár. The Place of Nothingness: The Japanese House and the Oriental World Views of the Japanese, in J. P. Bourdier and N. Alsayyad, Eds., *Dwellings, Settlements, and Tradition*. New York: Rowman and Littlefield, 1989, pp. 183–213.

Botand Bognár (Ed.), Japanese Architecture I, *AD Profile 73*, 58, 5–6, 1988.

Botand Bognár. An Architecture of Fragmentation: The Japanese Example, Reflections, *The Architectural Journal of the University of Illinois at Urbana–Champaign*, 5 (February 1988).

Botand Bognár. Celestial Abode out of the Industrial Landscape of the City: Yamamoto's 'Rotunda,' *JA+U, Japan Architecture and Urbanism*, February 1988, pp. 6–8.

Botand Bognár. *Contemporary Japanese Architecture – Its Development and Challenge*. New York: Van Nostrand Reinhold, 1985.

Botand Bognár, K. Frampton, and Kunio Kudo. *Nikken Sekkei 1900–1990: Building Modern Japan*. New York: Princeton Architectural Press, 1990.

Robin Boy. *New Dimensions in Japanese Architecture*, New York and London: Studio Vista, 1968.

R.J. Bowring. *Mori Ogai and the Modernization of Japanese Culture*. Cambridge: Cambridge University Press, 1979.

W.R. Braisted, Tr. *Meiroku Zasshi: Journal of the Japanese Enlightenment*, Cambridge, MA: Harvard University Press, 1976.

Piers Brendon. *The Dark Valley: A Panorama of the 1930s*, New York: Vintage, 2002.

Mitchell Bring and Josse Wayembergh. *Japanese Gardens – Design and Meaning* (1968), New York: McGraw-Hill, 1981.

Delmar M. Brown. *The Cambridge History of Japan, Vol.1: Ancient Japan*, Cambridge: Cambridge University Press, 1993.

S. Azby Brown. *The Genius of Japanese Carpentry: An Account of a Temple Construction*. Tokyo and New York: Kodansha International, 1989.

Dana Buntrock. Katsura Imperial Villa: A Brief Descriptive Bibliography with Illustrations, *Crosscurrents: East Asian History and Culture Review*, 1, 2, November 2012.

Richard F. Calichman. *Overcoming Modernity: Cultural Identity in Wartime Japan*, New York: Columbia University Press, 2008.

Norman F. Carver, Jr. *Japanese Folkhouses*. Kalamazoo, MI: Documan Press, 1987.

Ernst Cassier. *The Philosophy of Symbolic Forms, Vol. IV*, Eds. John Michael Krois and Donald Phillip Verene, Trans. John Michael Krois, New Haven: Yale University Press, 1996.

Basil Hall Chamberlain. Kojiki: Records of Ancient Matters, Presented at the Asiatic Society of Japan, Kobe, 1882. Reprinted by Tuttle Publishing, 1981.

Ching Yu Chang. Japanese Spatial Conception 1–11, *JA, The Japan Architect*, 3, 1985.

Ching Yu Chang. Japanese Spatial Conception: a Critical Analysis of its Elements in the Culture and Traditions of Japan and its Post-War Era, University of Pennsylvania, Phd Thesis, 1982, University Microfilms International.

Hyunjung Cho and Chunghoon Shin. Metabolism and Cold War Architecture, *The Journal of Architecture*, 19, 5, 2014.

John Clammer. *Contemporary Urban Japan: A Sociology of Consumption*. Oxford and Malden: Blackwell Publishers, 1997.

John Clark. Okakura Tenshin and Aesthetic Nationalism, *East Asian History* 29, Institute of Advanced Studies Australian National University, Editor Geremie R. Barme, June 2005.

William H. Coaldrake, *Architecture and Authority in Japan*, Nissan Institute, London: Routledge, 1996.

Ralph Adams Cram. *Impressions of Japanese Architecture and the Allied Arts*, New York: Dover, 1966.

Amanai Daiki. The Founding of Bunriha Kenchiku Kai: "Art" and "Expression" in Early Japanese Architecture Circle, 1888–1920, *Aesthetics* 13, 2009, The Japanese Society for Aesthetics, Osaka University of Arts, Osaka, Japan.

Francesco Dal Co. *Tadao Ando – Complete Works*. London: Phaidon, 1995.

Peter N. Dale. *The Myth of Japanese Uniqueness*, Abingdon: Routledge Revivals, 1986.

Thomas Danielli. *After the Crash: Architecture in Post-Bubble Japan*, New York: Princeton Architectural Press, 2008.

Peter Davey. *Arts and Crafts Architecture*, London: Phaidon, 1997.

William E. Deal and Brian Ruppert. *A Cultural History of Japanese Buddhism*, Chichester: Wiley Blackwell, 2015.

Takeo Doi. *The Anatomy of Dependence*, Tokyo, Kôdansha, 1973.

R.P. Dore. *Land Reform in Japan*, Oxford: Oxford University Press, 1959.

Andreas Dorpalen. *The World of General Haushofer*, New York: Farrar and Rinehart, 1984.

John W. Dower. *Embracing Defeat: Japan in the Wake of World War II*, New York: Norton, 1999.

John W. Dower. *War Without Mercy: Race and Power in the Pacific War*, New York: Pantheon Books, 1986.

Gary L. Ebersole. *Ritual Poetry and the Politics of Death in Early Japan*, Princeton, NJ: Princeton University Press, 1989.

Peter Eckersall. *Performativity and Event in 1960s Japan: City, Body, Memory*, Basingstoke: Palgrave Macmillan, 2013.

Walter Edwards. Event and Process in the Founding of Japan: The Horse-rider Theory: Archaeological Perspective, *The Journal of Japanese Studies* 9, 2, Summer 1983, pp. 265–295.

Nold Egenter. Rice in Japan: You Are What You Eat, *The Economist*, December 24, 2009.

Heino Engel. *Measure and Construction of the Japanese House*. Rutland, VT and Tokyo: Charles E. Tuttle Company, 1985.

Dallas Finn. *Meiji Revisited, the Sites of Victorian Japan*, Tokyo: Weatherhill, 1998.

Kenneth Frampton, Ed. *A New Wave of Japanese Architecture*, New York: Institute for Architecture and Urban Studies, 1978.

Kenneth Frampton. Arata Isozaki: A.D.A., Tokyo: Edita, 1991.

Kenneth Frampton and Kunio Kudo, Eds. *Nikken Sekkei: Building Modern Japan, 1900–1990*, Princeton, NJ: Princeton University Press, 1990.

Kenneth Frampton. Tadao Ando: The Museum of Modern Art, New York: Harry. N. Abrams, 1991.

Louis Frederic. *Japan Encyclopedia*, trans. Kathe Roth, Cambridge, MA: The Belknap Press of the Harvard University Press, 2002.

Mildred Friedman, Ed. *Tokyo: Form and Spirit*, Minneapolis, MN: Walker Art Center, 1986.

Hiromi Fujii. *The Architecture of Hiromi Fujii*, New York: Rizzoli, 1987.

Michio Fujioka. *Japanese Residences and Gardens*, Tokyo and New York: Kodansha International, 1983.

Hiroshi Fujioka. The Search for Japanese Architecture in Modern Ages. *Japan Foundation Newsletter*, Xiroshi V, 3, 1987.

Toshio Fukuyama. *Heian Temples: Byodo-in and Chuson-ji*. Tokyo: Heibonsha/Weatherhill, 1976.

Yukio Futagawa, Ed. Text by Teiji Itoh. *Traditional Japanese Houses*. New York: Rizzoli, 1983.

Stylianos Giamarelos. Interdisciplinary Reflections and Deflections of Histories of the Scientific Revolution in Alberto Pérez-Gómez's Architecture and the Crisis of Modern Science, *Journal of Architectural Education* 69, 1, 2015, pp. 17–27.

Carol Gluck. *Japan's Modern Myths: Ideology in the Late Meiji Period*, Princeton, NJ: Princeton University Press, 1985.

Sarah Williams Goldhagen and Rjean Legault, Eds. *Anxious Modernism: Experimentation in Postwar Architectural Culture*. Montreal: Canadian Center for Architecture; and Cambridge, MA: MIT Press, 2000.

Erica Goode. How Culture Molds Habits of Thought, *The New York Times*, August 8, 2000.

A. Goto. *The Japanese People Seen from the Sea Side: History of Japan with a Focus on the People Living in the Coastal Areas*, Tokyo: Kodansha, 2010.

Barrie B. Greenbie. *Space and Spirit in Modern Japan*. New Haven and London: Yale University Press, 1988.

Walter Gropius, Kenzo Tange and Yasuhiro Ishimoto. *Katsura: Tradition and Creation in Japanese Architecture*. New Haven: Yale University Press, 1960.

Koichi Hamada. Japan 1968: A Reflection Point During the Era of the Economic Miracle, Economic Growth Center, Yale University, Discussion Paper #764, 1966.

E. Hamaguchi. A Contextual Model of the Japanese . . . , *Journal of Japanese Studies*, 11, 2, 1985.

E. Hamaguchi. Towards a Theoretical Dialogue Between Asia and the West, *Japan Foundation Newsletter*, XIV, 4, 1987.

Ryuichi Hamaguchi. History of Modern Architecture, Special edition of *JA, The Japan Architect*, June 1966.

Hiroshi Hara and David B. Stewart. *Hiroshi Hara*, Tokyo: A.D.A. Edita, 1993.

Hiroshi Hara. *100 Lessons: Learning from Villages*, Tokyo: GA Architect, 1987.

Hiroshi Hara. Architectural Environments for Tomorrow, in *Architectural Environments for Tomorrow*, Kazuyo Sejima and Ryue Nishizawa, Eds., Tokyo: Access, 2011.

Harry Harootunian. *Japan in the World*, Durham, NC: Duke University Press, 1993.

Harry Harootunian. *History's Disquiet*. New York: Columbia University Press, 2000.

Harry Harootunian. *Overcome by Modernity: History, Culture, and Community in Interwar Japan*, New York: Princeton University Press, 2002.

Befu Harumi. Watsuji Tetsurô's Ecological Approach: Its Philosophical Foundation, in Kalland, A. Asquith, Pamela J., *Japanese Images of Nature: Cultural Perspectives*, London: Curzon, 1997.

Itsuko Hasegawa. *Itsuko Hasegawa*, London: Academy Editions, 1993.

Itsuko Hasegawa. *Selected and Current Works. The Master Architect Series*. Victoria: Mulgrave, 1997.

Masao Hayakawa. *The Garden Art of Japan*, Tokyo: Heibonsha/Weatherhill, 1973.

Tatsusaburo Hayashiya, M. Nakamura and S. Hayashiya. *Japanese Arts and the Tea Ceremony*. Tokyo: Heibonsha/Weatherhill, 1974.

Martin Heidegger. *On the Way to Language*, trans. Peter D. Hertz, New York: Harper and Row, 1971.

Kenneth Henshall. *A History of Japan from Stone Age to Superpower*, Basingstoke: Palgrave, 1994.

Sadao Hibi. *Japanese Detail: Architecture*. San Francisco, CA: Chronicle Books, 1989.

Kiyoshi Hirai. *Feudal Architecture of Japan*. Tokyo: Heibonsha/Weatherhill, 1973.

Wontack Hong. *Relationship Between Korea and Japan in Early Period: Paekche and Yamato Wa*, Pan Korea Books, 1988.

Wontack Hong. *Ancient Korea-Japan Relations: Paekche and the Origin of the Yamato Dynasty*, Seoul: Kudara, 2012.

F.L.K. Hsu. *Iemoto: The Heart of Japan*, New York: Halsted Press, 1975.

F.L.K. Hsu. The Japanese: Portrait of Change, *Special Issue, Japan Echo*, XV, 1988.

Mark Hudson. *The Ruins of Identity: Ethnogenesis in the Japanese Islands*, Honolulu: University of Hawaii Press, 1999.

Mark Hudson and Gina L. Barnes. Yoshinogari. A Yayoi Settlement in Northern Kyushu, *Monumenta Nipponica* 46, 2, Summer, 1991, pp. 211–235.

Edmund Husserl. *Ideas Pertaining to a Pure Phenomenology and to a Phenomenological Philosophy*, Book 1, trans. F. Kersten, The Hague: Martinus Nishoff, 1983.

Mitsuo Inoue. *Space in Japanese Architecture*, trans. Hiroshi Watanabe, New York and Tokyo: Weatherhill, 1985.

Timothy Insoll, Ed. *The Oxford Handbook of the Archaeology of Ritual and Religion*, Oxford: Oxford University Press, 2011.

Junya Ishigami. *Small Images*, Tokyo: LIXIL Publishing, 2008.

Junichi Ishizaki. Tracing the Genealogy of Modernism and Materiality in the Works of Raymond, Yoshimura and Masuzawa, Hiroshi Matsukuma, "Modern Houses," *Japan Architect* 22, 2, Summer 1996. Special Issue.

Arata Isozaki. Arata Isozaki: Works in Architecture, RIBA Architecture Center, 1995.

Arata Isozaki. *Japan-ness in Architecture*. Cambridge, MA: MIT Press, 2006.

Arata Isozaki. *The Island Nation*, London: Academy Editions, 1996.

Arata Isozaki. Theme Park, *South Atlantic Quarterly*, 92, 1, Winter 1993.

Arata Isozaki. Of City, Nation, Style, in Masao Miyoshi, (Ed.), *Postmodernism and Japan*, Durham, NC: Duke University Press, 1989.

Arata Isozaki. *Katsura Villa: Space and Form*, New York: Rizzoli, 1987.

Arata Isozaki. Floors and Internal Spaces in Japanese Vernacular Architecture, the Phenomenology of Floors, *RES* 11, Spring 1986, pp. 54–77.

Arata Isozaki. City Demolition Industry, Inc., in Kenneth Frampton (Ed.), *A New Wave of Japanese Architecture*, New York: IAUS, 1978.

Arata Isozaki. Rhetoric of the Cylinder. *JA, The Japan Architect*, April 1976, pp. 61–63.

Arata Isozaki. The Metaphor of the Cube. *JA, The Japan Architect*, March 1976, pp. 27–32.

Teiji Itoh. MA: Space–Time in Japan. Catalogue for the Exhibition at the Cooper–Hewitt Museum, New York, 1979.

Teiji Itoh. *Traditional Domestic Architecture of Japan*, Tokyo: Heibonsha, 1974.

Teiji Itoh. *Space and Illusion in the Japanese Garden*. New York and Tokyo: Weatherhill/Tankosha, 1973.

Toyo Ito. What Was Metabolism? Reflections on the Life of Kiyonori Kikutake, Lecture, November 10, 2012. Graduate School of Design, Harvard University, Cambridge, MA.

Toyo Ito. Blurring Architecture, Milano: Edizioni Charta, 1999.

Toyo Ito. Japan. *Archis* May 1999, Rotterdam, The Netherlands.

Toyo Ito. *Toyo Ito Architectural Monograph* No. 41. London: Academy Editions, 1995.

Toyo Ito. Toyo Ito 1986–1995. *El Croquis*, 71, 1994.

Toyo Ito. Japan: A Dis-oriented Modernity, Special Issue of *Casabella* 608–609, January-February 1994.

Toyo Ito. The Architectural Image of the Microelectronic Age, in Toyo Ito, *JA Library*, Summer 2, 1993, pp. 4–7.

Toyo Ito. Architecture Sought After by Android, *JA, The Japan Architect*, June 1988, pp. 9–13.

Toyo Ito. Toyo Ito, *SD, Space Design* 09/1986, Tokyo: Kajima, 1986.

Toyo Ito. Japan: Climate, Space and Concept, *Process Architecture* 25, 1981.

Toyo Ito. Japanese Houses I, II, III, *GA, Global Architect Houses*, 4, 14, and 20, Tokyo, 1978, 1983, 1986.

Fredric Jameson. *Postmodernism, or, The Cultural Logic of Late Capitalism*, Durham, NC: Duke University Press, 1991.

Japan i Dag (Japan Today). Louisiana Museum, Denmark: Humlebaek, 1995.

Hidenobu Jinnai, Ed. Ethnic Tokyo, *Process Architecture* 72, 1987.

Philip Jodidio. *Tadao Ando: Complete Works*, Taschen Verlag, Cologne, 2004.

John E. Joseph. *Saussure*, Oxford: Oxford University Press, 2012.

Jiro Kamishima. Modernization of Japan and the Problem of "IE" Consciousness, *Acta Asiatica*, 13, 1967.

Gergory J. Kasza. *The State and Mass Media in Japan, 1918–1945*, Berkeley: University of California Press, 1988.

Toshihiko Kawagoe. Agricultural Land Reform in Post-War Japan: Experiences and Issues, World Bank Policy Research Working Paper 2111, May 1999.

Noboru Kawazoe. *Contemporary Japanese Architecture*, Tokyo: Kokusai Bunka Shinkokai, 1965.

Noboru Kawazoe *et al. Metabolism 1960: The Proposals for a New Urbanism*, Bitjsutu Shuppan Sha,1960.

Jackie Kestenbaum. *Emerging Japanese Architects of the 1990s*, New York: Columbia University Press, 1991.

J. Edward Kidder, Jr. *The Lucky Seventh: Early Horyu-ji and Its Time*. International Christian University, Hachiro Yuasa Memorial Museum, 1999.

Makoto Kikuchi. Development and Environmental Control: Takashi Asada and the High Rise City, Artificial Land, and Extreme Architecture in the 1960s, *10+1*, 50, Final Issue, 2008, pp. 96–113.

Yuko Kikuchi. *Japanese Modernization and Mingei Theory, Cultural Nationalism and Orientalism*, London: Routledge Curzon, 2004.

Yuko Kikuchi. The Myth of Yanagi's Originality: The Formation of Mingei Theory in its Social and Historical Context, *Journal of Design History*, 17, 4, 1994.

Kiyonori Kikutake. *Kiyonori Kikutake: Tradition to Utopia*, Milan: L'Arca Edizioni, 1997.

Kiyonori Kikutake. *Concepts and Planning*, Tokyo: Bijutsu Shuppansha, 1978.

Joyce Kilmer. *Trees and Other Poems*, New York: George H. Doran Co., 1914.

Hiroaki Kimura. Modernism and Indeterminacy, *JA, The Japan Architect* 6, Spring 1992.

Waro Kishi. The Future of the Game, *JA, The Japan Architect*, 14, Summer 1994.

Waro Kishi. About Modernism in Architecture. *JA, The Japan Architect*, 6, Spring 1992.

Atsushi Kitagawara. JA, The Japan Architect 8, 92:04.

Nishida Kitarô. *An Inquiry into the Good*, trans. Abe Masao, New Haven: Yale University Press, 1990.

Kishio Kurokawa. *The Architecture of Symbiosis*, New York: Rizzoli, 1988.

Wilhelm Klauser. *Riken Yamamoto*, Boston and Berlin: Birkhäuser Basel, 1999.

Rudolph Klein. *Tadao Ando: Architect Between East and West*, Budapest: Pont, 1995.

Akira Komiyama. Sakakura Associates: Half a Century in Step with Postwar Japanese Modernism in Process, *Architecture* 110, May 1993.

Nikolai Kondratieff. *Long Wave Cycle*, trans. Guy Daniels, Boston: E.P. Dutton, 1984.

Rem Koolhaas and Hans Ulrich Olbrist. *Project Japan: Metabolism Talks*, Cologne: Taschen, 2011.

J. Victor Koschmann. *Revolution and Subjectivity in Post-War Japan*, Chicago: University of Chicago Press, 1996.

Udo Kultermann. *Kenzo Tange*, Barcelona: Gustavo Gili, 1989.

Udo Kulterman, Ed. *Kenzo Tange 1946–1969: Architecture and Urban Design*, London: Pall Mall Press, 1970.

Udo Kultermann. *New Japanese Architecture*, New York: Tubingen, 1960.

Kengo Kuma. *Studies in Organic, Kengo Kuma & Associates*, Tokyo: Toto, 2009.

Kengo Kuma. *Kengo Kuma: Geometries of Nature*, Milan: L'Arca Edizioni, 1999.

Kengo Kuma. Kengo Kuma, *JA, The Japan Architect* 38, 1999.

Kengo Kuma and Luigi Alini. *Kengo Kuma: Works and Projects*. Milan: Electa, 2005.

Kisho Kurokawa. *Metabolism in Architecture*. Studio Vista. 1997.

Kisho Kurokawa. *Kisho Kurokawa: Selected and Current Work*, Mulgrave: Images Publishing, 1995.

Kisho Kurokawa. *The Philosophy of Symbiosis*, trans. Jeffrey Hunter, London: Academy Editions, 1994.

Kisho Kurokawa. *New Wave Japanese Architecture*, London: Academy Editions/Ernst & Sohn, 1993.

Kisho Kurokawa. *From Metabolism to Symbiosis*, New York: John Wiley & Sons, 1992.

Kisho Kurokawa. *From Metabolism to Symbiosis*, London: Academy Editions and New York: St. Martin's Press, 1992.

Kisho Kurokawa. New Wave Japanese Architecture, originally the transcript of his lecture at the Academy Forum in 1992, and first published as *Kisho Kurokawa: From Metabolism to Symbiosis*, London/New York: Academy Editions/St.Martin's Press, 1992.

Kisho Kurokawa. *Intercultural Architecture: The Philosophy of Symbiosis*, Washington, D.C.: American Institute of Architects Press, 1991.

Kisho Kurokawa. *Kisho Kurokawa: The Architecture of Symbiosis*, New York: Rizzoli, 1988.

Kisho Kurokawa. *Rediscovering Japanese Space*, Tokyo and New York: Weatherhill, 1988.

Kisho Kurokawa. *Kisho Kurokawa: Recent Works*, Tokyo: Process Architecture, 1986.

Kisho Kurokawa. *Metabolism in Architecture*, London: Studio Vista, 1977.

Takeo Kuwabara. *Japan and Western Civilization*, Tokyo: University of Tokyo Press, 1983.

Wolf Ladjinsky. *Agrarian Reforms as Unfinished Business, The Selected Papers of Wolf Ladjinsky World Bank Research Publications*, Oxford: Oxford University Press, 1977.

Le Corbusier. *Journey to the East*, Cambridge, MA and London: MIT Press, 1987.

David Leatherbarrow. *Uncommon Ground: Architecture, Technology and Topography*. Cambridge, MA & London: MIT Press, 2000.

Claude Levi-Strauss. *The Elementary Structures of Kinship*, Ed. Rodney Needham, trans. J.H. Bell, J.R. von Sturmer, and Rodney Needham, Boston: Beacon, 1970.

Zhong-Jie Lin. *Kenzo Tange and the Metabolist Movement: Urban Utopias of Modern Japan*, London: Routledge, 2010.

Zhong-Jie Lin. From Megastructure to Megalopolis: Formation and Transformation of Mega-Projects in Tokyo Bay, *Journal of Urban Design* 12, 1, February 2007, pp. 73–92.

Seiji M. Lippit. *Topographies of Japanese Modernism*, New York: Columbia University Press, 2002.

Arnulf Lüchinger. *Structuralism in Architecture and Urban Planning*, Stuttgart: Karl Kramer Verlag, 1981.

C.D. Lummis. Introduction, Japanese Critiques of Technological Society, *Journal of Social and Political Theory*, 8, 3, Fall 1984.

C.D. Lummis. *The Psychological World of Natsume Soseki*, Cambridge, MA: Harvard University Press, 1981.

Jean-François Lyotard. *The Postmodern Condition: A Report on Knowledge*, Minneapolis, MN: University of Minnesota Press, 1979.

Gavan McCormack. Breaking Japan's Iron Triangle, *The New Left Review*, 13, January–February 2002.

Gavan McCormack. *The Emptiness of Japanese Affluence*, London: Routledge, 2001.

Gavan McCormack. Manchukuo: Constructing the Past, *East Asian History*, 2, December 1991.

Peter McNeil. Myths of Modernism: Japanese Architecture, Interior Design and the West, c.1920–1940, *Journal of Design History* 5, 4, 1992.

Brian J. McVeigh. *The Nature of the Japanese State*, London: Nissan Institute/Routledge Japanese Studies Series, 1998.

Fumihiko Maki, B. Bognar, A. Krieger, *et al. Fumihiko Maki: Buildings and Projects*, New York: Princeton Architectural Press, 1997.

Fumihiko Maki. On Maki Architecture/Maki on Architecture, Exhibition Catalogue for "The Architecture of Fumihiko Maki: Modernity and the Construction of Scenery," Victoria and Albert Museum, 2001.

Fumihiko Maki. Modernism at the Crossroads, *Japan Architect* 58, 311, March 1983.

Fumihiko Maki. Japanese City Spaces and the Concept of Oku, *JA, The Japan Architect*, May 1979, pp. 51–62.

Fumihiko Maki. The Theory of Group Form, *JA, The Japan Architect*, February 1970, pp. 39–42.

Fumihiko Maki. Investigations in Collective Form. St. Louis, MO: University of Washington Press, 1964.

Michael F. Marra. *Essays on Japan: Between Aesthetics and Literature*, E.J. Brill, 2010.

Miwa Masahiro. *Japanese Designers at Home and Abroad*, Tokyo: Process Architecture, 1983.

Miyoshi Masao and H.D. Harootunian, Eds. *Japan in the World*, Durham, NC: Duke University Press, 1993.

Miyoshi Masao and H.D. Harootunian, Eds., *Authenticating Culture in Imperial Japan: Kuki Shûzô and the Rise of National Aesthetics*, Berkeley: University of California Press, 1996.

Tomoya Masuda. *Living Architecture: Japan*, New York: Grosset and Dunlap, 1970.

Shinenori Matsui. *The Constitution of Japan: A Contextual Analysis*, London: Hart, 2011.

Yasumitsu Matsunaga. *Kazuo Shinohara*, New York: Institute for Architecture and Urban Studies and Rizzoli International, 1982.

Robert Matthew. *Japanese Science Fiction: A View of a Changing Society*, London: Routledge and Nissan Institute of Japanese Studies, University of Oxford, 1989.

Dirk Meyhöfer. *Contemporary Japanese Architects*, Cologne: Benedikt Taschen, 1994.

Hiroshi Minami. *The Psychology of the Japanese People*, Toronto: University of Toronto Press, 1971.

Sonoda Minoru. *The World of Shinto*, Tokyo: International Shinto Foundation, 2009.

R.H. Mitchell. *Censorship in Imperial Japan*, Princeton, NJ: Princeton University Press, 1983.

R.H. Mitchell. *Thought Control in Pre-War Japan*, Ithaca, NY: Cornell University Press, 1976.

Adachi Mitsuaki. *Kunio Maekawa: Sources of Modern Japanese Architecture*, Tokyo: Process Architecture, 1984.

Masao Miyoshi and Harry D. Harootunian, Eds. *Japan in the World*, Durham, NC: Duke University Press, 1993.

Masao Miyoshi and Harry D. Harootunian, Eds. *Post-modernism and Japan*. Durham, NC: Duke University Press, 1989.

Seiichi Mizuno. *Asuka Buddhist Art: Horyu-ji*, Tokyo: Heibonsha/Weatherhill, 1974.

Patricia Monaghan. *Encyclopedia of Goddesses and Heroines, Africa, Eastern Mediterranean, Asia*, Vol. 1, Greenwood: ABC-CLIO, 2010.

Mori Art Museum. Metabolism: City of the Future, Dreams and Visions of Reconstruction in Postwar and Present day Japan, Exhibition September 17, 2011 to January 15, 2012.

T. Morris-Suzuki. Concepts of Nature and Technology in Pre-Industrial Japan, *East Asian History* 1, June 1991.

Teijiro Muramatsu. Ventures into Western Architecture, in Chisaburoh F. Yamada (Ed.), *Dialogue in Art: Japan and the West*. Tokyo and New York: Kodansha International, 1976.

Teijiro Muramatsu, Hiro Sasaki, and Hiroki Onobayashi. History of Modern Japanese Architecture, 1840–1945, special feature issue of *JA, The Japan Architect*, June 1965.

Hermann Muthesius. *Style-Architecture and Building-Art: Transformations of Architecture in the Nineteenth Century and Its Present Condition*, Chicago: University of Chicago Press, 1996.

T. Najita and H.D. Harootunian. Japanese Revolt Against the West: Political and Cultural Criticism in the Twentieth Century, in *The Cambridge History of Japan, Vol. 6, The Twentieth Century*, Cambridge: Cambridge University Press, 1988.

Mari Nakahara, *et al.*, Eds. *Crafting a Modern World: The Architecture and Design of Antonin and Noemi Raymond*, Princeton, NJ: Princeton University Press, 2006.

Naofumi Nakamura. Meiji-Era Industrialization and Provincial Vitality: The Significance of the First Enterprise Boom of the 1880s, *Social Science Japan Journal* 1, 2, 2000, pp. 187–200.

Oscar Newman, Ed. *CIAM '59 in Otterlo*, Stuttgart: Krämer, 1961.

Raymond Nickerson. Confirmation Bias: A Ubiquitous Phenomenon in Many Guises, *Review of General Psychology*, 2, 2, 1998.

Kazuo Nishi and K. Hozumi. *What is Japanese Architecture?* Tokyo and New York: Kodansha International, 1985.

Yasuhiko Nishizawa. *Itsuko Hasegawa*, Architectural Monographs No. 31, London: Academy Editions, 1994.

Yasuhiko Nishizawa. Modern Architecture in Early Showa Japan: The 1920–1945 Period, *Space Design (SD)* 286, 7, July 1988.

Gunter Nitschke. Rock Flower: Transcience and Renewal in Japanese Form, *Kyoto Journal* 50, Transcience Perspectives on Asia, June 2002, pp. 2–12.

Gunter Nitschke. *From Shinto to Ando: Studies in Architectural Anthropology in Japan*, London: Academy Editions, and Berlin: Ernst and Sohn, 1993.

Gunter Nitschke. *The Architecture of Japanese Gardens*, Cologne: Benedikt Taschen Verlag, 1991.

Gunter Nitschke. 'MA': The Japanese Sense of Place, *AD, Architectural Design*, March 1966.

Kevin Nute. *Frank Lloyd Wright and Japan: The Role of Traditional Japanese Art and Architecture in the Work of Frank Lloyd Wright*, London: Chapman & Hall, 1993.

Mitsuo Ohkawa. Modernism in Wooden Construction 1930–1950: Japanese Approaches Transform Materials, *Space Design (SD)* 432, 9, September 2000.

Emiko Ohnuki-Tierney. *Rice as Self: Japanese Identities Through Time*. Princeton, NJ: Princeton University Press, 1993.

Kakuzo Okakura. *The Book of Tea*, reprint, Tokyo and North Clarendon, VT: Tuttle, 1989.

Naomi Okawa. *Edo Architecture: Katsura and Nikko*, Tokyo: Heibonsha/Weatherhill, 1975.

Sokyo Ono. *Shinto: The Kami Way*, Tokyo and North Clarendon, VT: Tuttle, 1992.

Minoru Ooka. *Temples of Nara and Their Art*. Tokyo: Heibonsha/Weatherhill, 1974.

Ken Tadashi Oshima. *International Architecture in Interwar Japan: Constructing Kokusai Kenchiku*, Seattle: University of Washington Press, 2010.

Ken Tadashi Oshima. Antonin Raymond. *Japan Architect* 33, Spring 1999 Special Issue.

Ken Tadashi Oshima. Den'en Chofu: Building the Garden City in Japan, *Journal of the Society of Architectural Historians*, 55, 2, June 1996.

Ken Tadashi Oshima. Modernism in Japan 1950s–1970s, in *Kenchiku Bunka* 49, 567, January 1994.

Hirotaro Ota. Japan: Climate, Space and Concept, *Process Architecture* 25, Tokyo, 1981.

Hirotaro Ota, Ed. *Japanese Architecture and Gardens*, Tokyo: Kokusai Bunka Shinkokai, 1966.

Robert Treat Paine and Alexander Soper. *The Art and Architecture of Japan*, New Haven and London: Yale University Press and Pelican History of Art, 1958.

Richard T. Pearson. Japan, Korea and China: The Problem of Defining Continuities, *Asian Perspectives*, 19, 1, pp. 176–187.

Juliet Piggott. *Japanese Mythology*, London: Hamlyn, 1969.

Gino K. Piovesana. *Recent Japanese Philosophical Thought*, Tokyo: Enderle, 1968.

Henry Plummer. *Light in Japanese Architecture*, Tokyo: A+U Extra Edition, 1995.

Herbert E. Plutschow. *Introducing Kyoto*, Tokyo and New York: Kodansha International, 1979.

Paolo Polledri, Ed. *Shin Takamatsu*. San Francisco: MOMA and New York: Rizzoli, 1993.

Richard Pommer. The New Architectural Supremacists, *Artforum*, October 1976.

Peter Popham. *Tokyo: The City at the End of the World*, Tokyo and New York: Kodansha International, 1985.

K.B. Pyle. *The New Generation in Meiji Japan: Problems of Cultural Identity 1885–1895*, Stanford: Stanford University Press, 1969.

Mark Ravina. *Land and Lordship in Early Modern Japan*, Stanford, CA: Stanford University Press, 1999.

Antonin Raymond. *An Autobiography*, Tokyo: Tuttle, 1973.

Antonin Raymond. Notes on Architecture in Japan. Cultural Nippon, IV, July 1936.

Kurt G. Raymond, F. Helfrich, and William Whittaker. *Crafting a Modern World, The Architecture and Design of Antonin and Noemi Raymond*, New York: Princeton Architectural Press, 2003.

Edwin O. Reischauer. *Japan: The Story of a Nation*, Tokyo: Tuttle, 1990.

Jonathan M. Reynolds. *Maekawa Kunio and The Emergence of Japanese Modernist Architecture*, Berkeley and Los Angeles: University of California Press, 2001.

Jonathan M. Reynolds. Ise Shrine and a Modernist Construction of a Japanese Tradition. *The Art Bulletin* 83, 2, June 2001, pp. 316–341.

Jonathan M. Reynolds. Japan's Imperial Diet Building: Debate Over the Construction of a National Identity. *Art Journal* 55, 3, Fall 1996.

Paulo Riani. *Contemporary Japanese Architecture*, Florence: Centro Di Edizioni, 1969.

J. Thomas Rimer, Hiroyuki Suzuki and Jonathan Chaves, *Shisendo: Hall of the Poetry Immortals*, Tokyo: Weatherhill, 1991.

J. Thomas Rimer, Ed. *Culture and Identity: Japanese Intellectuals During the Interwar Years*, Princeton, NJ: Princeton University Press, 1990.

Robert M. Rodden, Floyd John, and Richard Laurino. Exploratory Analysis of Firestorms, Stanford Research Institute, Office of Civil Defense, Department of the Army, Washington, D.C. 1965.

John M. Rosenfield. Introduction, in Yutaka Mino, Ed., *The Great Eastern Temple: Treasures of Japanese Buddhist Art from Todai-ji*, Bloomington: Indiana University Press, 1986.

Michael Franklin Ross. *Beyond Metabolism: The New Japanese Architecture*, New York: McGraw Hill, 1978.

J. Barkley Rosser, Jr. and Marina V. Rosser. *Comparative Economics in a Transforming World Economy*, Chicago: Irwin, 1996.

Sophie Roulet and Sophie Soulie. *Toyo Ito: The Architecture of the Ephemeral*, Paris: Editions due Montieur, 1991.

Jay Rubin. From Wholesomeness to Decadence: The Censorship of Literature Under the Allied Occupation, *Journal of Japanese Studies*, 11, 1, Winter 1985.

Jay Rubin. *Injurious to Public Morals: Writers and the Meiji State*, Seattle: University of Washington Press, 1984.

Riitta "Ri" Salastie. *Living Tradition of Panda's Cage? An Analysis of the Urban Conservation in Kyoto*, Helsinki: Helsinki University of Technology, 1999.

Serge Salat, Francoise Labbe, and Fumihiko Maki. *Fumihiko Maki: An Aesthetic of Fragmentation*, New York: Rizzoli, 1988.

Jordan Sand. *The House and Home in Modern Japan: Architecture, Domestic Space, and Bourgeois Culture, 1880–1930*, Cambridge, MA: Harvard University Press, 2005.

Hiroshi Sasaki. *Japanese Architecture 2: Recent Developments*, Tokyo: Process Architecture, 1983.

Peter Cachola Schmal, Jochen Visscher, and Ingeborg Flagge, Eds. *Kisho Kurokawa: Metabolism and Symbiosis*, Berlin: Jovis Verlag, 2004.

Thomas Schneider. Traditionalism and Modernization: The Case for Mori Ogai, *Comparative Civilizations Review*, Boston College, 2012, p. 59–64.

Edward Seidensticker. *Tokyo Rising: The City Since the Great Earthquake*, Tokyo: Tuttle, 1991.

Edward Seidensticker. *Low City, High City: Tokyo from Edo to the Earthquake*, New York: Alfred A. Knopf, 1983.

Kiyosi Seike. *The Art of Japanese Joinery*, Tokyo and New York: Weatherhill, 1977.

Kazuyo Sejima. Kazuyo Sejima, 1988–1996, *El Croquis* 77, 1996.

Karen Severns and Koichi Mori. Magnificent Obsession: Frank Lloyd Wright's Buildings and Legacy in Japan 2005. Documentary.

Marcus Shaffer. Incongruity, Bizarreness and Transcendence: Ritual Machine vs. Technocratic Rationalism at Expo '70, in Globalizing Architecture Machine Traditions, Conference Proceedings of the 102nd Annual Meeting of the Associated Collegiate Schools of Architecture (ACSA), April 10–12, 2014, Florida International University, Miami.

Barrie Shelton. *Learning from the Japanese City: West Meets East in Urban Design*, London: Spon, 1999.

Ben-Ami Shillony. Politics and Culture in Wartime Japan, Oxford: Clarendon, 1981.

Hiroshi Shimizu. *Japanese Firms in Contemporary Singapore*, Singapore: NUS Press, 2008.

Kazuo Shinohara. The Context of Pleasure, *JA, The Japan Architect*, September 1986.

Kazuo Shinohara. Kazuo Shinohara: Complete Works in Original Publications, *JA, The Japan Architect* 93 Spring 2014.

Kazuo Shinohara. A Program from the Fourth Space, *JA, The Japan Architect*, September 1986.

Shigenori Shiratsuka. The Asset Price Bubble in Japan in the 1980s: Lessons for Financial and Macroeconomic Stability, in Indicators and Financial Stability, Conference Proceedings, IMF-BIF Conference on Real Estate, International Monetary Fund, Washington, D.C. October 27–28, 2003.

Donald Shively, Ed. *Tradition and Modernization in Japanese Culture*, Princeton, NJ: Princeton University Press, 1971.

Kuki Shûzô. *Observations on Japanese Taste: The Structure of 'Iki,'* ed. Matsui Sakuko and J. Clark, Sydney: Power Publications, 1996.

Kuki Shûzô. The Structure of 'Iki,' trans. Hosoi Atsuko and Jacqueline Pigeot, *Critique*, 29, 308, January 1973.

Miriam Silverberg. Constructing a New Cultural History of Pre-War Japan, in Miyoshi Masao, Y. Sugimoto, and J.P. Arnanson, Eds., *Japanese Encounters with Post-modernity*, London: KPI, 1995.

David Slawson. *Secret Teachings in the Art of Japanese Gardens: Design Principles, Aesthetic Values*, Tokyo and New York: Kodansha International, 1987.

Daniel Smihula. *Long Waves of Technological Innovations*, Bratislava: Studia Politica Slovaca, 2011.

Henry D. Smith, II. Tokyo as an Idea: An Exploration of Japanese Urban Thought Until 1945, *Journal of Japanese Studies* 4, 1, Winter 1978, p. 45–50.

Patrick Smith. *Japan: A Reinterpretation*, New York: Vintage Books, 1997.

Andre Sorenson. *The Making of Urban Japan: Cities and Planning from Edo to the Twenty-First Century*, London and New York: Routledge and Nissan Institute, Routledge Japanese Studies Series, 2002.

Manfred Speidel, Ed. *Team Zoo – Buildings and Projects 1971–1990*, New York: Rizzoli, 1991.

Roy Starrs. The Kojiki as Japan's National Narrative, in Edwina Palmer, Ed., *Asian Futures, Asian Traditions*, Folkestone, KT: Global Oriental, 2005.

David B. Stewart and Yatsuka Hajime. *Arata Isozaki Architecture 1960–1990*, New York: Rizzoli, 1991.

David B. Stewart. *The Making of a Modern Japanese Architecture, 1868 to the Present*, Tokyo: Kodansha International, 1987.

Louis Sullivan. *Kindergarten Chats and Other Writings*. New York: Dover, 2012.

Louis Sullivan. Yoshio Taniguchi, *The Japan Architect* 21, Spring 1996.

Daisetz T. Suzuki. *Zen and Japanese Culture*, Princeton, NJ: Princeton University Press, 1959.

Daisetz T. Suzuki. *Zen Buddhism*, New York: Double Anchor Books, 1956.

Hiroyuki Suzuki. The "Blown Roof" in Modern Japanese Architecture, *Japan Echo*, XIV, 1, 1987.

Hiroyuki Suzuki and Reyner Banham. *Contemporary Architecture of Japan*, New York: Rizzoli, 1985.

Kakichi Suzuki. *Early Buddhist Architecture in Japan*, Tokyo: Kodansha International, 1980.

Shin Takamatsu. *SD, Space Design* (01/1988). Tokyo: Kajima, 1988.

Shuji Takashina, Ed. Tokyo: Creative Chaos, *Japan Echo*, XIV, 1987.

Soshichi Uchii. Is the Philosophy of Science Alive in the East? A Report from Japan, Lecture at Kyoto University, March 14, 2002.

Yoseburo Takokoshi. *The Economic Aspects of the History of the Civilization of Japan*, (1930), London: Routledge, 2005.

Kyokichi Tanaka. Quest for Tokyo in the Future, *The Japan Architect*, 63, June 1988.

T. Tanaka. The Acceptance of Western Civilization in Japan, *East Asian Cultural Studies*, VI, March 1967.

Kenzo Tange. Creating a Contemporary System of Aesthetics, *The Japan Architect*, 65, January 1990.

Kenzo Tange. A Plan for Tokyo, *The Japan Architect*, 62, November/December 1987.

Kenzo Tange. Towards Urban Design, *The Japan Architect*, 46, 9–10/176, September/October 1971.

Kenzo Tange and Kawazoe Noboru. *Ise: Prototype of Japanese Architecture*, Cambridge, MA: MIT Press, 1965.

Junichirô Tanizaki. *In Praise of Shadows*, trans. T.J. Harper and Edward G. Seidensticker, New Haven, CT: Leete's Island Books, 1977.

Sakamoto Taro. *The Six National Histories of Japan*, Vancouver: University of British Columbia Press, 1991.

Bruno Taut. Houses and People of Japan, reprinted in Daedalos, 15, December 1994, pp. 62–76.

Bruno Taut. *Fundamentals of Japanese Architecture*, Tokyo: Hideya Takamura, 1937.

Charles Taylor. *Modern Social Imaginaries*, Durham: Duke University Press, 2004.

Karel Teige. *The Minimal Dwelling*, trans. Eric Dluhosch, Cambridge, MA: MIT Press, 2002.

Egon Tempel. *New Japanese Architecture*, New York: Praeger, 1969.

Yasuhiro Teramatsu, Ed. Shigeru Ban, *The Japan Architect* Special Issue, 30, 1998.

Watsuji Tetsurô. *Climate and Culture: A Philosophical Study*, trans. Geoffrey Bownas, Westport, CT: Greenwood Press, 1961.

Ming Tiampo. *Gutai: Decentering Modernism*, Chicago: University of Chicago Press, 2010.

Elise K. Tipton and John Clark, Eds. *Being Modern in Japan: Culture and Society from the 1910s to the 1930s*, Honolulu: University of Hawaii Press, 2000.

Shigeki Toyama. Reformers of the Meiji Restoration and the Birth of Modern Intellectuals, *Acta Asiatica*, 13, 1967.

Mark Treib and Ron Herman. *Guide to the Gardens of Kyoto*, Tokyo: Shufunotomo, 1980.

Alice Tseng. *The Imperial Museums of Meiji Japan: Architecture and the Art of the Nation*, Seattle: The University of Washington, 2008.

Shunsuke Tsurumi. *An Intellectual History of Wartime Japan*, London: Routledge, 1986.

Alexander Tzonis and Liane Lefaivre. *Architecture of Regionalism in the Age of Globalization, Peaks and Valleys in the Flat World*, London: Routledge, 2011.

Alexander Tzonis and Liane Lefaivre. *Critical Regionalism, Architecture and Identity in a Globalized World*, Munich: Prestel, 2003.

Makoto Ueda. The Architecture of Kameki Tsuchiura: A Reappreciation, *Space Design (SD)* 7, 382, July 1996.

Florian Urban. Japanese 'Occidentalism' and the Emergence of Postmodern Architecture, *ACSA Journal of Architectural Education* 65, 2, pp. 89–102, March 2012.

Paul Varley. *Japanese Culture*, Tokyo: Tuttle, 1974.

Robert Venturi. *Complexity and Contradiction in Architecture*, New York: Museum of Modern Art, 1966.

Maurizio Vitta, Ed. *Kiyonori Kikutake: From Tradition to Utopia*, Milan: l'Arca Edizioni, 1997.

Maurizio Vitta, Ed. *Shin Takamatsu: Architecture and Nothingness*, Milan: l'Arca Edizioni, 1996.

Gabriele Vorreiter. Japan, *The Architectural Review*, Special Issue, 1089, November 1987.

Paul Waley. Tokyo-as-World-City: Reassessing the Role of Capital and the State in Urban Restructuring, *Urban Studies* 44, 8, July 2007, pp. 1465–1490.

Hiroshi Watanabe. *The Architecture of Tokyo*, Fellbach: Editions Axel Menges, 2001.

Hiroshi Watanabe. *Amazing Architecture from Japan*, Tokyo and New York: Weatherhill, 1991.

Makoto Sei Watanabe. *Conceiving the City*, Milan: L'Arca Edizioni, 1998.

Yasutada Watanabe. *Shinto Art: Ise and Izumo Shrines*, Tokyo: Heibonsha/Weatherhill, 1974.

Roxana Waterson. *The Living House: An Anthropology of Architecture in South-East Asia*, 3rd Edition, Thames and Hudson: Oxford University Press, 1997.

Cherie Wendelken. Putting Metabolism Back in Place: The Making of a Radically Decontextualized Architecture in Japan, in Sarah Williams Goldhagen, and Rejean Legault (Eds.), *Anxious Modernisms: Experimentation in Postwar Architectural Culture*, Cambridge: MIT Press, 2002.

Pieter van Wesemael. *Architecture of Instruction and Delight, A Socio-Historical Analysis of World Exhibitions as a Didactic Phenomenon, 1798–1851–1970*, Rotterdam: 010 Publishers, 2001.

George M. Wilson and Leslie Pincus. In a Labyrinth of Western Desire: Kuki Shuzo and the Discovery of Japanese Being, *Monumenta Nipponica*, 103, 1, January 1998.

Ron Witte. *Toyo Ito – Sendai Mediatheque*, Munich and New York: Prestel Verlag, 2002.

Christopher Wood. *The Bubble Economy: Japan's Extraordinary Speculative Boom of the '80s and the Dramatic Bust of the '90s*, Atlantic Monthly Press, 1992.

Koji Yagi. *Japan: Climate, Space, and Concept*, Tokyo: Process Architecture, 1981.

Riken Yamamoto. *Cell City*, Tokyo: INAX Publishing, 1993.

Riken Yamamoto. *How to Make a City*, Luzern: Architekturgalerie Luzern, 2014.

Kunio Yanagita. *The Legends of Tono*, trans. R.S. Morse, Tokyo: Japan Foundation, 1975.

Kunio Yanagita. About our Ancestors: The Japanese Family System, UNESCO, Japanese Ministry of Education, 1970.

Masai Yasuo, Ed. *Edo/Tokyo Through Maps: Atlas Tokyo*, Tokyo: Heibonsha, 1986.

Hajime Yatsuka. Post–Modernism and Beyond, *JA, The Japan Architect*, 2, 1986.

Hajime Yatsuka. Architecture in the Urban Desert: A Critical Introduction to Japanese Architecture After Modernism, *Oppositions: A Journal for Ideas and Criticism in Architecture*, Peter Eisenman, Ed. Cambridge, MA: MIT Press for the Institute for Architecture and Urban Studies, 1981, pp. 21–27.

Shoei Yoh. *In Response to Natural Phenomena*, Milan: l'Arcaedizioni, 1997.

Ishihara Yoshinobu. *A Hidden Order: Tokyo Through the Twentieth Century*, Tokyo: Kodansha, 1989.

Molly Young, Tiny Spaces, *New York Times*, May 8, 2016.

David Young and Michiko Kimura. *Introduction to Japanese Architecture*, Hong Kong: Periplus Editions, 2004.

Index

Italic numbers refer to figures

"19 Article" constitution 21
21st Century Museum *193*, 194–195, *194*, 221
2004 House 204–205, *204*

Abe, Hitoshi 207, 211, 222–223, 241, 243, 259, *261*
Adorno, Theodor 131
aesthetic nationalism 49
Aichi Prefectural Government Office 58
Aida, Takefumi *136*
Aisaku Hayashi House 51
Allied Occupation 73–76, 100, 141, 165
alternative residence 38
Aluminum House 174–175
Amane, Nishi 49
Ama-no-Uzume 247
Amaterasu 9–10, 11, 247
American Architectural and Engineering Company 53
American Institute of Architects 2
Ando, Tadao 54, 165–172, 181, 194, 196, 207
Angelidou, Ioanna 4
Anti-Communist Pact 58
Aoki, Jun 136, 195–196, 211
Aomori Museum of Fine Art 195, *196*
apprenticeships 2
Arai, Chiaki 180–183
Architectural Institute of Japan 47
Arinobu Fukuhara House 51
Arita, Hachiro 44
Art Museum for the University 222
Arts and Crafts architecture 44, 229–230
Asada, Takashi 3–4
Asakusa Culture Tourist Information Center 190, *191*
Ashbee, Charles Robert 229
Ashikaga period 31
"Asia is one" theory 58

Asuka period 20–21
Atelier Bow-Wow 201, *202*
Atomic Bomb Dome 76
Atsuta Shrine 247
Awaji Island International Park City 170
Awaji Yumebutai International Conference Center 170–171, *171*
Awakening of the East (Okakura) 49
azaleas 220–221
Azuchi-Momoyama period 33–34

Bamboo house 189, *189*
Bank of Japan 47
Barthes, Roland 1
Bauhaus 232–233
BEANS Bookstore 235, *236*
Behaviorology 201
Behrens, Peter 65, 229–230
Being and Time (Heidegger) 144
Beistegui House 244
Benacerraf house 130
Benedict, Ruth 34
Beppu City Hall 63 237, *238*
Book of Tea, The (Kakuzō) 165
Boshin War 43
Bouno House 259, *261*
Brutalist style 85, 89, 90, 94, 257
Bubble Economy 141, 201
"Bubbletecture" group 211
BUMPS building 235, *235*
Bunriha Kenchiku Kai (Secessionist Architecture group) 64, 65
Burgess, William 47
Burke, Edmund 184, 257, 259
Buzen house 223, *227*

capitalism 44
Carson Price Scott Building 63
Case Study House Program 233
Cassirer, Ernst 99, 195
castle towns 37
Centennial Hall, Tokyo Institute of Technology *122*, 123, *123*, *124*, 125, *125*, 175, 207
Central Telegraph office 65
Central Telephone Office 61, *61*
chanoyu 35
chaos theory 126
Charter Oath (1868) 44, 46, 48
chashitsu 28
Cheng, Ji 28
Children's Center for Psychiatric Rehabilitation 259, *261*, *262*
Chokkura Plaza 190, *190*
Chosin Reservoir, Battle of 76
Church of St. Anselm 53, *53*
Church of the Light 169–170, *169*
Chūta, Itō 59, *59*
City in the Air initiative 147
Classic of Tea (Luyu) 34
Collective Form cluster 100, 102, 105, 144
Collezione 170, *170*
colonialism 44
colossal order 90
Commune at the Great Wall project 188–189, *189*
Complexity and Contradiction in Architecture (Venturi) 26–28
Conder, Josiah 46–48, 64
Constitution 48
Constructivism 155, 161
Convention of Kanagawa 43
Corbusier, Le: Ando and 165, 167, 172–173, 181; Aoki and 195; apprenticeships with 60, 92; Citrohan prototype by 65; Festival Hall and 94; Graves and 129; influence of 85–86; Ito and 177; Kishi and 244; *L'Esprit Nouveau* 1; Sejima and 191, 192, 193; Tange and 76; tensile structure and 82; *Vers Une Architecture* 60; during WWII 233; Yoshizaka and 93
Country and the City, The (Williams) 131
coup d'état attempt 57
Course in General Linguistics (Saussure) 130
"criterion of beauty in Japan" 50
Critical Regionalism 237, 239–241
Crystal Palace 112, 229, 234
Cubic Forest House 122

Daibutsuden 24
Dai-Ichi-Kangyo Bank 47
Dai-Ichi Seimei Building 73, *75*

Daimyo 37, 38
Daisen-in 28
Dai-tō-a Kyōeiken 44
Danchi 178
Dancing Trees, Singing Birds 249, *251*
Dannoura, Battle of 25
Davey, Peter 229
Deconstructivism 130–131
defensive borrowing 44
Deutsche Werkbund 230, 232
Dialectic of Enlightenment (Adorno and Horkheimer) 131
Dior stores 211, *213*
Discontinuous Unity 93
divine origin, belief in 9
Doctrine of the Three Stages of Development, The (Taketani) 98
Doken Kokka (Construction State) 2–3, 141
Dwelling Group Domain Theory 144

Eiffel Tower 229
Eisai 26, 28, 34
Elementary Structures of Kinship, The (Lévi-Strauss) 130
Emancipation of Farm Land 73
emotional encounter 121–122
Endo, Arata 51, 52
Endo, Shuhei 205, 207, 211, 264
Endoh, Masaki 216
Endoh Design House & MIA 216
engawa 219–227
Engels, Friedrich 98
Englishe, Haus, Das (Muthesius) 229
Ent-fernung 144
Environmental Education Center *209*, 211
Ernst Ludwig, Grand Duke 229
Euclidian geometry 161–162
Expo '70 111–119, 135, 161, 178

Farmland Adjustment Act 74
February 26 Incident 57
Feininger, Lyonel 232
Fillmore, Millard 43
Finite Element Method (FEM) 183
First Enterprise Boom 44
flatness 207, 211
F-town *210*, 211
fudo 98–99
Fuji Kindergarten 250, *252*
Fujimoto, Sou 138, *138*, 222, 253, 254–255, 258–259, 26, *262*
Fuji Television 143, *143*
Fujiwara period 25
Fukuda, Tomoo *112*
Fukuoka Cultural Center 47

Galerie des Machines 229
Garden of Fine Arts 170–171, *172*
gardens 28, 220–221
Gas Company Headquarters Building 63–64, *63*
Gazebo 178, 180
Geist der Gotik, Der (Scheffler) 232
Geku 11
Gemma Edict (1615) 37
Genmei, Empress 10
German Expressionism 64
Germany, dialogue with 58
Getty Museum 220–221
Gifu Kitagata Apartment Building 192–193, *192*
Gikai 28
Gilbert, Cass 52
Ginkaku-ji 32–33, *33*
Giri-On relationships 2, 4
Goethe, Johann Wolfgang von 240
Golden Hoard 31
Golden Twenties 231–232
Go-Sanjo 25
Go-Shirakawa 25
Gothic 232
Graves, Michael 129
Greater East Asia Co-Prosperity Sphere 49, 58, 85–86
Gropius, Walter 65, 155, 232–233
Guaranty Building 63
Gunjin Kaikan Building 58
Gunma Music Center 53, *54*, 195
Gunma Prefectural Museum of Modern Art 161

Hakusuki-no-e, Battle of 23
Hamaguchi, Osachi 57
Hamlet 178, 180, *180*
Hanselmann house 129–130
Hara, Hiroshi 144, 147–148, 187
Harada, Masahiro and Mao 215–216
Harumi Housing *108*, 109
Hasagawa, Itsuko 173–174
Hashihaka tomb 20
Hashimoto, Kingoro 57
Haushofer, Karl 58
Hegel, G. W. F. 98, 232
Heian period 24–25
Heidegger, Martin 144
Heien-Jinju Shrine 157
Heiji Rebellion 25
Heisei Boom 3
Hidden Order, A (Yoshinobu) 126
High Treason Incident 48
Hillside Terrace 105–106, *106*, 153, *154*, 159, 167
Himeji castle 38, *38*
himorogi 247–248

Hinoki 11–12, 207
Hirata, Akihisa 262, 264, *264*
Hiroshima Peace Center 3–4
Hiroshima Peace Memorial Park 76–77, *77*, 116
Hiroshi Nakamura & NAP Co. Ltd. 216
history, role of 4–5
Hitler, Adolf 233
Hōgen no Ran 25
Hojo-in, Uji 25
Horkheimer, Max 131
Horyu-ji 21–22, *22*
Horyu-ji Museum *162*, 163
Hosaka, Kenjiro 195
Hotakubo Daiichi 178, 180
"House and Garden" complex 202, *203*
House N 222, *226*
Houses and People of Japan (Taut) 60
House SH 216, *216*, *217*
House Under High Voltage Lines 122, 123
housing, social 178, 180, 193
Huizinga, Johan 136
Humanism 207
Husserl, Edmund 98
Hyakudanen 170

Ichiban-kan 131, *133*
ichi go ichi-e 35
Ideals of the East, The (Okakura) 49
Ieyasu, Tokugawa 33, 36–38, *36*
Ikaruga no Miya 21
Ikeda, Masahiro 216
ikkoku ichijo rei 37
Imagawa, Yoshimoto 36–37
Imperial Art Commission 49
Imperial Colors Incident 57
Imperial Crown style 58, 85–86
Imperial Hotel and Annex 51, *52*, 190
Imperial Palace 247
Imperial Rescript on Education 48
Imperial Villa 60
Ingalls Hockey Rink 82
International Design Conference 97
International House of Japan 92, *93*, 97
International Style 89
intersections, challenges of 61
Inter-University Seminar House 94, *94*, 237
Inui, Kumiko 211, 234, *234*
Investigations in Collective Form (Maki) 153, 155, 167
Irwin, Robert 220
Ise Shrine 11–13, *12*, 98, 163, 169, 183, 188, 207, 247
Ishigami, Junya 250, *252*, *253*, 254
Ishii, Kazuhiro 248
Ishikawa, Jozan 219

Ishimoto, Kikuji 64, 65
Ishizaka, Takeshi 214
Isozaki, Arata: Expo '70 and 113–114; flatness and 207; Gifu Kitagata Apartment Building and 192; Gunma and 195; Marxism and 119; Metabolism and 99, 132, 135–136; on modernism 58, 60; Sendai Mediatheque and 175–176; Tange and 100; work of 159–163; Wright and 52
Ito, Toyo 100–101, 174–178, 191, 207
Itten, Johannes 232
Iwato Boom 3
Izanagi 9–10, 11, 247
Izanami 9, 11, 247
Izumo Shrine Administrative Building 101, *102*, 247
Izumo Taisha, Shimane 11, 13

Jameson, Frederic 131, 138, 162
Japanese Guild of Crafts 50–51
Japanese Land Reform Act (1873) 44
Japanese Pavilion *92*
Japan Housing Corporation (JHC) 178
Japan Institute of Architects 2
Japan International Architectural Association 60
Japan-ness (Isozaki) 163
Japan-United States Mutual Cooperation and Security Treaty 119
Jencks, Charles 131, 134
Jiyu Gakuen School 51
Johnson, Philip 130, 215
jokamachi 37
Jomon 13–17, *14*
Juko, Murato 35
Jūkyo Shūgōron 144
Jurakudai Palace 34

Kaerumataike Dam 15
Kagawa Prefectural Office 77, *78*
Kagu-tsuchi 9
Kahn, Louis 165, 167, 172, 173, 177, 180–181, 244, 259
Kajima Corporation 2, 46
Kajima, Momoyo 201
Kakuzō, Okakura 165
Kamakura Museum of Modern Art *92*
Kamakura period 25
Kamiya, Koji *112*
Kammu 24
Kanagawa Institute of Technology (KAIT) 250, *252, 253*
Kanagawa Prefectural Government Building 58
Kandinsky, Wassily 64
Kanno Museum *210*, 211
Kant, Immanuel 184
Karesansui Zen gardens 28
Kasuien Annex 80

Katachi 98
Kataoka-Ishimoto Architectural Studio 65
Kataoka, Yashushi 65
Katayama, Tokoma 47
Katsumoto, Hosokawa 28
Katsura Rikyu 35–36, *36*, 98, 100, 163, 167, 183, 207
Kawai House *50*, 51, *51*
Kawzoe, Noboru 100
Kemmu, Emperor 31
Kikutake, Kiyonori 97, 98, 100, *101*, 106, 113, 173, 174
Kilmer, Joyce 4
Kimmei, Emperor 20–21
Kimura, Toshihiko 149
Kingo, Tatsuno *46*, 47–48
Kinkaku-ji 31–32, *32*
Kirin Plaza 184–185, *184*
Kirosan Observatory 188
Kishi, Waro 243–244, *243*
Kitakamakura 237, *239, 240*
Kitakyushu Municipal Museum of Art 161
Kiyomori, Taira 25
Kofun period 20
Kogei no Michi (Soetsu) 50
Kogyoku, Empress 22
Kojiki or Record of Ancient Matters, The 9, 10–11
kokudaka 38
Komatsu, Sakyo 112
Kondratiev, Nikolai 131
Korean War 75–76
Kotoku, Emperor 22
Kruger, Otto 229
Kuma, Kengo 121, 136–138, 187–190, 194
Kunstwollen 230
Kurashiki City Hall 77, *79*
Kurokawa, Kisho 13, 98, 100, 101, 114, 132–134, *134*, 149, 207
Kuwabara, Takeo 112
Kyororo Natural Science Center 207, *208*, 211
Kyoto International Conference Center 101, *103*, 116
Kyoto Station 148–149, *148*

Land Reform law 74–75
land reforms 73–75
Land Tax Revision Act (1873) 74
Language of Post-Modern Architecture, The (Jencks) 134
Lanvin boutique 212, *214*
Leach, Bernard 49–50
Lévi-Strauss, Claude 130
London Naval Treaty 57
Long, Richard 258–259
"Looptecture" series 211
Loos, Adolf 1
Lotus beauty salon 236, *237*

Lotus Sutra Hall 23
Louis Vuitton stores 195–196, *197*, 211, *212*
Lutyens Edwin, 129
Luyu 34
Lyotard Francois, 130–131

M2 Building 136–138, *137*, 187
Ma 163
MacArthur, Douglas 69, 73, 74–76
"Machine Age" 229
Maekawa House 86, *87*
Maekawa, Kunio 54, 85–90, *86*, 92, 97
Main Points of Education 48
Makawa, Kunio 109
Maki, Fumihiko 102, 105–106, 144, 153–159, 167, 207
Mamoru, Yamada 64, 65
Manchoukuo 57
Mandel, Ernest 131
mathematical city 126
Meier, Richard 220
Meiji, Emperor 43, 48
Meiji Restoration 1, 2, 37, 44, 48, 74
Memorial Cathedral for World Peace 80, *81*
Memu Meadows Experimental House 121
Mendelsohn, Erich 65
Metabolism movement 74, 76, 97–109, 111–112, 114, 119, 132–133, 153, 155, 187, 235
Metabolism: The Proposals for a New Urbanism 97
Metropolitan Festival Hall 86–89, *87, 88*, 94
Michelangelo 90
Midway, Battle of 68
mie-gakure 28
Mies van der Rohe, Ludwig 85, 130, 165, 191, 215, 232, 233
Mikimoto Ginza 2 178, *179*
Mikunisō 50
Mingei 50
mini-exhibitions 1
minimalism 66
Minimum Dwelling, The (Teige) 85
Ministry of Communication 60–64
Minka farmhouse 15, *15*
minshū-teki-na kōgei 50
Miyagi Stadium 241, *241*
modernism/Modernism: allegiance to 64–65; Ando and 167, 172–173; beginnings of 229; criticism of 144; in Germany 229–232; Isozaki and 160–162; in Japan 52, 57–58, 60–69; Maki and 106, 155, 157, 159; Metabolism and 101; Postmodernism and 130; reaction to 58; reinventing 229–244; role of 3–4; Sejima and 191, 192, 193–194; Shinohara on 125; suppression of 65; Tange and 76–77, 80, 82; in United Kingdom 233–234; in United States 233; *see also* Postmodernism

Modern Movement 85
Morigo Office Building 66–67, *66*, 207, *208*
Morris, William 49–50, 229, 230
Mosaic House 202, *203*
Motoe, Masahige 259
Mount Fuji Architects Studio 215–216, *254*, 255, 259
Mozu-Furuichi Tomb cluster 20
mujokan 99
Murano, Togo 65–68, 76, 80, 207, 211
Muromachi period 31
Musashino Library 222, *224, 225*
Museum of Brazilian Sculpture 257, *258*
Museum of Fruit 173, 174
Museum of Wood 194
Muthesius, Hermann 229–230

Nagoya City Hall 58
NA House *253*, 254–255
Nakagin Capsule Tower 101–102, *103, 104*
Nakagyo *243*, 244, *244*
Nakamura, Hiroshi 212, 236, 249–250, *251*
Nakatomi no Kamatari 22
Nakayama, Hideyuki 202, *204*
Nakaya Ukichiro Museum of Snow and Ice 194–195
Nandaimon gate 23, 163
NAP 236
Nara period 23–24
National Art Center 149, *149*
nationalism 48
National Museum of Modern Art 155, *157*, 159
National Museum of Western Art 94, *95*
Natural Ellipse House 216, *216*
nature 4, 247–255
Nibani-kan 131–132, *132*
Nihonbashi house 243–244, *243*
Nihon Shoki (Chronicles of Japan) 10–11
nijiriguchi 35
Nippon Electric Research Laboratory 63
Nisbett, Richard 126
Nishida, Kitaro 49
Nishiyama, Uzo 112, 113
Nishizawa, Ryue 121, 191, 193, 202, *203*
Nissei Theatre 80, *80, 81*
Nitschke, Gunter 99
Nobunaga, Oda 33–34, 35, 36–37
Nochi Kaiho 73
"Norm versus Form" 230
Notoyasu, Matsudaira 36–37
NYH house 222, *223*, 234, *234*

Obasyashi 46
Obasyashi Gumi 2
Odawara Performing Arts and Cultural Center 183

Ofunato Civic Cultural Center (Rias Hall) *181, 182,* 183
Ogai, Mori 49
Ogasawara Museum 193–194
Ohashi, Tomio 123, 144
Ohnishi, Maki 191
Oita Medical Hall 161
Okada, Shin'ichiro 48
Okakura, Kakuzo 49
Okakura, Tenshin 58
Okamoto, Taro 117–118
Olbrich, Joseph Maria 64
Olympic Complex 4
Omiwa Jinja 20
Omotesando *177,* 195–196
Onbashira Festival 248
one-castle-one-province edit 37–38
Onin War 31, 33
Ōno Yasumaro 10
Origin 1 *184*
Origin series 184
Osaka: Central Public Auditorium 47–48, *47;* Nakanoshima *47;* Post Office 63
Otaka, Masato 102, 105, 106
Otake house 236, *238*
Otani, Sachio 3–4, 101, 114, 116

Pankok, Bernhard 229
parametric modeling, rejection of 4
Parthenon 12–13
Paulista School 257
Pelletire, Louise 207
Peng, Kaiping 126
Pérez-G ómez, Alberto 207
Perret, Auguste 52
Perry, Matthew C. 43
Pet Architecture (Atelier Bow-Wow) 201
Plaza-Symbol Zone 112–114
Plocek House 130
Portsmouth Treaty 48
Positivism 99
Postmodernism 125, 129–138, 162; *see also* modernism/Modernism
Postmodernism, or, The Cultural Logic of Late Capitalism (Jameson) 131
prefabrication 234–235
property rights 73–74, 99
Public Party of Patriots 44
public space Togugawa regime and 38–39
Purgin, W. N. 229

Raku bowls 35
Raymond, Antonin 52–54, *53, 54,* 85, 153, 167
Reader's Digest Building 53, *53*

Reigl, Alois 230
Reihoku Town Hall 223, *227*
"Re-modeling the Japanese Archipelago" Program 3
retrenchment 44, 48
reverse course 75
Reynolds, Jonathan 61
rice cultivation 10, 13, 15–16, 20, 74
Ring House 248–249, *249, 250*
Rocha, Mendes de 257, *258*
Rokumeikan 47
Romanticism 214, *215*
Rotunda 178, 180
Ruskin, John 229, 240–241
Russo-Japanese War 48
rust, controlled 207, 211
Ryoan-ji *26,* 28, 165, *166,* 194

Saarinen, Eero 82
Saijō-ji *27,* 28
Saishunkan Seiyaku Women's Dormitory 191–192
Saitama Museum 134–135
Sakaida Artificial Ground development 105, 106, *107*
Sakakura, Junzo 92–93, 97, 114, 116
Sakamoto, Ryoma 48–49
SAKO Architects 214
Sako, Keiichiro 214, 234–235
Sakoku, policy of 43
Sakura House 215–216, *215*
Sakurakai 57
Samurai 37, 44
SANAA 191, 194, 202
San Francisco, Treaty of 73, 76
Sangatsu-do 23
sankin kotai 38–39
Saragaku commercial complex 262, 264, *264*
Sasaki-Gishi Medical Services Offices 241, *242,* 243
Saussure, Ferdinand de 130
Scheffler, Karl 232
Schmidt, Karl 229
Second Sino-Japanese War 57
Sejima, Kazuo 191–195, 202, 221
Sekigahara, Battle of 37
Sendai Mediatheque 175–177
Sen no Rikyu 35
Shanghai, Battle of 57
Shanghai Ceasefire Agreement 57
Shaw, Richard Norman 48
Shikibu, Murosaki 24, 36
Shimizu Kentetsu 2, 46
Shimoda, Kikutaro 58
Shimonoseki, Treaty of 48
Shinohara, Kazuo 121–126, 173, 175, 178, 187, 207, 259

Shinohara School 121–126
Shinokenchikukarenmei 64, 65
Shinshichi, Takeuchi 58
Shinto 10–13, 73
Shin-Yatsushiro Monument 211, *213*
Shisendo 219–220, *220*
Shisen no ma 219
Shizuoka Press and Broadcasting center 108, *108*
shoin zukuri 26
Shomu, Emperor 23, 24
Shonandai Cultural Center and Civic Theatre 173–174
shoshin 98
Shoso-in 23–24
Shoten, Iwanami 65
Shotoku Yatsumimi 21–22
Showa Restoration 57
Silver Hut, Museum of Architecture 175, *175*
Sino-Japanese War 47, 48
Sky House 100, *101*, 106
Smithson, Peter 77
Snyderman house 130
Soami 28
Soetsu, Yanagi 49–50
Soga no Iname 20–21
Sony Tower 101, 102, *105*
Sore Kara (Soseki) 49
Soseki, Natsume 49
Sousha 64
South Manchurian Railway sabotage 57
space frame roof 112, *112*
Spiral 155, *156*, 159
Springtecture 205, *205*
Staatliches Bauhaus 232
State Buddhism 24
Steel Hut, Museum of Architecture *174*, 175
Stirling, James 130
Stone Museum 190, 194
Stones of Venice (Ruskin) 229
Stresemann, Gustav 231
Structuralism 130–131
sublime 184, 257–264
sukiya 35–36, 65
Sullivan, Louis 63, 90
Suppose Design 236
Suppose Design Office 121, 223, *227*
Susano-o-no-Mikoto 9–10, 11, 247
Sutemi, Horiguchi 64–65

Taika reforms 22–23
Taisei Kentetsu 2
Taisu 46
Takamatsu Gymnasium 82–83, *83*
Takamatsu, Shin 183

Takamatsusuka mound 20
Takamori, Saigo 44, *45*
Takara pavilion 114, *116, 117*
Takauji, Ashikaga 31
Takei-Nabeshima Architects (TNA) 248
Takenaka Komuten 2, 46
Taketani, Mitsuo 98
Takeyama, Minoru 131–132, *132*, 133
Tale of the Genji (Shikibu) 24, 35, 36
Tanaka Kakuei, 3
Tange, Kenzo: Expo '70 and 112, 113, 118; Fuji
    Television building by 143, *143*; Hiroshima Peace
    Memorial Park and 3–4, 76–77, 80; Isozaki and 160,
    161; Maki and 153, 155; Metabolism and 100–101;
    Raymond and 54; Taniguchi and 163; Tokyo
    Metropolitan Goverment Building by 141, *142*, 143;
    work of 106, 108; World Design Conference and 97;
    Yoyogi National Gymnasium and Swimming Pool and
    82–83
Taniguchi, Yoshiro 63, 163
Tanijiri, Makoto 15, 223, 236–237
Taut, Bruno 60, 65
Taylor, Charles 233
Tazaemon Yamamura House 51
tea ceremony 34–35
Teige, Karel 85
teikan yoshiki 58, 60, 85–86
Television Asahi Headquarters 158–159, *159*
Temmu, Emperor 10, 23
Tepia 157–158, *158*, 159, 207
Tetsuro, Watsuii 98–99
Tezuka, Takaharu and Yui 249–250, *252*
Three-Power Pact 58
Times buildings 167, *168*
TNA Architects 202
Todai-ji 23–24, *23*
TOD's Omotesando 177, *177*
Tokyo: Apartments 138, *138*, 259, *260*; Bunka Kaikan
    86; Central Post Office 61, *62*; Imperial Museum 58,
    59; International Forum 143; Marine Tower 89–90,
    89, 90; Metropolitan Art Museum 90, *91*; Metropolitan
    Government Building 141, *142*, 143; Olympic Stadium
    82–83, *82*; Peace Exhibition and Memorial Tower 64;
    Train Station *46*, 47
Tomohiro Museum 221–222, *221, 222*
Toneri, Prince 10
Toshiba 114, *114, 115*
Toshihito, Hachijo 35–36
Toshitada 36
Tower of the Sun 117–118, *118*
Tower of Winds 176, *176*, 207
Town Centre Hall 223
Toy Block houses 136, *137*

Toyotomi, Hideyoshi 33–34, *34*, 35–36, 37
Tree House *254*, 255
tree metaphor 177
Tsuchiura, Kameki 51–52, 153
Tsukamoto, Yoshiharu 201
Tsukiji Hongan-ji 58, *59*, 60
Tsukiyomi-no-mikoto 9
Tsukuba Civic Center 135–136, *135*, *136*, 162
Tsunami Disaster Preventive Control Center *209*, 211
Tsuyoshi, Inukai 57
Typisierung 230
Tzonis 237, 239–241, 243

Ueda, Shunzo 259
Ueno Park 44, *45*
Uji 19
Umeda Sky Building 144, 147–148, *147*
Unite de Habitation 93, 165, 192
universalized technology 167

van der Velde, Henry 230
Venturi, Robert 129, 138, 181, 259
Versailles, Treaty of 231
Vers Une Architecture (Corbusier) 60
Vietnam War 119
Vinoly, Rafael 143

wabi chai style 35
wabi-sabi, 207 211
Wacoal Kojimachi Building *134*, 135
Wainwright Building 63
Wakakusa-Gran temple 21
Watanabe, Jin 58, *59*, 86
Water-Glass House 188
Wedding Tower 64
Weimar Republic 230–233

Western influence 44, 46, 49, 60
Westin Awaji Island hotel 170
Westin Miyako Hotel 67–68, *67*, *68*
West Plaza of Shinjuku Station 92–93
White U house 175
Williams, Raymond 131
Wooden House 259, 262, *263*
wood/trees 247–255
World Design Conference 97
World War I 230–231
World War II 3, 68–69, 99–100, 233
Wright, Frank Lloyd 51–53, *52*, 153, 165, 190

Yamaguchi, Bunzo 63, 64
Yamamoto, Riken 178–180, 193, 214
Yamanashi Broadcasting and Press Centre *107*, 108
Yamoto 19–23
Yamoto International Office Building 144, *145*, *146*
Yasui, Takeo 63–64, *63*
Yatsushiro Municipal Museum 175
Yayoi 13–17, 19
Yokomizo, Makoto 234
Yokomizu, Tomohiro 221–222
Yomiuri Miyagi Guest House 222–223, *226*
Yonago City Auditorium 77, *79*, 80
Yoritomo, Minamoto 25–26, 31
Yoshida, Tetsuro 60, 61–63, 93–94
Yoshimitsu 31–32
Yoshinobu, Ishihara 126
Yoshizaka, Takamasa 92, 237
Yoyogi National Gymnasium and Swimming Pool 82
Yuanye (*The Craft of Gardens*; Cheng) 28
Yusuhara Vistor's Center 188, *188*

Zen Buddhism 26–28